A HISTORY OF HATE IN OHIO

CONTENTS

A HISTORY OF HATE IN OHIO

Then and Now

MICHAEL E. BROOKS
AND BOB FITRAKIS

Introduction by Marilyn K. Howard

TRILLIUM, AN IMPRINT OF
THE OHIO STATE UNIVERSITY PRESS
COLUMBUS

Trillium, an imprint of The Ohio State University Press.

Library of Congress Cataloging-in-Publication Data

Names: Brooks, Michael E., author. | Fitrakis, Robert J., 1955– author. | Howard, Marilyn K.

Title: A history of hate in Ohio : then and now / Michael E. Brooks and Bob Fitrakis ; introduction by Marilyn K. Howard

Description: Columbus : Trillium, an imprint of The Ohio State University Press, [2021] | Includes bibliographical references and index. |

Summary: "*A History of Hate in Ohio* covers the history of white supremacy and hate groups in the state of Ohio from the colonial era into the twenty-first century"—Provided by publisher.

Identifiers: LCCN 2021006532 | ISBN 9780814258002 (paperback) | ISBN 9780814281406 (ebook)

Subjects: LCSH: Ohio—Race relations—History. | White supremacy movements—Ohio—History. | Racism—Ohio—History. | Hate groups—Ohio—History.

Classification: LCC F500.A1 B76 2021 | DDC 305.8009771—dc23

LC record available at https://lccn.loc.gov/2021006532

Cover design by Christian Fuenfhausen
Text design by Juliet Williams
Type set in Adobe Sabon

♾ The paper used in this publication meets the minimum requirements of the American National Standard for Information Sciences—Permanence of Paper for Printed Library Materials. ANSI Z39.48-1992.

ILLUSTRATIONS

ACKNOWLEDGMENTS

While authors get bragging rights when a book is completed, there are many people behind the scenes who contribute to its production. Thanks to Tony Sanfilippo from The Ohio State University Press for the original idea for this book, and also for incredible patience in bringing this effort to publication despite a myriad of setbacks, not the least of which was the COVID-19 pandemic. Thanks to my co-author, Robert Fitrakis, whose experience in documenting hate groups spans decades and who provided many timely and sensible suggestions along the way.

Several of my students assisted with the book. Thank you to Alyssa Kapelka, who helped me dig through archival materials. Thanks as well go out to Jacob Mach, reader of an early draft, who made editorial recommendations that improved the final version. Thanks to Travis Wright and Robert Carlock, who listened to me think out loud and provided valuable feedback. And no historian can be successful without archivists, several of whom were exceptionally helpful: Nick Pavlik of Bowling Green State University's (BGSU's) Center for Archival Collections, Julianna Witt of the American Jewish Archives, and Robin Wheelwright Ness of the John Hay Library at Brown University.

A shout-out to departmental colleagues at BGSU who provided useful suggestions: Rebecca Mancuso, Benjamin P. Greene, and Ruth

Wallis Herndon. Nicole M. Jackson was especially generous with her time and expertise, providing clarity and historiographical sources many times. Thanks to Jolie A. Sheffer and graduate students in the "1960s in Contemporary American Culture" course for asking astute questions during a presentation I gave.

Finally, thanks to my patient and super-smart wife, Kimberlyn Ross Brooks, who endured another book process and whose ability to quickly diagnose solutions to problems far outside her fields of expertise never ceases to amaze me.

—Michael E. Brooks

Like any book project, a debt is owed to a great deal of people. I would like to first acknowledge Tony Sanfilippo, Director of The Ohio State University Press, who had the original idea for this book after the incident at Charlottesville that signified an escalation of white supremacist activity in the country. Tony persevered through the pandemic to make sure this project was completed. I would also like to thank my co-author, Michael E. Brooks, who provided the historical framework in the text and great insight into the less-known history of white supremacy and racism in Ohio. I want to acknowledge my late Columbus State Community College colleague Judy Gentry, who co-wrote with me the first academic paper on white supremacy in Ohio and did the hard work of developing a CD-ROM identifying existing hate groups in the state during the 1990s. I would like to thank my "Little Sister," Marilyn Howard, for agreeing to write the introduction to this book. Dr. Howard has dedicated her long career to exposing white supremacy in its many forms. The photographers Paul Becker and Allen Zak deserve special thanks for risking their safety being on the front lines to capture and record these ugly moments in Ohio's history. I thank Kirk Bampton for an excellent job proofing and suggesting editorial changes in the initial manuscript draft. Finally, the project would have never been completed without the persistent support and assistance of my wife, Suzanne Patzer. She has endured another tedious project and deserves much credit for its completion.

—Bob Fitrakis

ACRONYMS

88	Neo-Nazi code for the eighth letter of the alphabet twice—HH, or Heil Hitler
ACLU	American Civil Liberties Union
AFSCME	American Federation of State, County and Municipal Employees
AIP	American Independent Party (George Wallace and his 1968 presidential campaign)
ARA	Anti-Racist Action
ANP	American Nazi Party (George Lincoln Rockwell's neo-fascist group)
AWNP	American White Nationalist Party
CAK	Coalition Against the Klan (Central Ohio)
CAR	Committee Against Racism (Central Ohio)
CCBC	Coalition of Concerned Black Citizens
CCRC	Columbus Community Relations Commission
CCC	Council of Conservative Citizens
CNP	Council for National Policy
COTC	Church of the Creator

CWP	Communist Workers Party
FOP	Fraternal Order of Police
INCAR	International Committee Against Racism
KKK	Ku Klux Klan
NAACP	National Association for the Advancement of Colored People
NAAWP	National Association for the Advancement of White People (William F. Miller) or North American Alliance of White People (successor group to Miller's NAAWP)
NCCS	National Christian Conservative Society (Robert W. Annable)
NKKK	National Knights of the Ku Klux Klan (also known as "Georgia Klan")
NSM	National Socialist Movement
NSWPP	National Socialist White People's Party (successor to the ANP)
NSRP	National States Rights Party
NYA	National Youth Alliance, precursor to neo-Nazi group National Alliance
OSS	Ohio State Skinheads
PLP	Progressive Labor Party
POER	Police Officers for Equal Rights
RAHOWA	Neo-Nazi term for a racial war (RAcial HOly War)
RCP	Revolutionary Communist Party
RWDS	Right Wing Death Squad
SCLC	Southern Christian Leadership Conference
SDS	Students for a Democratic Society
SHARP	Skinheads Against Racial Prejudice
SPLC	Southern Poverty Law Center
TUFF	Those United to Fight Fascism
UCC-Ohio	United Citizens Council of Ohio (Robert W. Annable)
UKA	United Klans of America (also known as "Alabama Klan")
WWP	Workers World Party

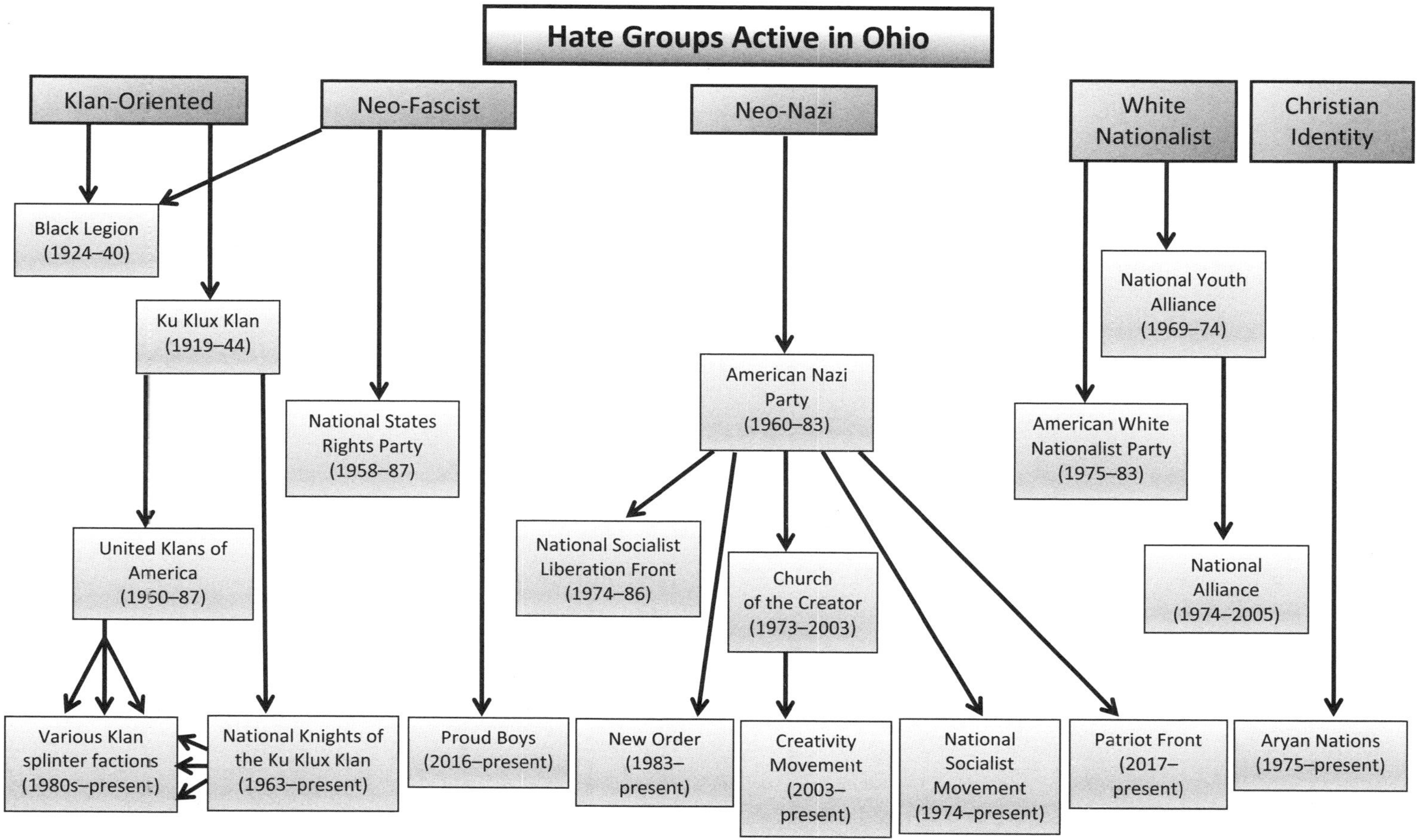

FIGURE 0.1. Hate groups active in Ohio

A Note on the Graphic Content of the Book

This book examines the history of white supremacy and hate groups in Ohio. The authors have elected to maintain historical accuracy in the language used by persons, texts, and videos quoted in the book. As a result, the book contains racial, ethnic, and homophobic slurs and terminology, and it also contains graphic depictions of violence, including lynching and genocide. Some readers may find the content in this book to be offensive and/or traumatizing.

INTRODUCTION

MARILYN K. HOWARD

Many people, even those who are college educated, are surprised to learn that slavery, racism, prejudice, and discrimination exist north of the Mason-Dixon Line. Indeed, racial segregation is primarily a Northern construct. Even the pious Puritans and Pilgrims participated in the slave trade and found it so profitable that they quickly managed to reconcile it with their religious beliefs. Northerners, scholars, and teachers for the most part seem perfectly comfortable with this fairy tale.

According to the Southern Poverty Law Center (SPLC), white supremacy terrorist organizations are growing most quickly outside the South, and 31 of these groups call Ohio their home. The picture of a terrorist in the minds of most Americans is that of a young Muslim man. Yet, according to the Federal Bureau of Investigation (FBI), most of their work in domestic terrorism since October 2019 is linked to white supremacy groups, and membership in these groups is growing fastest in the urban North. Even so, the FBI was slow to recognize this as a domestic problem and a threat to national security.

Race as we think of it in America today has its roots in the Atlantic slave trade. (It should be noted that anthropologists say there is no scientific basis for race.) Mercantilism in Europe drove the age of exploration and the formation of empires. Explorers traveled to East Asia seeking raw materials and goods to take back to their countries. Muslim traders, however, held fast to the monopoly they had in Asia. Europeans were forced to begin to explore different routes that would allow them to bypass Muslims. They eventually settled on the west coast of Africa as the route they frequented in their quest for goods.

The expansion of European empires highlighted a huge problem: a lack of workers. Indigenous people in the various New World regions were used, but they quickly proved to be a poor choice as they succumbed to diseases brought over from Europe. Unused to the tropical climate, Europeans were quickly deemed unfit as a workforce, too. The Europeans began to consider enslaved Africans the answer to their problem.

This discovery proved to be fortuitous. Africans had been enslaved and traded as slaves for centuries. They also had experience with keeping livestock and working in agriculture. Finally, they were accustomed to the tropical heat and resistant to tropical diseases. But slavery in Africa existed under different conditions. The enslaved were mostly prisoners of war, or on the losing side of a family or village dispute. They sometimes had the right to marry and own land. Their slave status was not passed on to subsequent generations. It was only when Africans were brought to the Americas and the British colonies that their condition of slavery changed. Of the 11,300,000 Africans brought over to the Americas, only about a half-million ended up in the British colonies.

Beginning in 1619, when the first Africans were brought over to Jamestown in Virginia, the colonies, customs, and laws changed gradually changed so that slavery became the natural condition of Black people. The colonists also introduced two new elements to the condition: human beings were treated as property or chattel, and the enslaved status of the mother became the enslaved status of the child.

Primarily because of geography, slavery never became deeply entrenched in the New England colonies. A short growing season and extremely cold winter weather kept the colonists from planting the kind of labor-intensive crops grown in the middle and southern colonies. But the institution definitely touched the region. Ships from the slaveholding colonies brought much-needed goods to the area. Even though New Englanders mostly used Native Americans for slaves, the Pilgrims and Puritans were certainly aware of the African slave trade. Still, there were few Africans in this area.

Massachusetts was the first colony to legalize slavery, and other New England colonies followed suit. By the beginning of the 1700s, the African slave population had increased dramatically. Slaves still had a number of rights, though; they could attend the Puritan churches, marry, and receive a jury trial if they were accused of criminal activity. Even so, some clergymen begin to question the morality of slavery.

The Framers and other social elites also recognized the dichotomy between their struggle for freedom from the British—which they often compared to slavery—and the fact that many of them engaged in human trafficking. The revolutionary spirit of 1776 and the subsequent war presented an opportunity to abolish the practice. The Northern colonies began to develop gradual manumission plans. The process proceeded in fits and starts, but it was a first step.

The Great Awakening, a multidenominational movement of religious revivals that took place from the 1730s through the 1780s, also affected the enslaved. The Awakening taught that salvation was available to all regardless of race or color. The emotional preaching and singing reminded many of them of their religious practices in Africa from which they had been separated. Many slaves converted during this period, and some became preachers. Slave owners feared the power the Awakening had for enslaved persons, and often blocked them from practicing their religion. This forced them to practice their faith secretly in hush harbors and the like.

The egalitarian spirit of the Great Awakening and the American Revolution gave Black people hope that they would be freed and slavery abolished. They joined both the Patriots and British Loyalists in a calculated effort to gain their freedom. The royal governor of Virginia, John Murray, the Earl of Dunmore, promised freedom to Blacks who fought on the side of the Loyalists. But it was not to be. Loyalists deserted their Black allies as their position in the conflict deteriorated. Few Black Loyalists gained their freedom; some were even sent back to slavery. Even though white colonists gained their freedom from the British, that freedom did not touch the enslaved. But after the war, there was interest in some of the states in abolishing slavery.

During the Constitutional Convention of 1787, slavery was the elephant in the room. It quickly became clear that if slavery was abolished, the Southern states would not agree to the new Constitution. Gouverneur Morris, a delegate from Pennsylvania, introduced a plan for gradual emancipation of the enslaved with compensation for slave owners. The idea was vetoed. There were also arguments over how the enslaved would be counted for purposes of determining each state's representation in the lower congressional chamber. Already the small Northern states were worried that they would be vulnerable in a new governmental system because they did not have large numbers of slaves. And what would be done about runaway slaves? A loose network of people opposed to slavery was already in operation and assisting them.

The delegates ultimately decided that each enslaved person would count as three-fifths of a person for the purposes of apportioning seats in the House of Representatives and the collecting of taxes. Second, Congress would make no moves to abolish the international slave trade before 1808. Finally, a provision was inserted in the new document that required the states to return fugitive slaves to their owners. The delegates had protected the institution of slavery and the slave trade without using the words *slave, slaves,* or *slavery.*

By the first decade of the nineteenth century, all Northern states had either abolished slavery or developed plans for the gradual emancipation of slaves. The five states carved from the Northwest Territory had forbidden slavery. Yet free Blacks in the North were not deemed citizens, and many of those states wrote laws that discriminated against Blacks. For example, they were barred from joining the national militia, and they could not even carry and deliver mail in the new country.

The abolition of slavery, however, did not mean that the region was interested in Black equality. Free Blacks in the North faced fierce opposition from whites as they tried to build families and communities. Before the turn of the nineteenth century, free Black men had at least some rights. As the number of free Blacks grew, the North responded with race-based legislation designed to ensure they remained on the margins of society.

Blacks knew to expect a daily barrage of verbal abuse; individual acts of violence and mob violence were not unheard of. Occasionally, Black homes, churches, and schools were burned down. African Americans also knew that the law would not protect them; as a societal institution, it assisted in their debasement and marginalization.

By the 1830s change was in the air. American society was becoming more democratic. Literacy increased, more people attended schools, and republican marriage—a union bound by love rather than economics or the joining of two great families—became more popular. Individualism flourished. The republican virtues of the Framers—and the Framers themselves—were dying. This period is referred to as the age of Jacksonian Democracy, after Andrew Jackson, the two-term Democratic president from Tennessee, and it ushered in the Era of the Common Man.

Jackson was the first man elected to the presidency who did not come from an elite family. Although he championed the common man, that did not include Blacks. He was openly racist and owned more than 150 slaves in his lifetime. Said to be a cruel master, he took some of his slaves to the White House. Yet he detested the planter elite—those men who held a large number of slaves—and resented their hold on politics.

Despite its being the Era of the Common Man, life for African Americans in the North was becoming increasingly more difficult. White northerners may have barred slavery, but they had no intention of living in a society in which Blacks were their equals. Segregation is a Northern invention. Just as in the South, white Northerners believed that Blacks were inferior, and they readily supported phrenology, a new pseudoscientific field that claimed it could rank different races based on the size of their skulls. This gave white Northerners scientific "proof" of Blacks' inferiority, and segregation helped preserve their whiteness.

Still, free Blacks continued moving into the North. White Northerners met their stubborn refusal to accept their inferior status by using established customs and the law to make the lives of Blacks more unbearable. They ensured that the law clearly designated Blacks as an inferior race, and that Blacks could expect no protection or consideration from it. They criminalized blackness, and developed a dual justice system in which Blacks were arrested and imprisoned far more than whites for even the most minor offenses.

At the same time that the common man was gifted with universal male suffrage, Blacks in the North were being stripped of the right to vote. White Northerners also excluded Blacks from political life, guaranteeing that no politician need give the slightest thought to anything even remotely related to Blacks. This foretold the battle against Black citizenship that would define so much of the 1850s.

Free Blacks in the North also continued to be the targets of white mob violence into the middle of the nineteenth century. Some of that violence happened in Cincinnati, Ohio, in the southwestern part of the state. It shared a border with Kentucky, a slave state, and as in other Northern states, white natives, European immigrants, and Blacks jockeyed for low-skilled or unskilled work. In that combustible mixture were runaway slaves and the whites who helped them. In the 1830s and 1840s Cincinnati whites formed mobs and wantonly destroyed Black neighborhoods and property belonging to abolitionists. Blacks in Massachusetts, Rhode Island, New York, and Philadelphia were also victimized by white mobs.

One of the clearest examples of Northern racism and its toleration for white mob violence were the Draft Riots in New York during July 1863. Whites in New York City were angry about the draft, which they viewed as unfair. A white man with money could literally pay a poor white man to take his place in the Union Army. Whites were also angry about what they began to see as a war that was being fought on behalf of defeating slavery. White mobs made up of criminals and ethnic whites took their frustration out on Blacks, roaming through Black neighborhoods unmolested, looting and burning. Some Blacks were even lynched. It took federal troops days to quash the violence.

White politicians did not hesitate to blame African Americans for the mayhem. They denounced public officials who supported a war against slavery in the most vitriolic of language. Legislators in Indiana, Illinois, and New Jersey were all led by Democrats who railed against the prospect of four million freed slaves moving into their states.

By 1862 the Civil War looked to be a stalemate. President Abraham Lincoln warned the Confederate States of America that he would free their slaves on January 1, 1863, if they did not lay down their arms and rejoin the Union. Ignored by Southerners, he issued the Emancipation Proclamation, which also provided for the entrance of Black enslaved and free men into the Union Army. The army found it difficult to recruit white officers to helm Black regiments; it did not appear to be a good career move. Black troops lacked equipment and supplies, and training conditions were poor. They also had to contend with being paid less than white soldiers. Even though once in combat most Black troops fought valiantly, it made no difference to white Northerners. They were no more reconciled to Black freedom at the end of the war than they had ever been.

The Republican Party may have been the party of Lincoln, but he himself was ambivalent about the place of Blacks in American society. While he abhorred slavery as an institution, he was not in favor of Black equality. He used the n-word, and made Blacks the brunt of jokes and stories. As a lawyer, he had helped a Black client prove her freedom, but he had also argued a case on behalf of a slave owner trying to reclaim his property. Lincoln did come to believe that some Black men should have the right to vote, but there had to be conditions, chief among them education. Still, at the time of Lincoln's assassination in 1865, there was no clear plan for how to handle four million newly freed Blacks. It fell to Andrew Johnson, Lincoln's vice president, a Southerner, and a slave owner, to define Reconstruction.

A careful reading of the Reconstruction Amendments to the US Constitution will clearly show that white Northerners conferred Black freedom on the one hand while taking it away with the other. The Thirteenth Amendment abolished slavery "except as punishment for a crime of which the party shall be duly convicted." That loophole allowed the development and maintenance of neoslavery in the South at the same time that it allowed Northerners to claim that they had abolished slavery. The Fourteenth Amendment conferred citizenship on African Americans and guaranteed the equal protection of the law. But Northern legislatures continued to pass laws that stripped Blacks of their citizenship and thus made a mockery of equal protection. The Fifteenth Amendment neither confers suffrage on Blacks nor guarantees that it will be protected. Most Northern legislators were not in favor of expanded voting rights for Black men, and so they merely developed a set of circumstances by which they could not be denied the vote. Once again racism and discrimination in the North blunted the efforts of African Americans to fully function as free people.

In the presidential election of 1876, the Republican, Rutherford B. Hayes, squared off against the Democrat, Samuel Tilden. Disputed Electoral College votes in Florida, Louisiana, and South Carolina made it difficult to determine the exact number of electoral votes earned by each candidate. A congressional committee was established to determine which candidate would receive the disputed votes, and it resulted in a so-called corrupt bargain. Hayes's emissaries let it be known that if he won those votes and thus the presidency, he would pull Northern troops out of the South and let the Confederate states return to home rule. The 12-year window of Reconstruction slammed shut with a loud bang. The former states of the Old Confederacy, along with the help of a very conservative Supreme Court that struck down federal civil rights laws, was able to wipe out any last vestige of rights for Blacks.

Northern cooperation was essential in helping the planter elite regain control in the South. Northerners continue to be deeply invested in erasing their role in promoting and supporting a society based on white superiority and Black inferiority. Delay, denial, and indifference have proved to be as powerful as police dogs and fire hoses.

It has been a colossal mistake to have ignored the history of white racial violence in the North. Doing so has allowed Northerners to assure themselves that they had no role in or responsibility for America's racist past, and therefore no need do anything about repairing its damage. It has also allowed white terrorist organizations to spread virtually unchecked while they indoctrinate young people in the ways of racial hate. Finally, it has facilitated the election of a president who is an unabashed racist and who uses that to consolidate his own power and sow even more racial discord in America. The specter of white supremacy was especially evident in the failed insurrection at the Capitol building in January 2021.

Brooks and Fitrakis have joined the cadre of historians, journalists, and social scientists who today are exposing the scourge of white supremacist ideology and violence. Their message is a powerful and necessary corrective as we work to heal the soul of America.

THEN

A History of Racism and Bigotry in Ohio

MICHAEL E. BROOKS

There is a present-day tendency among the general public in the states that remained part of the Union during the Civil War that the North was somehow immune to the malignant racism that underlay the institution of slavery that emerged in the American South. This is a dreamy revision of history that mythologizes the North as a benign, even friendly place that welcomed persons of color and other marginalized populations. This is particularly the case with many white Ohioans, who learn a rosy, sanitized version of their state's history in fourth grade.[1] After all (or so goes this view), no state had greater participation in the Underground Railroad, and many of the leading American abolitionists at one point called Ohio home.

This distorted depiction of Ohio history is akin to the illusory vision of the US as a melting pot of native-born peoples and immigrants, groups harmoniously forged into a unique culture based on freedom, opportunity, and individualism. The history of Ohio, with its fertile lands and burgeoning industrial centers, is often remembered fondly (if inaccurately) by many present-day Ohioans as a place that opened its arms to people from all over the world: immigrants who found new prospects in a state relatively free from bigotry and intolerance, and former slaves seeking freedom and a new start in life.

Each of these narratives, of course, possesses nuggets of truth. Ohio was indeed a major center of abolitionist activity, not the least of which was the participation by idealistic Ohioans in the Underground Railroad. Helping runaway slaves was a criminal activity under the federal Fugitive Slave Act of 1850, and people aiding runaway slaves faced potential jail sentences of six months and a $500 fine. For foreign-born persons, Ohio has certainly provided settings where newly arrived immigrants could find gainful employment and opportunities to build new lives in America.

This book is divided into two sections, with lengthy contributions from two specialists in the scholarship of white supremacy. Historian Michael Brooks examines the history of racism in Ohio from the colonial era through the 1960s. Political scientist and journalist Robert Fitrakis covers the more recent history of white supremacy from the 1970s through the present day. While each author brings different methodological and disciplinary approaches to this book, the result is the first full-length study of Ohio's long and complicated history of racism and white supremacy.

The first section of the book focuses on the less-known history of racism, intolerance, and bigotry in early Ohio history. While the history of high-profile examples of white supremacy such as the Ku Klux Klan and the Black Legion figure prominently in this story, there are historical undercurrents of racism and intolerance that are arguably even more pernicious in the state's past and present. Brooks argues that everyday racism and bigotry might be less visible, or at least less likely to be documented, but these forms of intolerance have a long history in the state of Ohio. This first section also provides the first comprehensive study of organized white supremacist activity in Ohio during the 1960s, a period when racism in Ohio in many ways mirrored Southern racism. The appeal of neo-Nazi groups among white Ohioans also demonstrated significant growth in the 1960s.

The second half of the book examines organized white supremacy in the late twentieth and early twenty-first centuries in Ohio. Fitrakis begins with the emergence of the Aryan Nations and offshoots of the group in the 1970s, explaining their connections to Ohio. He documents the growing interconnections between Klan and neo-Nazi groups, two white supremacist traditions that once had little overlap. Fitrakis also documents the concurrent emergence of antiracist groups in Ohio, especially moving forward from the 1980s.

We begin with an attempt to define what we mean by the use of the term *white supremacy* in this book. In some uses of the term in this book, we use *white supremacy* to refer to specific racist ideologies promoting the idea that persons of European descent (especially from northern Europe) are superior to people from other races (such as found in the ideologies of the Ku Klux Klan). We might also use the term *white supremacy* to refer to systems of structural or systemic racism in which white people possess privileges that others lack, regardless of the absence or presence of conscious racial hate or prejudice (such as the institutional racism associated with the Jim Crow era). Finally, *white supremacy* may also refer to general beliefs held by mainstream, native-born whites in the supposed inferiority of other ethnic and racial groups, the sort of lower-level bigotry known in the present day as "everyday racism"[2] or the related "casual racism."

The term *white supremacy* emerged in the nineteenth century, and it did not become widespread in mainstream American discourse until the modern civil rights movement of the 1950s and 1960s. However, ideas of white superiority certainly date back several centuries, and these racist constructs are closely related to the emergence of the transatlantic slave trade. Thus, while we may use the term *white supremacy* to refer to specific historical behaviors, practices, or laws, people in different historical periods would have found other ways to describe beliefs that by twenty-first-century standards would be considered racist.

Racism and white supremacy have sometimes been depicted as occurring along a spectrum, with more overt forms of racism on one end (such as belonging to the Ku Klux Klan) and less overt forms of racism on the other end (such as holding on to a racist stereotype, or holding an unconscious bias against members of another group). We are taking a somewhat broad view of white supremacy in this book, examining overt behaviors associated with white supremacy in the form of organized advocacy as well as less obvious, "everyday" forms of racism. As we will see, white supremacy has taken many forms over the course of Ohio's history, and it continues to fester in Ohio into the twenty-first century.

Struggle for Control of the Ohio Country

Ohio's history of bigotry and intolerance begins with the earliest documented interactions between Native Americans and white settlers in the Ohio Country prior to statehood. The term *Ohio Country* is somewhat ambiguous, and Europeans and white colonists used it to describe the land north of the Ohio River that included (depending on the person defining the term) parts of present-day Ohio, Indiana, Michigan, Pennsylvania, and West Virginia. Competition for the Ohio Country led to violent conflict between natives and newcomers that lasted many decades, even after statehood. Underlying this conquest and slaughter was a belief that Europeans—by supposed virtue of their superior culture, enhanced biology, or divine right—were entitled to the lands held by Native Americans.

Europeans in general believed Native Americans to be a degraded, heathen, and ignorant people who failed to make industrious use of the lands they occupied. Influential American writer Philip Freneau expressed this view in a 1782 article regarding the reasons why the new US should settle the trans-Appalachian territories that it would soon acquire in the peace treaty with Britain that ended the Revolutionary War. He observed that Indians lacked the agricultural and industrial knowledge possessed by the Americans; moreover, he argued that Native Americans exhibited "so little resemblance in the features of the mind to what the civilized world calls a man that they scarcely deserve the name."[3]

The colonial period in Ohio Country featured extreme violence perpetrated by all sides. This was a highly contested region—for natural resources like animal pelts as well as future settlement by Eastern whites—and the struggle for control of the region led to many atrocities. However, a distinction should be made in sorting out the violence: Native Americans generally believed their white opponents were humans like themselves (albeit humans who were greedy and desired land not given to them by the Great Spirit), while many whites viewed Indians as alien beings (or even subhuman) who were fair game for extermination.

Many scholars of Native American history have argued that westward expansion by the US was aided in large measure by a desire to exterminate Indian groups as a means to control territory. Even if some whites did not advocate the wholesale slaughter of Native Americans, noted one scholar of genocide studies, many or most

Anglo-Americans "shared a fundamentally genocidal conviction that sooner or later, Indians should and would disappear from the region."[4]

Certainly Native Americans in the Ohio Valley and lower Great Lakes in the late eighteenth and early nineteenth centuries believed that extermination was part of the American agenda in the trans-Appalachian regions. Native American scholar Jeffrey Ostler's work demonstrated that "Delawares and other Indians in this region continued to believe that the United States and its people intended to destroy them"[5] despite statements to the contrary by white treaty negotiators. This belief in a white campaign of genocide—driven at its core by values of white supremacy—led many Indian groups to oppose westward expansion by white settlers out of a sense of self-preservation.

And Native Americans had plenty of concrete reasons to arrive at the conclusion that white settlers meant them harm. For example, we might consider the case of the Lenni Lenape (Delaware) Indians in east-central Ohio in the 1780s. Many of the Lenni Lenape had converted to Christianity, due in large measure to missionary efforts led by Moravian missionary David Zeisberger, who founded a series of towns where hundreds of Christian Lenape lived. Chief among these were the villages of Schoenbrunn, Salem, Lichtenau, and Gnadenhutten. German for "Tents of Grace," Gnadenhutten was located roughly halfway between Fort Detroit (held by the British) and Fort Pitt (held by the Americans).

These Christian converts found themselves caught between the British and the rebel Americans as the Revolutionary War broke out. The Lenape professed neutrality and peaceful intentions, hoping to avoid having to choose sides in the war, a choice many Indian peoples were forced to make. British-allied Indians forced the Christian Lenape to march to an area known as "Captive Town," located on the Sandusky River to the northwest. Due to poor rations at Captive Town, many Lenape returned to Gnadenhutten hoping to salvage some of the harvest they were forced to leave behind.

Unfortunately for the Christian Lenape scavenging for harvest remnants at Gnadenhutten in March 1782, their paths crossed with those of a group of 160 Pennsylvania militia seeking revenge for some raids committed by different Indians. The militia members took a vote and decided overwhelmingly to slaughter the Lenape. Soldiers bound and imprisoned the Indians, crushed their heads with mallets,

FIGURE 1.1. Depiction of Gnadenhutten Massacre. Courtesy of Ohio History Connection, AL02709.

scalped them, and then burned the building in which they had been held. In all, some 96 Christian Lenape were murdered by the white militia, including 34 children (see Figure 1.1).[6]

Word of the horrors perpetrated by white militia at Gnadenhutten spread quickly among the Indians of the Ohio Country. If the Americans would murder even peaceful Indians who had converted to Christianity and adopted white customs, what would they do to Indians who resisted white trans-Appalachian settlement? A 1792 document that highlights a conversation with Aupaumut, a Christian Indian ambassador to a variety of peace talks with the Americans, succinctly encapsulates the fear of extermination by whites that Indians held. Aupaumut argued that white missionaries would "Christianize number[s] so as to gain their attention, then they would [kill] them, and have killed of such 96 in one day."[7] This statement came a full decade after the Gnadenhutten Massacre, illustrating the power this tragedy had over Native–newcomer relations in the Ohio Country.

The end of the Revolutionary War marked the legitimacy of the new American Republic, and the 1783 Treaty of Paris resulted in Britain ceding most of its claims to North American territories between the Appalachians and the Mississippi River. In particular, the Americans looked immediately to the Ohio Country as the next major destination for white settlement. This desire by whites for westward expansion into lands held by Native Americans set up a lengthy period of conflict known today as the Northwest Indian War, lasting from roughly 1785 to 1795.

Native Americans successfully defended their lands in two major campaigns by the US in 1791 and 1792 before finally being defeated by the Legion of the United States, led by American general "Mad" Anthony Wayne. The pivotal battle for control of the Ohio Country occurred along the Maumee River at the Battle of Fallen Timbers in 1795. The total number of civilian and combatant casualties in this decade-long war—which varied from low-level skirmishes to full-scale military campaigns—will never be known with any degree of certainty, though deaths on each side unquestionably ran at least into the thousands.

The hostilities between white settlers and Indian groups in the Ohio Country—along with the federal government's initial inability to effectively assert itself in the region—led some settlers to incentivize the slaughter of Native Americans. A 1794 circular advertisement offered the following bounties for Indian scalps; signatories ("subscribers") of the contract received somewhat higher bounties for delivering Indian scalps than did nonsignatories:

> For every scalp, having the right ear appendant, of the first ten Indians who shall be killed . . . by those who are subscribers to the said articles, shall, whenever collected, be paid the sum of one hundred and thirty-six dollars; and for every scalp of the like number of Indians, having the right ear appendant, who shall be killed within the time and limits aforesaid, by those who are not subscribers shall, whenever collected, be paid the sum of one hundred dollars.[8]

After the American government and white settlers finally crushed Native American resistance via formal military campaigns, paramilitary activity, and vigilantism, most remaining Indian communities were forcibly relocated away from Ohio in the first half of the nineteenth century. A region once populated with tens of thousands of Native Americans was conquered by the new American government, and white settlers rapidly poured in to stake a claim for the "new" lands. Moreover, as historian Kristopher Maulden noted, federal officials "institutionalized anti-Indian violence on the frontier" and "placed the U.S. Army at the head of westward expansion for the next century."[9]

Even after wars of extermination and subjugation with Native Americans died down, a sort of cultural violence emerged. Reformers, led by missionaries, began to gain traction in the nineteenth century with the idea that Indians could be "rehabilitated." This was a shift away from direct slaughter and toward the destruction of Native American culture. Consider the following quote by George Manypenny, a nineteenth-century writer pondering the "Indian question"; Manypenny was an Ohioan who served as the director of the Bureau of Indian Affairs in the 1850s and whose views on Native Americans were shaped by his years of interactions with Indians in Ohio:

> The Indian women must cease to do the outdoor work, and confine themselves to domestic duties and the cares of the house and the family. The labor in the garden and the field must be done by the men and boys. To the nomad, this change will be a great innovation; but the step being taken by one, others will follow, and, with proper prompting and encouragement, accessions will continually be made to the ranks of labor . . . As the habit of roaming must cease, and all Indians have their fixed homes, the young of both sexes will always be within reach, and then an inviting and interesting field will be open, not only for the work of the agent, but for the Christian missionary.[10]

For white officials like Manypenny, Native Americans needed to assimilate into mainstream white American culture. Even traditional gender roles and methods of subsistence needed to be jettisoned, to be replaced by ways of life radically different from their own cultural heritage. In some ways cultural death is just as destructive to Indian groups as genocide by whites: the net result in both cases is a loss of tribal members and collective memory. Underlying the cultural and physical violence lay an ideology of white supremacy, a belief system that European culture was superior and destined to rule the American continents.

Ohio's Black Laws

From the earliest days of statehood, Ohioans exhibited extreme hostility to Blacks living in the state. Delegates to the state's constitutional convention in November 1802 could have extended voting rights to Black Ohioans; instead, they chose to limit suffrage to white males. Convention president (and future Ohio governor) Edward Tiffin cast the deciding vote against Black suffrage at the constitutional convention. The new state of Ohio had an opportunity to set a progressive precedent for the rest of the country, but it chose an exclusionary path with regard to Black suffrage.

Early Ohio was dominated by white settlers from Virginia and Kentucky, and much of the state's non-Indian population was concentrated in the southern part of the state. Many of the first white Ohioans thus came from states where slavery was legal, and even if they did not come from families that owned slaves, white settlers in southern Ohio likely arrived with the same prejudices and biases found in their states of origin. Moreover, whites who engaged in commercial activity likely had business connections in those states, giving them reason to be sympathetic to issues faced by white business and plantation owners in Virginia and Kentucky.

It is not surprising, then, that among the earliest legislative acts in the newly formed state of Ohio could be found numerous measures designed to "regulate black and mulatto persons"[11] and/or escaped enslaved persons. The so-called Black Laws of 1804 and 1807 severely restricted the rights of free Blacks in Ohio while creating obstacles for free persons of color to move to Ohio and providing penalties for aiding, harboring, or employing an escaped slave.

In 1804 the Ohio legislature decreed that persons of color could not reside in Ohio unless they possessed a certificate of freedom that was registered by a county clerk; the clerk would require a "fair certificate from some court with the United States" attesting to the person's status as a freeman.[12] Ohioans were forbidden to hire African Americans who did not carry an official registration document. Employers who violated this law were subject to a fine of between ten and 50 dollars, and they would also be assessed a fine paid to the owner of the supposed slave. In addition, the law allowed local judges to order the arrest of unregistered Blacks and return them to their purported owners. To incentivize enforcement of the legislation, the 1804 act permitted half the fine for employing an unregistered Black worker to be collected by the informant of the "offense."[13]

The 1804 laws, however, failed to pacify Ohioans with fears about free persons of color in the state. The state legislature in 1807 decided to amend the earlier Black Laws in favor of stricter measures to constrain the movement and activities of African Americans in Ohio. In addition to securing a bond of $500, the new law required African Americans to furnish a "freehold surety" (see Figure 1.2) signed by at least two Ohio residents who guaranteed their good behavior and who would agree to pay for their support should they be unable to support themselves. The cost of a registration certificate was raised from 12.5 cents to one dollar. At the same time, a fine of $100 was authorized against anyone who would "employ, harbor, or conceal" a person of color who did not possess a registration certificate. Similar to the 1804 law, this fine would be split between the informant and the government. Finally, the law contained a provision outlawing that a Black person "be sworn or give evidence" in a legal case where a white person was involved.[14]

A recurrent and thorny issue in Ohio history has been the education of Black children with such pervasive bigotry and racism present. Well into the 1960s there was strong resistance among various segments of the white population to efforts by the state to desegregate Ohio's public schools. As early as 1829 Ohio legislators attempted to tackle the issue; however, legislative solutions have never been able to pacify those who opposed the education of Black children in Ohio public schools.

The first Ohio public school acts (1821 and 1825) did not mention race as a qualifier for public school enrollment, using instead the term *householder* to refer to the basis on which children could attend public schools in Ohio. The 1829 act, however, specifically indicated that "nothing in this act contained shall be so construed as to permit black or mulatto persons to attend the schools hereby established, or compel them to pay any tax for the support of such schools." The act made allowances for districts that chose to offer education for Black children, noting that local trustees retained the ability to assess taxes "for the education of said black and mulatto persons therein."[15]

The 1829 public school act likely reflects existing conflict regarding Black children sharing educational facilities with white children. This legislation was amended by a similar 1832 act, which noted that funds raised by state public school taxes were to be used "for the instruction of the white youth of every class and grade, without distinction," and that no taxes could be levied on the property of persons of color for the support of schools. The census taken to govern the distribution of state funds could only include only white

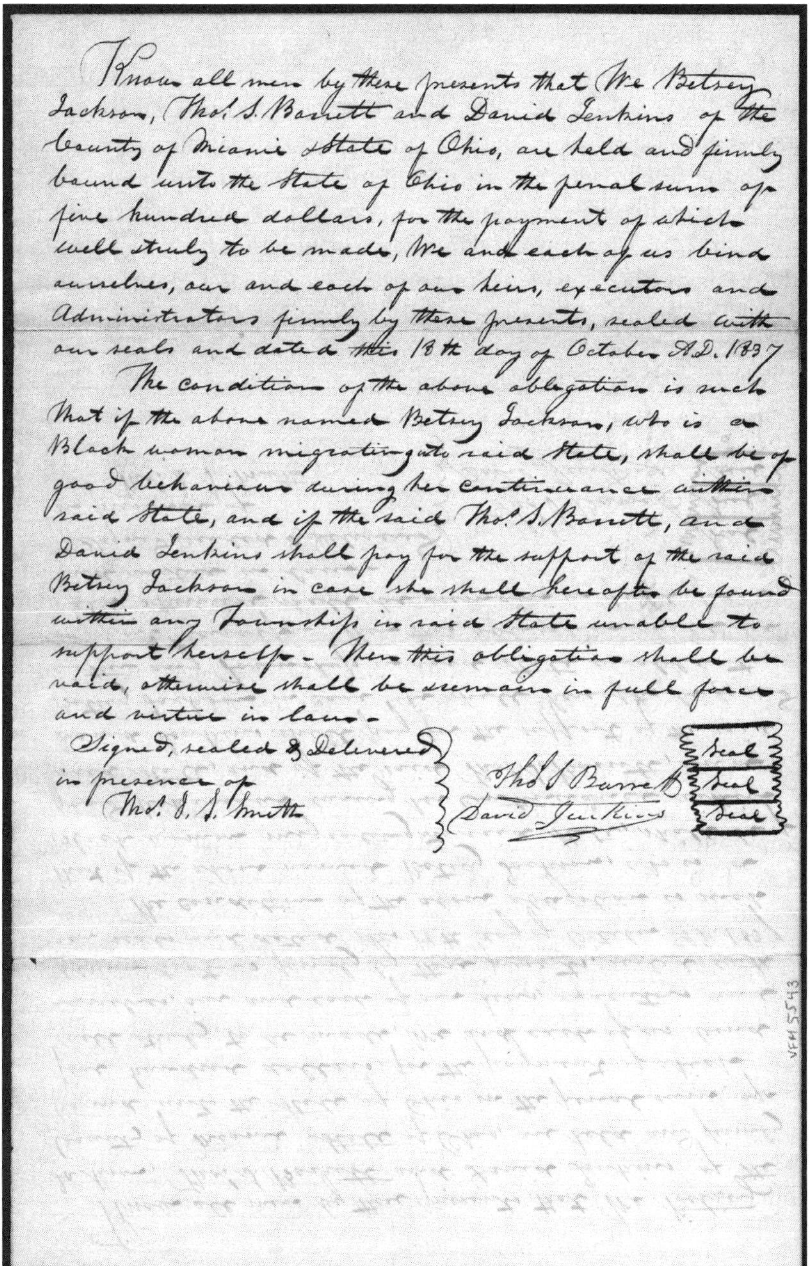

Know all men by these presents that We Betsey Jackson, Thos. S. Barrett and David Jenkins of the County of Miami State of Ohio, are held and firmly bound unto the State of Ohio in the penal sum of five hundred dollars, for the payment of which well truly to be made, We and each of us bind ourselves, our and each of our heirs, executors and Administrators firmly by these presents, sealed with our seals and dated this 18th day of October A.D. 1837

The condition of the above obligation is such that if the above named Betsey Jackson, who is a Black woman migrating into said State, shall be of good behaviour during her continuance within said State, and if the said Thos. S. Barrett, and David Jenkins shall pay for the support of the said Betsey Jackson in case she shall hereafter be found within any Township in said State unable to support herself — Then this obligation shall be void, otherwise shall be & remain in full force and virtue in law —

Signed, sealed & Delivered in presence of
Thos. J. S. Smith

Thos S Barrett — Seal
David Jenkins — Seal
Seal

VFM 5543

FIGURE 1.2. Example of a freehold surety bond from Miami County, 1837. Courtesy of Ohio History Connection, VFM5543_02.

children.[16] These racial distinctions appeared again in later Ohio laws passed in 1834 and 1838.

Racial animosity in southern Ohio escalated in the decades before the Civil War; in particular, Irish residents of Cincinnati directly competed with African Americans for employment, especially in jobs along the docks. Conflict led to countless violent attacks by whites against free Blacks in Ohio in this period. The most severe of these was a deadly 1829 riot in Cincinnati in which whites forced many hundreds of Black residents out of the city. The pretense for the mass expulsion was the supposed violations of the Black Laws by Black residents.

Growth of the Black population in Cincinnati had been steady during the 1820s. There were about 1800 more Black residents as of the 1830 census than there had been during the 1820 census. However, the percentage of Black residents in Cincinnati was only 9.4 percent in 1830, a growth from the 3.9 percent of Cincinnati residents who were Black during the 1820 census. Similarly, the Irish American population grew during this decade, though at a lower rate than that for African Americans.

However, there are additional long-term and short-term causes of the 1829 Cincinnati riot. African Americans and Irish Americans competed for the same low-wage, unskilled positions. White artisans concerned about the decline in trades-based employment due to industrialization sought to scapegoat Blacks for their misfortunes. Some whites sought to use public safety as a mask for their racist views by claiming that Blacks lived in unsafe housing; this concern, of course, ignores the fact that poor whites were just as likely to live in dilapidated shanties as poor Blacks. Moreover, the emergence of building codes in Ohio is really a twentieth-century phenomenon, as the Ohio legislature first approved construction regulation in 1911.[17] White residents began circulating petitions that no politician would be elected who did not agree to end growth of the Black population in Cincinnati. However, many council members were business owners and wealthy elites who profited from cheap labor, and they were thus unwilling to drive African Americans out of town.

The threat of political fallout, however, forced Cincinnati's city council to act. The city directed Black residents to register, present certificates of freedom, enroll the name of a bondsman, or leave the city. Cincinnati's Black residents were given 30 days to comply, and they attempted to buy time for a mass relocation to Canada. Historian Nikki Taylor wrote that persecuted Blacks no longer considered the Queen City to be safe: "Stalked by the black laws, economic repression, and social inequality, Cincinnati no longer seemed to be the Promised Land."[18]

Blacks in Cincinnati were in a tenuous position in the late 1820s. Most whites wanted to see them removed from the city, and even business leaders and elites—those whose financial well-being depended on Black labor—were at best ambivalent about the Black population in Cincinnati, and many white elites were openly hostile to Black residents. The editor of *Liberty Hall,* a Cincinnati-based newspaper, offered the following assessment of the situation: "The rapid increase of our black population, to say nothing of slavery, is of itself a great evil . . . The city is filled with night walkers, lewd persons, and those who lounge about without any visible means of support, especially the negro house gamblers."[19]

It is worth considering at this point the views of John Malvin, a free Black man who arrived in Cincinnati in 1827 from Virginia. He arrived in Ohio with high hopes, but the reality of life for a person of color in nineteenth-century Ohio was quite harsh:

> I thought coming to a free state like Ohio that I would find every door open to receive me, but from the treatment I received by the people generally, I found it little better than Virginia . . . I found that every door was closed to the colored man in a free state except the jails and penitentiaries.[20]

Malvin faced numerous color-based barriers during his time in Ohio. He bought a boat in the 1830s with the hope of making enough money to pay off debts he had incurred in gaining the manumission of his father-in-law. However, when he applied for a license to operate the vessel as a freight carrier, a local official refused to issue the necessary license; fortunately for Malvin, a higher-ranking bureaucrat overruled this decision.[21] In another instance of intolerance, Malvin helped build a Baptist church, but later found that Black church members would be relegated to pews in a Black-only section of the church.[22]

White city officials refused the three-month extension requested by Black leaders. Meanwhile, working-class and poor whites refused to listen to calls for calm, and they began armed raids into Black neighborhoods. Between August 15 and August 22, white mobs burned and demolished Black houses, and up to 1,500 Black residents were driven outside the city limits.

In the aftermath of the 1829 riot, the city fined white mob leaders, and city officials released all detained African Americans, but the damage was done: hundreds of Black Cincinnati residents made a trek northward (in at least two steams of migration) to start a settlement in Ontario, Canada, which they named Wilberforce after the British abolitionist William Wilberforce.[23] Neither the city of Cincinnati nor the Ohio legislature would agree to provide any funding for the Black refugees who moved to the Wilberforce settlement. Finally, it was members of the Quaker religious group who donated money to help purchase land for the settlement, but this unwillingness on the part of the city or state to provide financial help to the persecuted Blacks of Cincinnati left a lengthy legacy of strained race relations in the Queen City.

A similar fate awaited African Americans in the city of Portsmouth, located about 100 miles up the Ohio River from Cincinnati. The city was a port town with strong connections to Virginia and Kentucky, and a sizable population of African Americans grew there in the decades after statehood.[24] Gradually white intolerance toward the Black residents of Portsmouth began to increase, and likely the 1829 Cincinnati rioting influenced the sequence of events that emerged in Portsmouth. In its January 21, 1831, edition, the *Portsmouth Courier* published the following announcement regarding the status of persons of color in the city:

> The citizens of Portsmouth are adopting measures to free the town of its colored population. We saw a paper, yesterday, with between one and two hundred names, including most of the house-holders, in which they pledged themselves not to employ any of them who have not complied with the law. The authorities have requested us to give notice that they will hereafter enforce the law indiscriminately.[25]

Interestingly, the 1831 expulsion of 80 to 100 Black residents of Portsmouth by white authorities was not the first forced removal of African Americans in the history of the area. At a meeting on March 2, 1818, the trustees of Wayne Township (then the location of the city of Portsmouth) authorized a special payment to the township's constable. The treasurer was ordered to pay the constable "$4.18 for the fees in warning out blacks and mulatto persons of the township."[26] Of course, so long as there were employers willing to hire Black laborers, efforts to expel Blacks often turned out to be temporary in their effectiveness.

Advocates of repealing the Black Laws made repeated efforts to get the Ohio legislature to take up the issue. Unfortunately, there remained stiff resistance among Ohio voters and politicians to get rid of these legislative acts. A committee report to the 1832 Ohio legislature held that Blacks "form a distinct and degraded caste and are forever excluded by the fiat of society and the laws of the land from all hopes of equality in social intercourse and political privileges." The legislators concluded that the presence of Blacks in Ohio led to the "demoralization" of whites who interacted with them, and that African Americans would, by definition, be "imposing on the community the burden of an idle population [and] fill our jails with criminals."[27]

Even when Blacks owned property, they faced persecution and intimidation. On June 10, 1846, a group of 383 formerly enslaved persons departed from a plantation in Virginia for Mercer County, Ohio, a region in the western part of the state that borders Indiana. They had once been owned by John Randolph, who stated in his will that they should be emancipated; moreover, he provided funds to purchase for these people land in the state of Ohio. Randolph intended that these people have a fresh start as free persons of color in a state where slavery had been outlawed. He decreed that each of his former slaves should receive a parcel of at least ten acres of land.[28]

The newly freed people traveled from the western part of Virginia to western Ohio, and made much of the journey on foot. The group faced harassment at various places on their trek, including a confrontation when they stopped for water at the city of Piqua. The new arrivals were met by German settlers when they arrived in in Mercer County in 1846. The white residents of the community, as a form of protest against the migration and settlement in Mercer County of formerly enslaved persons, passed the following resolutions:

> *Resolved,* That we will not live among Negroes, as we have settled here first, we have fully determined that we will resist the settlement of blacks and mulattoes in this county to the full extent of our means, the bayonet not excepted.

> *Resolved,* That the blacks of this county be, and they are hereby respectfully requested to leave the county on or before the first day of March, 1847; and in the case of their neglect or refusal to comply with this request, we pledge ourselves to remove them, peacefully if we can, forcibly if we must.
>
> *Resolved,* That we who are here assembled, pledge ourselves not to employ or trade with any black or mulatto person, in any manner whatever, or permit them to have any grinding done at our mills, after the first day of January next.[29]

The armed white mob forced the Randolph freedpersons to leave Mercer County and travel south to Piqua, where they took up residence on a farm owned by a sympathetic white resident. Some members of the group relocated in the general region between Troy, Piqua, and Cincinnati. Others were taken in by individual farmers of both races, trading their labor for food and shelter. A few appear to have joined a community administered by Augustus Wattles in Mercer County that was initially set up to provide vocational education to Black children. Others joined a small community of Black settlers known as Carthagena.[30]

Local reactions to the expulsion (both for and against) soon appeared in newspapers. The editor of the *St. Mary's Sentinel* offered his approval, claiming that the well-being of the white farmers would be destroyed by the would-be Black settlers "as thoroughly as the settling of a cloud of locusts upon the fair lands of Egypt . . . No more blacks will be permitted to settle among our people."[31] However, the *Sydney Aurora* denounced the evictions, arguing that "what makes the thing worse is the fact that a number of those who were fiercest in their opposition to the blacks, loudest in their threats to shoot . . . were the very men who sold them land, received wages for constructing the buildings, and actually pocketed a large amount of money for provisions."[32]

White residents denied the group the right to settle in Mercer County, and the land that was purchased on their behalf was essentially stolen from them. The last attempt to collect damages for the stolen land occurred in 1907, but ultimately the US Supreme Court ruled that the statute of limitations had expired, so the descendants of the Randolph Freedpeople were unable to receive compensation for the thousands of acres denied the formerly enslaved people.[33] Not only did white supremacy rear its head in Mercer County in 1846; it did so while pocketing tens of thousands of dollars in funds reserved for ex-slaves.

Ohio legislators sought to strengthen the Black Laws after a series of court cases that called into question their constitutionality. The intent and effect of the 1839 legislation was to exclude Black Ohioans from citizenship as well as basic civil rights enjoyed by white Ohioans. The General Assembly argued that it was "unwise, impolitic, and inexpedient, to repeal any law now in force, imposing disabilities upon black and mulatto persons, thus placing them upon an equality with the whites." Moreover, the act claimed that repealing the Black Laws "indirectly inviting the black population of other States to emigrate to this State, to the manifest injury of the public interest."[34] Thus the Black Laws served two purposes: to restrict the activities of the Black population of Ohio and to discourage Blacks in other states from moving to the state.

The 1848 election afforded Black Ohioans a brief opportunity to push for legislative change, especially with regard to the onerous Black Laws. In particular, a group known as the State Convention of Colored Men was influential in pressuring the state legislature to repeal the Black Laws. The measures to bring about repeal also benefited from backroom deals made between the new Free Soil Party and the Democratic Party regarding the election of Samuel Chase as a new member of the US Senate. However, provision related to Black suffrage, Black service on juries, and the refusal of the state to allow Blacks to receive poor relief remained on the books.[35]

The convention delegates who met in 1850 and 1851 to revise the Ohio state constitution had an opportunity to put into place the forward thinking of Ohio abolitionists and others concerned with legal equality. However, while the new constitution addressed some structural issues in state government and shifted some authority away from the legislature, the document avoided any sweeping changes, and it supported the status quo in many ways. This was especially the case with regard to conditions for Black Ohioans. As convention delegate James Loudon of Brown County argued, "Ohio was a state for white men. The negroes were intruders amongst us."[36]

One of the main issues that concerned Black Ohioans going into the convention was that of suffrage. Since the close balloting related to the issue in the 1803 constitutional convention, African Americans in Ohio had been deprived of the vote for nearly half a century. Delegates briefly debated Black suffrage, but the motion to allow Black Ohioans the right to vote was soundly defeated by a vote of 75 to 13. A similar measure to allow women the right to vote was defeated 72 to 7.[37] In some ways this document was quite backward-looking at a time when Ohio was emerging on the national stage as an economic and political powerhouse.

The repeal of the 1804 and 1807 Black Laws by legislators, however, did not end legal discrimination against African Americans in Ohio. In fact, restrictive racial legislation continued to be introduced (and frequently passed) by Ohio legislators. One example of this can be found in an 1859 law that codified emerging practices regarding biracial Ohioans seeking the suffrage rights held by whites.

The Ohio legislature passed a measure in April 1859 that denied those persons of color who were "less than one-half Negro blood" the right to vote. Previous court rulings in the 1830s and 1840s had allowed some biracial Ohioans to vote in elections, and these court rulings left it to individual judges to determine whether a person was "less than one-half Negro blood." The act took the measure out of the hands of individual judges, mandating that any person with a "distinct and visible admixture of African blood" be barred from the right to vote by local judges.[38] Local election officials in Ohio used the new law, and in one notable case tried to thwart a man who was seven-eighths white and one-eighth Black. The Ohio Supreme Court found the admixture law unconstitutional in the case *Anderson v. Millikin*.[39] While later court cases upheld the ruling, the bill marks yet another grim chapter in Ohio's history of white supremacy.

The issue of biracial suffrage re-emerged again in Ohio during the postwar Reconstruction era, despite efforts by Republicans in the state legislature (via referendum and also legislative proposals) to introduce universal male suffrage.[40] In April 1868 the Ohio legislature passed yet another law barring any person "having a distinct and visible admixture of African blood" from voting in Ohio elections. In the case *Monroe v. Collins*, the Ohio Supreme Court unanimously ruled against this new law. The court argued that the 1868 law imposed "unreasonable burdens of proof" on prospective voters and placed harmful burdens on the "kind and amount of evidence" that voters had to produce at polling places.[41]

A highly intrusive Ohio law was passed in 1861 titled "An Act to Prevent the Amalgamation of the White and Colored Races," and this act banned interracial marriage. Ohio legislators, in response to perceived fears by many white Ohioans (even abolitionists) that runaway enslaved persons (and potentially, down the road, emancipated Blacks) would flood the state, passed this bill. The law also owed something to political wrangling between Ohio Democrats and Republicans during the Civil War. During this period the Democratic Party in the North was generally hostile to legislation regarding racial equality, whereas the Republican Party during the Civil War and Reconstruction took the lead in promoting such legislation.

The act was even more intrusive than earlier Black Laws, which affected primarily political and economic spheres in the lives of Black Ohioans (lack of suffrage, limits on court presence, registration and surety bonds). The 1861 act interfered with the most personal of relationships, and it exerted state authority in spheres previously avoided, even by white officials accustomed to exercising power over the lives of Black residents of the state. The law read as follows:

> [I]t shall be unlawful for any person of pure white blood to intermarry with or have illicit carnal intercourse with any negro, or person having a distinct and visible admixture of African blood; or for any negro or person having a distinct and visible admixture of African blood to intermarry with or have illicit carnal intercourse with any person of pure white blood; and any person offending against either of the provisions of this section shall be deemed guilty of misdemeanor, and on conviction thereof, shall be fined in any sum not exceeding one hundred dollars, or be imprisoned in the jail of the county for any period not exceeding three months, or both, at the discretion of the court.[42]

The law also set forth penalties for individuals (such as ministers or county clerks) who performed a marriage ceremony or issued a marriage license involving persons from different races; this extended the illegality even further:

> That any person who shall, knowingly, solemnize a marriage forbidden by this act, or any probate judge who shall, knowingly, issue a license for the solemnization for any marriage forbidden by this act, shall be deemed guilty of misdemeanor, and on conviction thereof, shall be fined in any sum not exceeding one hundred dollars, or be imprisoned in the jail of the county

> for any period not exceeding three months, or both, at the discretion of the court.

The wording of this statute was slightly modified in 1877, though it remained essentially unchanged. Ohio's laws against interracial marriage remained on the books until 1887. While it is unclear how often these laws were enforced, or whether some parts of the state were more likely than others to prosecute individuals for their violation of the law, it is clear that enforcement continued nearly until the law's rescission.

The *Perrysburg Journal* provided an 1890 example of prevailing white attitudes regarding interracial marriage in its coverage of the marriage of a Toledo couple. What is most striking in the article are the language choices used by the reporter. A Black man named Charles Harris, described by the *Journal* as "said to be very repulsive," married a "quiet, modest girl named Katie Albert." The reaction of the mother of the bride on receiving the news was "pitiful." The mother's efforts to find her daughter and "effect a separation" were thwarted because "the dusky chap had hid his white wife and she could not be found." Yet despite the fact that the woman was supposedly concealed, the *Journal* somehow managed to receive (or fabricate) quotes allegedly from the new couple, creating a sort of cautionary tale for those who might seek to break mainstream white social norms regarding race:

> The girl was clearly in love with the negro, repulsive, spotted and black as he is, and was told by him that she would be compelled to give up all her white associates and relatives and move exclusively in the colored society, to which she replied that she didn't care, saying "I love you and am willing to become your wife."[43]

Another example of the application of Ohio's antimiscegenation law involved the 1884 case of a Black man named Robert Bailey. The Toledo native had married a white woman named Carrie Haymier, and it appears that Bailey was charged in conjunction with court cases against Haymier for public drunkenness. Bailey's attorney argued that the Ohio law violated the Fourteenth Amendment, but the judge in the case argued that—at least theoretically—the law applied to both races. This, of course, was little solace to Bailey, who received both "a $100 fine and two months at hard labor in the Toledo workhouse."[44]

Long after interracial marriage had been decriminalized, though, individual judges and county clerks routinely denied marriage licenses to biracial couples. An example of this phenomenon occurred in 1904 in the city of Hamilton. The Butler County probate judge refused to issue a marriage license to a Black man named James Stewart, who wanted to marry a white woman named Ella Reuter. The pair eventually traveled to Cincinnati to obtain a license.[45] Interestingly, the *Cincinnati Enquirer* described the couple as a "Strange Pair" in the headline; it is unclear whether the description referred to the interracial nature of their marriage or the fact that Stewart was 80 and Reuter was 53 at the time of the marriage.

A similar fate awaited George Williams and Myrtle Scott of Cincinnati, who wanted to get married in 1912. They obtained a marriage license but "had considerable difficulty getting the ceremony performed" at the courthouse. The first attempt was with a magistrate identified as "Squire Yeatman" (likely Cincinnati attorney and justice of the peace W. Meredith Yeatman), but this official "declined to officiate, as he is opposed to unions of the white and colored races."[46] The pair eventually found a magistrate who would perform the ceremony.

The passage of a civil rights bill in Ohio in 1884 somewhat allayed fears among Black Ohioans after the US Supreme Court in 1883 overturned the landmark 1875 Civil Rights Act,[47] which provided enforcement mechanisms to address violations of the Thirteenth, Fourteenth, and Fifteenth Amendments. The 1884 Ohio Public Accommodations Act outlawed racial discrimination in "inns, public conveyances, restaurants, and places of amusement." Potential damages to the claimant and the fine for a violation were each set at $100. Those determined guilty of racial discrimination were subject to a jail sentence of up to 30 days.

Unfortunately, the law was rarely enforced. A recurrent source of displeasure voiced by African Americans in Ohio during the late nineteenth and early twentieth centuries was the unwillingness of local law enforcement to adhere to the limited protections guaranteed them under state law. In addition, the law only permitted individuals to seek redress, and if (for example) a restaurant refused service to a group of ten Black patrons, each of the ten would have to file an individual claim against the restaurant owner. Theoretically, a Black Ohioan would have to file claims against every entity that engaged in racial discrimination against that person, which would be a cumbersome process.

An example of the hardened late nineteenth-century white attitudes in Ohio against African Americans can be found in the case of Mattie Allen, a young Black woman hired in 1887 as a sales clerk at Weisman's dry goods store in Columbus. The owner specifically hired Allen to "gain for him the colored patronage," telling a reporter that Allen possessed the necessary skills to be successful. Unfortunately, Weisman rescinded his offer of employment to Allen after his white clerks "said that they would quit rather than work with a colored lady."[48]

Similarly, a group of white coal mine workers in Coshocton took a vote in 1888 and announced that they would no longer work with Black miners. Observers said the white workers "would either work the mine with whites alone, or they would run the last Negro out of town." When mine officials refused their demands, a mob of "about thirty whites caught Mr. Patterson [a black mine worker] recently and beat him unmercifully."[49] While one white leader of the mob was arrested, he was later acquitted of all charges in the violence.

Nativism and Ohio in the Nineteenth Century

Ohio similarly has had a lengthy history of intolerance toward religious minorities, especially Roman Catholics and Jews. Anti-Catholicism and anti-Semitism have historically been closely linked to nativist sentiments in the US, and Ohio was prominent in most national bigotry movements, such as the Know-Nothing Party, the American Protective Association, and the National Protective League.

Cincinnati was an ideal setting for the nativist movement to take a strong hold in the 1850s. This was a major city whose rise to prominence owed much to immigrants, especially the Germans and the Irish. Cincinnati was profoundly split over the question of slavery, and in the 1850s a considerable number of antislavery German Protestants left the Democratic Party in favor of the new Republican Party.[50] Nativists and immigrants were also divided over local issues like temperance, with immigrant groups resentful of efforts to ban or tightly regulate the sale of alcohol. On April 2, 1855, which happened to be an election day, Cincinnati erupted in waves of violence against immigrants. Anti-immigrant mobs rampaged through the Over-the-Rhine neighborhood, a German area of the city. The rioters destroyed ballot boxes in an attempt to negate the votes of immigrants. Mobs stormed into other Irish and German areas, and nativists were especially uneasy about the presence of armed German militias in Cincinnati. Officials later that summer arrested Charles Rowecroft, the British consul in Cincinnati, for alleged recruitment of German militia members for the British Army, a violation of the Neutrality Act of 1818.[51] This was a sensational trial that led to national interest in the case, and the incident stoked anti-German sentiments in the state.

Strong anti-Catholic sentiments began to emerge in Cincinnati in the 1830s. Prominent Presbyterian minister Lyman Beecher, who became the first president of Lane Theological Seminary in the city, denounced Catholics in sermons and in his writings. Shortly after his arrival in Cincinnati, Beecher authored the nativist tract *A Plea for the West.* Beecher called on the government to "to check the influx of immigrant paupers, thrown upon our shores by the governments of Europe, corrupting our morals, quadrupling our taxation, and endangering the peace of our cities, and of our nation."[52] Beecher feared the creation of a new Vatican in America, and he believed Cincinnati—with its large Irish Catholic population—was a natural choice for a papal seat. Beecher warned that "there can be no liberty in the presence of such masses of dark mind [i.e., Irish Catholic immigrants], and of such despotic power over it in a single man."[53]

An 1854 editorial in the *Canton Repository* extolled the virtues of the Know-Nothings, which the writer described as "purely a moral and patriotic institution," while lambasting immigrants and Catholics as threats to the American political system. The author argued that "the mass of our naturalized citizens are ignorant and cannot understand our institutions." Since immigrants were "unacquainted with our institutions," observed the writer, "they must not meddle in our household affairs [i.e., politics]." Moreover, noted the editorial's author, the Know-Nothings were desperately needed to counteract the "ends and designs" of the American Catholic Church, which were "no less that the destruction of our free political institutions."[54]

By 1854 Cincinnati had become an important base for the Know-Nothings, an anti-Catholic, anti-immigrant, antiradical secret society that became a major political force and was renamed the American Party in 1855. Cincinnati's first Know-Nothing lodge debuted in the spring of 1854, and by July it had met in at least seven halls in the city, each supporting a number of neighborhood factions of the nativist group.[55] Official participation in the Know-Nothing Party of Ohio increased from 50,000 members in October 1854 to 120,000 members in June 1855, with the southwest part of the state the leading region of party activity.[56] While the Know-Nothings as a party would fade into obscurity with the rise of the Republican Party and the sectional conflict that led to the Civil War, the anti-immigrant and anti-Catholic sentiments remained a near-constant for many decades.

Anti-Catholic (and, by extension, anti-immigrant) sentiments flared up again in 1869 during an attempt by Catholic leaders to obtain state funding for parochial schools. What became known as the "Cincinnati Bible War" began as a discussion about the possible merger of parochial and public schools in the Queen City. For several decades Catholic leaders in Cincinnati had protested a number of practices in the city' public schools, such as daily readings from the Protestant King James Bible, the use of Protestant prayers and hymns in the classroom, and the use of textbooks that depicted Catholics negatively. Catholic leaders in Cincinnati (and in other major cities such as New York and Philadelphia) argued that the public schools could more accurately be defined as sectarian schools with a decidedly Protestant spirit. Since Protestants controlled the curriculum (so goes the argument), the state should split tax revenues with schools operated by other faith traditions. In some ways this debate is similar to the present-day debate over school vouchers for charter schools operated by religious entities.

In 1868 student enrollment in Cincinnati schools was roughly 60 percent in public and 40 percent in parochial and private schools. Cincinnati school board president H. L. Wehmer argued that "a greater effort should be made to make the Public Schools less objectionable to the Catholics if we desire to avoid an irrepressible conflict."[57]

The initial 1869 discussions regarding a possible merger between the public and Catholic school systems was led by F. W. Rauch, a member of the board who happened to be Catholic. Both sides agreed on a nonsectarian curriculum, repealing the use of the Bible as a school text and eliminating the use of opening prayers and hymns. Catholic leaders requested two additional concessions; the first related to continuation of employment for licensed teachers in Catholic schools, and the second was a request to continue to use the schools for weekend religious education.[58]

The public learned of the preliminary agreement, and reaction to the proposals was harshly critical. Many Protestants viewed this as a Catholic conspiracy to eradicate the Bible from the public schools, "leaving the students of these godless institutions devoid of moral direction and religious instruction."[59] The debate became one centered on the defense of the Bible from a devious papacy rather than a simple merger between parochial and public school systems.

Sensing the futility in trying to continue the merger talks, Catholic leaders quickly decided to exit the preliminary agreement. However, the proposal to eliminate religious instruction in Cincinnati public schools remained on the table, and pro-Bible forces ramped up their defense of the inclusion of religious teaching in the schools. After the school board voted to remove religious instruction from the curriculum, pro-Bible supporters filed for and received a temporary injunction against the measure. However, the ban on religious instruction was ultimately upheld by the Ohio Supreme Court in 1873 in the case *Minor v. Board of Education of Cincinnati.*

Pro-Bible supporters were angered, and this perceived injustice hardened existing anti-Catholic and anti-immigrant sentiments. An example of this can be found in an 1875 letter to the editor of the *Athens Messenger* by a reader signing the name of "Veritas":

> The Popish priesthood are becoming more bold and outspoken in their designs and purposes to crush out our liberties, and to wipe out our Free School system, and set up in its stead a system of parochial schools, wherein funds of the State will be appropriated for the education of children into the Catholic religion . . . There is danger ahead for the country, and it will be well for all Protestants to be careful how they support a power that may, in the not far future, strike the glorious liberties of our Republic out of existence.[60]

The 1887 state Republican platform, of which William McKinley was a committee member, held that party officials "view with alarm the unrestricted emigration from foreign lands as dangerous to the peace and good order of the country and the integrity and character of its citizenship." Thc platform urged Congress to pass "such laws and establish such regulations as shall protect us from [those] who come among us to make war upon society to diminish the dignity and rewards of American workingmen and to degrade our labor to their level. Against all these our gates should be closed."[61] While the platform can be partly viewed as an attempt to appeal to workers, one cannot ignore the overt anti-immigrant rhetoric in the text.

Civil War Era Ohio: Free-but-Unfree

Despite the rhetoric of freedom for enslaved persons increasingly espoused by Northern politicians during the Civil War—as well as the political power wielded notable Radical Republicans from Ohio like Benjamin Wade—Ohio in the Civil War years was a state where African Americans occupied a place of inferior social, economic, and political status. There were a few notable exceptions, such as the formation of the 127th Ohio Volunteer Infantry, Ohio's first Black regiment (later renamed the 5th US Colored Troops), but even Black soldiers willing to put their lives on the line for the Union cause faced discrimination and harassment. In fact, the formation of the 5th USCT owed more to a desire by the governor of Ohio to avoid a draft than it did to any idealistic notions of racial equality.[62]

Tensions related to the war exacerbated race relations in Ohio. An 1862 letter to the editor of the *Portsmouth Times* denounced the idea of emancipating enslaved persons. This letter is an example of the hardened opinions that many Ohioans—especially from the southern part of the state, but by no means exclusively southern Ohio—regarding emancipation. The anonymous author posited that if Kentucky hypothetically ended slavery, southern Ohio would be the principal destination for freedmen:

> The people don't want them—the laboring class don't want them . . . This is the white man's government, and when we want to elevate anyone, let it be the white man and the white man's children . . . It is our business and interest to see that our state is not filled with free negroes. We have too many now. Fewer negroes and not so many abolitionists is what we need . . . Thousands of lazy, illiterate negroes roaming over the State of Ohio would be a disadvantage to both white and black.[63]

This view is in keeping with an observation made by Harriet Beecher Stowe, author of the best-selling abolitionist novel *Uncle Tom's*

Cabin. She noted that many "well-meaning people can form no idea of immediate emancipation but one full of dangers and horrors." Stowe argued that many Northern whites "imagine the blacks free from every restraint of law, roaming abroad a terror and nuisance to the land."

The editor of the *Toledo Commercial* newspaper provided a response to the sentiments of the types of people who most strongly opposed the presence of African Americans in Ohio. This editor represented the moderate (for the period) mainstream Northern white views regarding Black migrants to Ohio:

> Should the rebels succeed, even for a brief period, in effecting a separation of the Union, the necessary result would be a general stampede of the slaves from the disloyal into the loyal states. But freedom would be their only object in coming to the North. Give them that where they are, and they will certainly stay in the South, or emigrate to a still warmer climate.[64]

In short: many moderate whites in the North favored emancipation, but only because they believed emancipated persons would remain far away in the South.

Population growth in Ohio for the decade from 1860 to 1870 was quite robust, as the state's population grew by 13.9 percent in that decade. The Black population grew by over 57 percent in that decade, from 40,015 persons (1860) to 63,213 persons. However, that growth of a little more than 23,000 African Americans is but a small fraction of the 325,749 total new Ohioans in the decade. Still, many Black migrants to Ohio began their new lives in cities, where they were more visible and more likely to encounter hardened racial attitudes from whites, especially whites of lower socioeconomic status who often competed with them for laborer jobs.

The city of Toledo experienced a wave of race-related mob violence in July 1862. On the morning of July 8, white dock workers went on strike over the issue of Black stevedores being employed to load and unload ships. Especially galling to the white workers was the fact that the company began paying Black workers the same wages. Yet, prior to this period, African Americans had been employed as dock workers without significant conflict beyond typical interpersonal squabbles that might arise between individuals in any group of workers.[65]

The strikers were joined by other white protesters, and the group evolved into a violent mob. They attacked Black dock workers, who were forced onto a ship named the *New York* to seek refuge. White strikers made "free use of stones, brick-bats, and other similar missiles"[66] in their successful efforts to drive Black workers off the Toledo docks. In the initial melee on the docks, "two negroes had an arm broken and one had his head split open."[67] After several unsuccessful attempts by the police chief and a local priest to disperse the crowd, white rioters roamed the city looking for Blacks to target with violence. Numerous houses in "the back part of the city" owned by Black families were damaged by rioters, with one home completely demolished. Black pedestrians were attacked at random throughout the city of Toledo, including one Black man who was "discovered on Monroe Street, chased, and finally overtaken and beaten in a severe manner."[68] Another Black man sought refuge from a white mob in the office of a lawyer, and the angry crowd was so violent that the man had to be "conveyed to jail for safe keeping."[69]

After destroying yet another house occupied by a Black family, one white mob turned to a house occupied by a "quiet, industrious negro woman" and destroyed her residence. Even worse, the mob then attacked the home of a German family because there were two Black children hidden inside away from the violence. The rioters demanded that the Black children be released to the mob, "declaring it their purpose to kill them." Fortunately, the German family whisked the children out the back door before the rioters learned they were gone. The mob then moved back toward downtown Toledo, "and every house inhabited by colored people was more or less damaged."[70]

The *Toledo Blade,* citing a Cincinnati writer who happened to be in Toledo at the time, argued that the Toledo riot owed much to demagogues who egged on the rioters. The *Blade* reported that there were persons shouting to rioters to "clean out the niggers," that the war was "only a war of capital against white labor," and that rioters could improve wages by driving away Blacks and abolitionists. In short, argued the *Blade,* the cause of the riot was "men in our very midst ready to incite the ignorant to lawlessness and violence."[71]

However, at least one Toledo resident expressed views inconsistent with mainstream interpretations of the causes of the 1862 Toledo riots. The author of a letter to the editor of the *Napoleon North-West,* identified only as "S. E.," blamed the Toledo violence on African Americans and abolitionists. The "tide and flood of negroes poured upon Toledo" was the root cause of the violence, according to the letter's author, who claimed that the Black arrivals were "idle, indolent, and following no particular avocation but theft and plunder." The author took great exception to the way African Americans presented themselves in public, claiming that Blacks were "haughty and indolent in demeanor, strutting along the sidewalks like so many peacocks, and oftentimes obliging white men and women to leave the sidewalks and let Cuffee pass."[72]

The "tide and flood of negroes" commentary by "S. E." does not seem to be supported by demographic data. In 1860 Black Toledoans represented about 1.7 percent of the city's population, while by 1870 that share had increased to only 1.9 percent. By actual census count, the number of back Toledoans increased from 229 persons to 612 persons in a decade that saw Toledo's overall population increase more than two times, with a total growth of nearly 20,000 people.[73] Toledo's modest increase in African Americans from 1860 to 1870 can hardly be a contributory cause of racial conflict.

Another example of mob violence based on racial attitudes held by whites can be found in a series of attacks on African Americans in Cincinnati in July 1862. A decline in commerce along the Ohio River emerged during the war, and jobs in Cincinnati for manual laborers fell sharply. The economic downturn increased frustration among workers, especially those who had been employed as roustabouts and stevedores. Relations between the Irish and African Americans were particularly strained, as these two groups composed most of the dock workers in Cincinnati.[74] It is not surprising that the earliest signs of the riot could be found in a fight between several Irish and Black levee workers on July 10, 1862, over rumors that Black stevedores were willing to work for lower wages.[75]

The violence in Cincinnati was of greater duration and intensity than the Toledo riot, spanning eight days and resulting in several fatalities. White mobs temporarily managed to drive almost all the Black population out of the city of Cincinnati and into the countryside to seek safety. The mob violence against African Americans coincided with fears of a Confederate invasion of Cincinnati. Much of the Cincinnati police forces had been deployed to Lexington, Kentucky, to assist in the defense against Confederate troops moving into the region.

Ohioans fought in a civil war that became tied directly to the issue of legal equality and an end to slavery. However, at the same time, persons of color in Ohio faced widespread discrimination, cruel harassment, and even deadly violence. The high moral ground and lofty principles staked out by the Lincoln administration in the Emancipation Proclamation did not get reflected especially well in Ohio in the century after the end of the Civil War.

Ohio in the Era of Jim Crow

The term *Jim Crow law* refers to state and local legislation that enforced racial segregation, and these laws were particularly common in the South after Reconstruction. The period runs from roughly 1877 (the end of Reconstruction) until the 1960s, with the passage of the Civil Rights Act of 1964 and the Voting Rights Act of 1965. The phrase *Jim Crow* is derived from a minstrel song-and-dance routine known as "Jump Jim Crow," featuring a caricature of an African American played by a white actor in blackface. The character was typically portrayed as lazy, feckless, and less than human, and thus unworthy of political and social equality. Over time the phrase *Jim Crow* became a negative code word for "black person," and by the 1890s the term began to refer to segregation legislation.[76] The Northern state of Ohio, however, was not immune to the racial segregation and discrimination (both formal and informal) that have traditionally been associated with Southern states in the Jim Crow era.

Minstrel shows, incidentally, had wide appeal in Ohio in the nineteenth century and even well into the twentieth century. Minstrels typically featured white actors in blackface portraying standard stereotypes of Black Americans held by mainstream whites. The white actors in blackface sang songs and performed dance routines derived from Black traditions while serving to reinforce and perpetuate white supremacy through the racist caricatures. Some minstrel shows also included white characters who reflected degrading nativist stereotypes about groups such as Irish, German, Italian, or Chinese immigrants.

An example of the typical local amateur minstrel show in Ohio can be found in the city of New Philadelphia, which hosted an annual minstrel program for many years in the late nineteenth and early twentieth centuries. The show was promoted in the years before the First World War by a man named Sebastian Hare and his son George. The local Elks fraternal organization and a community musical group

FIGURE 1.3. Illustration of racist caricatures in minstrel show printed in *New Philadelphia Daily Times*, 1911

known as the Great Eastern Band joined forces to produce the minstrel show. The 1907 show featured in a skit the "Coonville Colored Band," a small ensemble in which "no two instruments played the same tune at the same time."[77] The 1911 show presented "quaint coon songs, and some that weren't so quaint." A reviewer of that show praised local singer Norman Parr's ability as a "coon shouter," referencing a parody of a Black vocal style.[78]

A review of the 1911 New Philadelphia minstrel show included an illustration that illuminates the demeaning caricatures of Blacks found in minstrelsy (see Figure 1.3). The image was titled "Just a Few Types of New Philadelphia Minstrel Boys in Big Show," and it contained six blackface cartoon characters. The first was a Black beggar, sad-faced, with hat in hand as if asking passersby for spare change. Two blackface characters perform dance routines, one a happy-go-lucky simpleton and the other a frowning oaf. Two musicians appear in the image, one seated playing a banjo and the other a buffoon playing what appear to be castanets. The last figure is an unkempt and somewhat bewildered-looking blackface soldier. All the caricatures seem servile, and all are patronizingly depicted as dim-witted and of a low position in the social hierarchy.

While such shows are considered racist and offensive by the standards of mainstream twenty-first-century American culture, many white Ohioans even during the height of the civil rights movement defended the "tradition" associated with donning blackface and strutting, singing, and dancing like the demeaning characters they believed accurately represented Black Americans.

Such was the case in the city of Port Clinton in 1964, where the local Jaycees organization encountered some resistance to their annual minstrel show. Jaycee president Ronald Chapman defended the "traditional form of art," which he believed should not be considered offensive because the "Jaycees have talked with Negro citizens and they have not objected to the show." Chapman also insisted that minstrel shows were an acceptable form of entertainment because there had "never been any trouble between Negro and white citizens in Port Clinton."[79] Chapman's rationale about the caricatures of Black Americans offers additional insight into whites who continued to support minstrel shows in the 1960s:

> Perhaps in our show we will cast a "black-faced character" as slow or as a ladies man or as a drinker. That character will tell his story or pull his jokes in the manner a real person of that particular type might do it, but the character might be characteristic of all people . . . Each race or group has people of that type within its ranks and that's just the way things are. . . . As for black face itself, again this is just a traditional form of entertainment. If a minstrel show cannot be presented of people made up in the traditional manner, then we might as well throw out the minstrel show idea entirely.[80]

Yet, clearly by the 1960s, some whites were beginning to question the racist underpinnings of minstrel shows featuring blackfaced actors. Exemplary of the shift in recognizing the demeaning stereotypes was Mattie Carpenter of Mansfield, who recounted in a 1964 editorial letter her experiences. Carpenter had been a member of the Mansfield amateur minstrel show, and at times traveled back and forth from her home to the theater while made up in blackface. On several occasions she encountered a young boy who yelled racial epithets at her, thinking she was a Black resident of the town. She complained to the child's mother, who shrugged off the incident, arguing that her children "learn about Black Sambo in school." Carpenter had an awakening of sorts: "Later on it burned me up to see this very boy in the minstrel show with his face black." Based on her experiences as a recipient of racial slurs and understanding the inherent racism involved in blackface minstrel shows, Carpenter argued that she no longer supported minstrels.[81]

Ohio had a complicated history during Reconstruction and the Jim Crow era. As a Northern state and a center of considerable abolitionist activity, Ohio played important roles in the development of groundbreaking legislative and constitutional changes. For example, Representative James Mitchell Ashley, of Ohio's 5th congressional district, introduced the first bill that led to the formation of the proposal for the Thirteenth Amendment, which abolished slavery and involuntary servitude. Yet Ohioans were deeply divided over passage of the Fifteenth Amendment, which prevents state and federal governments from denying a citizen the right to vote based on that citizen's race, color, or "previous condition of servitude." The measure passed in the Ohio state senate by only one vote and in the state house by only two votes.

Interestingly, despite the vote to accept the Fifteenth Amendment, there remained a clause in the Ohio state constitution limiting voting rights to "white male citizens of the United States." This was a holdover from the 1802 constitution that was not removed in the 1851 constitution. Voters had an opportunity to strike this phrase from the 1912 constitution, but the effort to eliminate the phrase "white male" was defeated, and it was not until 1923 (with the successful women's suffrage movement) that the phrase "white male" was struck from the state's constitution. Yet, even in 1923, over 420,000 Ohioans voted to retain the phrase "white male," slightly less than 45 percent of the voters who cast a ballot on that proposal.[82]

African Americans in Ohio faced a number of legal barriers to equality in the late nineteenth and early twentieth centuries. Chief among these were the segregation of public schools, unfair treatment in obtaining employment, and segregation in public accommodations. In addition, Blacks in Ohio continued to face occasional harassment and even mob violence in the state, underscoring the notion that they were "free but unfree."

While not quite exhibiting the levels of racial violence that emerged in the South in the Jim Crow era, Ohio nonetheless did not escape the phenomenon of racial attacks on Black Ohioans, up to and including lynching. Of course, like any extralegal activity, lynchings are difficult for historians to document, since the perpetrators of this type of mob violence could ostensibly be charged with murder (though admittedly in Jim Crow–era American history, lynchings were notoriously underprosecuted).

One study documented 25 incidents involving white mobs seeking to lynch Blacks. Twelve of these incidents resulted in the killing of a Black Ohioan who—for a variety of reasons—managed to become the target of mob violence.[83] The peak year for lynchings in Ohio appears to have been 1894, which featured six documented instances of racially oriented mob violence; four of these cases resulted in the deaths of African Americans, and two of these mobs were so dangerous that Governor William McKinley needed to order the Ohio Militia to quell the violence.[84] At any rate, the issue of lynchings in Ohio was significant enough for the state legislature to pass a stringent antilynching law in 1896.

Another researcher studying lynchings in the Midwest contextualized Ohio's history of violence by white mobs. The author noted that the five Black lynching victims in Ohio during the 1890s might seem relatively small in number compared with the 27 recorded in Virginia in the same decade. However, given that Ohio's Black population in 1890 was less than one-seventh that of Virginia, "Ohio's rate of 5.7 victims per 100,000 of the population at risk [of lynching] exceeded Virginia's at 4.2."[85]

One of the most notorious large-scale riots led by an angry white mob erupted in the city of Akron in August 1900. The crowd had gathered around the city's municipal buildings demanding that police hand over a Black man named Louis Peck, who was being held on the charge of sexual assault of a small child. Peck, who had "a bad record in the East," had allegedly confessed to the crime, which occurred after a period where "he had been drinking heavily for a month."[86]

Interestingly, the confession offered up by Peck was of questionable value, as it was made to the "Prisonkeeper Washer" immediately after Peck's arrest. The rush to justice was certainly not unusual for the period, especially for a Black man accused of committing sexual assault against a young white girl, but the case was so poorly prosecuted that the governor of Ohio pardoned Peck in 1916. The governor's office argued that there was "grave doubt as to Peck's guilt," citing information provided by a former warden and other state justice administrators.[87] Among the problems with the case was that Peck was entirely without legal representation, as no attorney contacted would take his case.

The description of Peck in the *Akron Daily Democrat* is worth reviewing. The details about Peck are overshadowed by the overt racism in the description; the writer was seemingly unconcerned with what by today's standards would be highly objectionable racial stereotypes and presumptions:

> The negro is aged 30 years. His height is medium, and he is of stocky build. He has a sullen expression in his face, and his eyes

> are downcast. He wears a heavy moustache. His cheek bones are prominent, and his lips are of the full, negro type. In all, he is a man with few commendable traits in his appearance. He is a man who would ordinarily impress one as being a suspicious character.[88]

Likely influenced by sensational and inflammatory media coverage like that of the *Akron Daily Democrat,* a mob of 1,500 surrounded municipal buildings in Akron, demanding the release of Peck so that he could be hanged. Peck had already been moved to a jail in Cleveland, as authorities feared that "trouble of some sort would arise." The mob would not be pacified, and they gained entry to both the city jail and the county jail, located two blocks away.[89] They gained access to firearms after looting a local hardware store, where "guns and a large quantity of ammunition were secured" by the rioters.[90] The store owner estimated that 30 revolvers, 125 rifles, and 2,500 rounds of ammunition were seized by the rioters.

Two children were killed in crossfire between police and the white mob, and 20 people were reported injured from gunfire, thrown projectiles, and stampeding. Several municipal buildings were destroyed in fires deliberately set by the mob, and several private residences were also targeted, including that of the Akron police chief. Police officers managed to protect the chief's home and avoided major damage.[91]

Interestingly, the *Akron Daily Democrat* published an artist's sketch of Louis Peck on the front page of the paper the day after the riot (see Figure 1.4). The image does not seem to be especially biased, and it even depicts Peck in a jacket, tie, and hat. However, the caption under the image is highly biased: "NEGRO PECK, THE CAUSE OF ALL THE TROUBLE." In the eyes of the *Akron Daily Democrat,* the reason for the orgy of violence, looting, and arson in Akron was not the 1,500 white rioters but one Black man accused of a crime.

The city of Springfield experienced a pair of riots in 1904 and 1906 that spilled over from racial violence by white mobs against Black targets. The first riot began with a Black man accused of killing a white police officer. After Springfield police arrested the suspect, a white mob of perhaps 1,500 participants formed and proceeded to attack the jail. The prisoner was seized, dragged out of his cell, and hanged. The raging mob then moved to a part of Springfield known as the Levee, a heavily Black neighborhood located along the Mad

FIGURE 1.4. Illustration of Lewis Peck by *Akron Daily Democrat,* 1900

River. The mob torched numerous businesses and residences, wreaking significant damage in the Levee district.[92] Two years later, a white mob attacked the Levee in another wave of racial violence. Unlike the earlier riot, though, the mob seemed to lack a motive other than to attack African Americans, their homes, and their businesses. One observer noted that the white mob in 1906 "attacked the homes and businesses of African Americans who had no conceivable connection with vice or crime, such as an elderly minister and a funeral home."[93]

Ohio and the Ku Klux Klan

The history of the Ku Klux Klan is typically divided by scholars into three distinct phases, each with unique characteristics and areas of focus. The first phase of the Klan is associated with the political violence that took place in the South in response to Reconstruction, running from roughly 1865 to 1874. The Klan's second phase generally dates from 1915 to the end of the Second World War, while the third phase of the Klan emerges during the height of the American civil rights movement in the 1950s and 1960s through the present day.[94]

The first wave of the Ku Klux Klan was a terror-based vigilante organization that emerged in the South in the years after the Civil War. These were loosely connected bands of insurgents who used political violence to oppose what they viewed as Northern intrusion on Southern political rights. This first wave of the Klan particularly despised the postwar Reconstruction legislation that attempted to safeguard the newly guaranteed civil rights of recently freed Black slaves. This phase of the Ku Klux Klan did not emerge in Ohio after the Civil War, as it was primarily a phenomenon in former Confederate states and several of the wartime border states in which slavery had been abolished.

The origin of the name "Ku Klux Klan" to describe the political vigilantes in the postwar South is somewhat unclear. The founders of the first wave of the Klan combined the Greek word *kuklos* ("circle") with *Klan* to create the group's name. Numerous group rituals share similarities with Kuklos Adelphon, a Southern college fraternity operating in the decades before the Civil War. The fraternity faded in popularity by the 1850s, and by the 1870s Kuklos Adelphon no longer operated.[95]

This first wave of Klan activity directed its violence at politically active African Americans and white Republicans who desired to redesign the South after the Civil War. Although the government abolished the official organization of the first Klan in the 1870s (most notably by federal anti-Klan legislation in 1872), lynchings and other political violence by individuals who shared the philosophies of the Klan continued through the end of the century. During the last third of the nineteenth century, several thousand people were executed by members of the Klan or the group's sympathizers.

The Ku Klux Klan re-emerged in the early twentieth century in much of the US, including hundreds of thousands of Ohio KKK members. This rebirth owed much to sympathetic portrayals of the Klan in books, films, and other media. Of particular importance in the re-emergence of the Klan was *Birth of a Nation,* the 1915 film by D. W. Griffiths. The film was based on a 1905 novel by Thomas F. Dixon Jr. titled *The Clansman: An Historical Romance of the Ku Klux Klan.* In the film Griffiths portrayed African Americans as lazy, drunken, and immoral imbeciles. Conversely, the film depicted the Klan as gallant defenders of tradition and order in the postwar South.

Birth of a Nation helped mold a new reputation of the Ku Klux Klan as an upholder of principles and virtue, despite the historical reality of the group's use of violence and terror to push its political and social agendas. Many millions of Americans watched the film when it was released, spreading wide this thinly veiled pro-Klan propaganda. It was during this second phase of the Ku Klux Klan that Ohioans joined this white supremacist group in large numbers.

The creation of the second phase of the KKK was largely the work of the Atlanta-based huckster William Joseph Simmons, who stumbled through a variety of careers before attaining a degree of financial success as a recruiter for fraternal organizations like the Woodsmen of the World. Simmons was inspired by the portrayal of the Klan in *Birth of a Nation,* and he also found useful as a recruiting tool the 1915 mob lynching of Leo Frank. The killers of Frank, who included notable political figures, abducted him from a jail in Marietta and drove for hours along Georgia's back roads before lynching him.[96]

The original Klan unit that Simmons created included several members of the Leo Frank lynch mob, as well as two older men who claimed to be members of the first Ku Klux Klan. As part of their incorporation rituals, and to generate buzz for the new Klan, the group climbed Stone Mountain and set fire to a giant wooden cross that could be seen from a distance of several miles. This was the first use of the burning cross by a Klan group, as the earlier incarnation of the Klan did not burn crosses.

By 1920 the group that Simmons formed numbered only a few thousand members. Under the direction of Simmons, the group remained limited to the areas around Atlanta. Simmons then had the wisdom to hire two public relations specialists, Elizabeth Tyler and Edward Young Clarke, to promote the group and increase its membership. The pair's Southern Publicity Association led to rapid growth for the Klan, and membership skyrocketed.

FIGURE 1.5. Ku Klux Klan Ladies' Auxiliary Centennial Float in Akron, 1925. Akron-Summit County Public Library; General Photograph Collection, Centennial Parade—KKK LC_Centennial_34.

This rebirth of the Ku Klux Klan was as much a corporate success as it was a social, cultural, and political phenomenon. The Klan adopted an incentivized business model in which recruiters—local Klan contractors known as Kleagles—received a sizable portion of the initiation fees of new members in exchange for their recruitment efforts. From the initial ten-dollar membership fee, four dollars went to the recruiting Kleagle; one dollar went to the King Kleagle (regional recruitment leader); 50 cents went to the Grand Goblin (state recruitment leader); and the remaining $4.50 was remitted to the national office in Atlanta.[97] This revived Ku Klux Klan was essentially a multilevel marketing arrangement under the veneer of a hate group.

At the group's membership apex in the mid-1920s, as many as five million American men joined the Klan, and it became politically influential in many states. In Ohio, one of the Klan's strongholds, membership likely peaked in 1925 at over 300,000 Klansmen; some estimates suggest that as many as 400,000 Ohioans joined the Klan at its peak.[98] This figure does not include women's auxiliary Klan units (see Figure 1.5) nor Junior Klan organizations, and their inclusion could drive the total number of Klan-affiliated Ohioans well into the half-million range. One estimate by a leader of the women's auxiliary Klan claimed that over 100,000 women were members of the units around the state of Ohio.[99]

Attacks by Klan adversaries temporarily helped raise the popularity of the group. The period of highest membership growth appeared after a 1921 *New York World* exposé on Klan activities that led to a 1922 Congressional investigation. These events enhanced the appeal of the group as a patriotic means for mainstream white Americans to voice their political views.[100] This second phase of the Ku Klux Klan was broader in its outreach to tradition-inclined white American Protestants: the group expanded its targets to include Catholics, Jews, immigrants, and sometimes even labor and political activists. The re-emergent Klan also exhibited an ability to adjust to local conditions and tailor its appeal to local and regional concerns.

Understanding the views of members of the second phase of the Ku Klux Klan requires twenty-first-century readers to set aside present-day morality and to understand what was "normal" by the standards of the 1920s, at least "normal" for mainstream white Protestants. The Klan tapped into existing views held by mainstream white Protestants that follow these general notions:

- A racial hierarchy existed in which whites of Anglo-Saxon heritage were at the top;
- "Lesser" races needed to be controlled, taught, and supervised by whites;
- A Roman Catholic conspiracy existed to install the Pope as the supreme Earthy power;
- Jews dominated important industries such as banking and entertainment, and these powerful Jews sought to debase otherwise morally impeccable whites;
- America of the 1920s was in a state of moral, political, and social crisis;
- There were imminent threats to the American political system.

Some scholars attempt to minimize the importance of white supremacist ideology in Klan recruitment efforts during this period. Nonetheless, Klan recruitment materials are quite explicit in their promotion of white supremacy. For example, consider the case of *America for Americans,* a Klan pamphlet widely distributed in Ohio in the mid-1920s. The document's author argued that "the distinction between the races" was "decreed by the Creator," and that Klan members should swear to "be true in the maintenance of White

Supremacy."[101] It is misleading to suggest that Klan members of the 1920s did not understand that they were joining a white supremacist group.

The second phase of the Klan differed from its earlier forms in other ways. In addition to its new emphasis on nativism, the Klan also stressed its self-proclaimed role as a judge of public morality. One of the most important moral questions used by the Klan in the 1920s was that of Prohibition. Many Klan chapters tried to achieve public acceptance through legal, illegal, and extralegal efforts to assist law enforcement officials in reducing the underground alcoholic beverage market.

The revived-version Klan also featured a fraternal component. It was a group with complex structures, intricate symbolism, and secret rituals. Some new inductees to the Klan were likely lured by promises of financial, social, and political benefits that came with joining an organization that had millions of members. This was an era prior to public "safety nets" such as Social Security and unemployment compensation; many American men joined fraternal groups to protect their families in case of their accidental death or injury.

Public schools were a major area of emphasis for the second Ku Klux Klan, especially their use in furthering the organization's political agenda. Partly this was to support what Klan leaders viewed as critical American values, but it also served as a means to undermine Catholic parochial schools. In general the Klan possessed an obsessive animosity toward Catholicism; the group viewed Catholic schools as indoctrination centers for a supposed revolution that would establish a new Vatican in the US. Many Klan members also bought in to conspiracy theories that Catholic churches maintained stores of weapons for this revolutionary purpose, and that the Knights of Columbus secretly trained Catholic militias in preparation for a coming war with Protestants.[102]

The second phase of the Ku Klux Klan did not emerge without philosophical precursors. Racism, anti-Semitism, nativism, and anti-Catholicism each possess extensive lineages in American history. The resurgent Klan merely provided an opportune mode for white Americans (in particular white, Anglo-Saxon, Protestant males) to express these views.

The second wave of the Klan declined for a number of reasons. A sensational rape-murder trial in 1925 of a Klan official resulted in negative publicity for the group, and simultaneously other Klan officials were accused of mishandling or embezzling Klan funds. The group's decline in the late 1920s and early 1930s also reflects the instability associated with the Great Depression, as economic issues became greater priorities to most Americans than the moral crusade the Klan attempted to lead. In 1944 the Internal Revenue Service filed a lien for $685,000 in back taxes against the Klan, and the national organization literally went bankrupt.

The third wave of the Ku Klux Klan is associated with the emergence of the modern civil rights movement in the 1950s and 1960s. This era is noted for fragmentation, as dozens of small, localized groups adopted the name Ku Klux Klan in a period of reactionary political violence. There have been several attempts to unify the Klan under a national banner (most notably the David Duke period in the 1980s) but twenty-first-century Klan organizations lack the overarching unity that the Klan displayed in the 1920s. This third wave of the Klan was noted again for a greater propensity toward violence, including shootings, bombings, and lynchings. Civil rights activists were most frequently targeted for violent actions, though in recent decades Klan-directed violence has lessened. The emergence of the internet has aided Klan-oriented and other white supremacist groups, however, both providing a vehicle for marketing their message and serving to aid in recruitment. Internet use by white supremacist groups owes something to the anonymity that chat rooms and email permit, allowing information to be disseminated without the constraints typically imposed by traditional media.[103] These later phases of the Klan are covered in greater depth later in this book.

At the height of the Klan's power in the mid-1920s, all 88 counties in the state of Ohio had Klan chapters, and some counties had multiple chapters. As an example of how pervasive the group was, we might consider as a case study Wood County, a farming region in northwest Ohio. The county possessed a very small Black population, yet at its peak the Klan registered over 1,400 members in the mid-1920s.[104] To put this into perspective, the Klan managed to sign up about 15 percent of the total eligible population (white, male, native-born, Protestants who were over the age of 21). Klan activity began to get organized in early 1923, and quickly the group made inroads into Wood County.

On the night of October 4, 1923, the Ku Klux Klan flexed its organizational muscles in an event in the city of Bowling Green, a small town in the northwestern section of Ohio. The group drew between "fifteen and twenty thousand people" to a KKK recruitment event, according to a news item the next day in the Bowling Green *Daily Sentinel-Tribune.* The KKK parade, which contained several marching bands and Klansmen on horses, "stretched out over a distance of a half a mile." A fireworks display and the burning of "four huge crosses" brought the meeting to a close. The *Sentinel-Tribune* reporter estimated the center cross that Klan members burned to be over 40 feet in height, and the reporter detailed the careful methods he used to count the nearly 18,000 people who filled the Wood County Fairgrounds.[105]

The crowd at this Klan event was a gathering about two-fifths the size of the entire population of Wood County at the time. While perhaps half of those in attendance came from nearby counties, to objective estimates on the ground this was an unprecedented political event, and a spectacle never seen before (in terms of crowd size) in the county's history. But how did a fairly small Ohio farming region become such a hotbed of Klan activity in the 1920s?

Religious bigotry combined with white supremacy in the second wave of the Ku Klux Klan. As noted, millions of Americans joined the Klan during this period of national growth, and no state could equal the estimated 400,000 Klan members who joined Ohio's Klan chapters in the 1920s. Additionally, the Klan's innovative marketing and recruitment strategies ensured that millions of Ohioans would hear its messages. Klan members in the Columbus region even produced a feature-length film titled *The Toll of Justice,* which featured over 1,000 Ohio Klansmen as extras.[106]

The Klan also relied on policy to entice native-born white Protestants to join the group. The Klan in Ohio consistently focused on several key goals with regard to public schools. Klan members battled for the prominent display of the Bible and the American flag in public schools, and they concurrently tried to eliminate any influences they considered "alien" or "foreign." In particular, textbooks in public schools were scrutinized and subject to replacement based on the supposed "alien" or "un-American" ideologies that Klan members detected in them. A 1924 *Wood County Republican* editorial argued that consistent Bible-reading in public school classrooms was the perfect way to "Americanize the foreigners and enlighten the people." In addition, observed the writer of the editorial, the "enemies of true Americanism are doing everything possible to keep the Bible out of public schools."[107]

Three particular bills were introduced between the years 1923 and 1925 by Ohio legislators who were either Klansmen or Klan-endorsed. These included measures designed to force students in parochial schools to attend public schools (an overt salvo directed toward Catholics), to ban Catholics from being employed as teachers in public schools, and to make it illegal for ministers to perform a marriage ceremony between white and nonwhite persons. While all these proposals failed to be enacted by the Ohio legislature, they served as evidence of the increasing influence of the Ohio Ku Klux Klan in the political sphere.

This growing power and presence of the Klan in Ohio manifested itself on several occasions on the shores of Buckeye Lake in central Ohio. The leader of the Indiana Klan, D. C. Stevenson, owned a summer residence there, and in 1923 and 1925 two statewide Klan events were held at Buckeye Lake. About 75,000 people showed up for the 1923 event,[108] and between 75,000 and 100,000 people attended the Klan Konklave at Buckeye Lake in 1925.[109] As evidence of the importance of Ohio to the Klan, the 1925 event also doubled as a meeting of the organization's national officials.[110]

The Ku Klux Klan faded after the 1920s as a national group, and Ohio chapters dwindled to a handful of supporters here and there. However, white supremacy and religious bigotry in Ohio quickly found a new home to foster the ideologies of hate. Moreover, this new white supremacist organization was born and raised right here in the Buckeye State.

The Black Legion

Ohio had a prominent place in the history of a quasi-fascist secret society that emerged in 1924 as a faction of the Klan known as called the "Klan Guard." This group underwent several name changes, morphing from the "Black Guard" to the "Black Night Riders" before finally settling on the name "the Black Legion."[111] The group—initially based in Bellaire, Ohio—focused on vigilante nightriding actions to terrorize its perceived enemies and assert its place in American politics.

The Black Legion's printed materials offer insights into the hate-based ideology of the group; listed below are excerpts from the Black Legion's "Secrets":

> This organization was founded on Southern chivalry and is obligated to the preservation of the white race. The native-born white people of America are menaced on every side from above and below. If America is in the melting pot the white people are neither the aristocratic scum on top nor the dregs of society on the bottom which is composed of anarchists and Communists and all cults and creeds believing in social equality . . . We fight as guerrillas, using any weapon that comes to our hand, preferably the ballot. We regard as enemies of ourselves and our country all aliens, Negroes, Jews and cults and creeds believing in racial equality and owing allegiance to any foreign potentate.[112]

In many ways the Black Legion was simply a revised version of the 1920s Ku Klux Klan with an added emphasis on attacking what it considered to be radical leftist threats to traditional mainstream American values. The Black Legion's founder, a physician and former Klan leader named William Shepard, created the group after becoming frustrated with the Klan's overtly commercial nature, which seemed to emphasize growing Klan membership rather than direct action. Shepard recalled in 1936 that Klan leaders of the 1920s "weren't interested in men; they were interested in the $10 initiation fee."[113]

Shepard did not prove to be an effective organizer for the group, with only a handful of chapters scattered across the state of Ohio in its first few years. The onset of the Great Depression exposed Shepard's lack of gravitas even further, as Black Legion members became increasingly strident in their demands for a stronger organization. By 1932 day-to-day leadership was assumed by a new leader: Bert Effinger of Lima, an unemployed electrician who had been major-general in the Black Legion. Effinger appears to have used his administrative connections to get key Legion members appointed as foremen on Allen County relief works projects, generating loyalty among his officers and providing the Legion with a source of funding that could be used to trade jobs for Legion enrollment.[114]

Unlike Dr. Shepard, who possessed at least occasional elements of refinement and social grace, Effinger was gruff, coarse, and physically intimidating. Described by one observer as a "dour, humorless fanatic,"[115] Effinger set out to remake the Black Legion as a group whose very name would strike terror in the hearts of its enemies.

Effinger saw the mission of the Black Legion as serving the interests of the "good, white Protestant people," those wholesome Americans who were tormented by "Jewish moneylenders and the Catholic Pope" and "subverted by Communists and radicals 'who were going to let the niggers marry your daughter.'"[116] Effinger's vision for the group was a brawling, street-oriented paramilitary force that was more akin to the contemporaneous *Sturmabteilung* (SA) of Nazi Germany than to the comparatively tame Ku Klux Klan of the 1920s.

Effinger had a talent for developing like-minded lieutenants who were capable of recruiting new members and maintaining discipline among existing members of the Legion. In just two years Effinger's leadership was responsible for building the membership of the Black Legion to as many as 100,000.[117] The strength of the Legion was primarily in Ohio, Michigan, Indiana, and Illinois, but evidence exists that vibrant Legion units could also be found in Pennsylvania, West Virginia, and Kentucky. As indicated in a 1936 newspaper headline (see Figure 1.6), the group claimed to have millions of members, but its extreme secrecy prevents present-day researchers from achieving a definitive enumeration.

Effinger insisted on creating a group that used fear and intimidation not only for its enemies but also to keep its members in check. The initiation rituals involved were designed strike fear in new recruits.[118] Initiates swore to protect until death the group's secrecy and were required to arm themselves in order "to tear down, lay waste, despoil and kill our enemies."[119] In a typical induction ceremony near Lima in 1935, approximately three dozen new members pledged with "their hands over their hearts and their left hands on Bibles, while members held loaded pistols to initiates' heads."[120] The violent symbolism used by the Black Legion during induction ceremonies surely could not be lost on new recruits.

The Black Legion has been connected by scholars to a variety of violent crimes in the 1930s, including murder, attempted murder, assault, and arson. Some contemporary estimates suggest that as many as 50 people may have been executed by Legion hit squads,[121] though most scholars believe there were less than two dozen murder victims of the Black Legion. Most notorious of these criminal activities involved the death of a man named Charles Poole, who worked as a Works Progress Administration organizer. Poole was abducted from his home in Detroit by Black Legion members and murdered in

MANSFIELD NEWS-JOURNAL

FINAL EDITION

VOL. 52, NO. 69 — MANSFIELD, OHIO, TUESDAY, MAY 26, 1936 — PRICE THREE CENTS

'BLACK LEGION' CLAIMS 6,000,000

Grand Jurors Indict 13 in One-day Session

ROOMER CITED IN MOTHER'S DAY SLAYING

Charged With Second Degree Murder in Fatal Stabbing; 15 True Bills in All.

JURY IGNORES TWO CASES

8 Indictments Secret Pending Arrest of Accused; 28 Witnesses Quizzed.

Queen Mary, Floating Hotel DeLuxe, to Arrive in U. S. June 1

Tourist cabin stateroom

Lounge

Cocktail bar

The Queen Mary

Commodore Sir Edgar Britten

Cabin class swimming pool

Finds Old Master In Attic

SECRET ORDER AIMED TOWARD DICTATORSHIP

Prosecutor Hints Startling Developments Due in Far-Reaching Inquiry.

MORE DEATHS ARE PROBED

State-Wide Grand Jury Quiz Sought; Lima Man Revealed as High Official.

FOREST FIRE KILLS 5, RAGES ON IN JERSEY

Hundreds of Weary Men Fight to Halt Progress of Woodland Blaze.

Charles Mill Dam to Be In Operation by July 1

CITY STILL HAS WATER TROUBLE

Main Breaks Continue at Rate of 2 a Day, 'Muddy' Water Flows From Faucets.

Lucas Churches Take Up Pastor Problem Tonight

Guess There's Nothing This Guy Stops At

DEFENSE RESTS

Tub Murder Trial Nears Jury; Witness Fails Fiorenza.

FREE SUSPECTS

Police Release 4 Quizzed in Armory Burglary.

CRASH KILLS 6

Inquiry Opens in Air Mishap Mystery for 2 Days.

Lima "Chieftain" Defends Purpose Of Hooded Order

OUT OF JAIL

Bittinger, Son of Speaker, Freed on Bond.

BOARD PROBES FLIER'S DEATH

PRESIDENT HOME

23 CHILDREN DIE

WENT A BIT TOO FAR

BACK ON JOB

BEGINS AUDIT

CONFESS MURDER

TURN ABOUT

Veteran 'Flopper' Has 'Dream', Cuts City Hall Grass Before He 'Awakes'

Why He Did It Puzzles Not Only Him, but Police Officers.

QUEER MIXTURE

NOTICE TO PASTORS

FIGURE 1.6. 1936 front page of *Mansfield News Journal*

May 1936. Eleven members of the Legion were eventually convicted for their roles in Poole's murder.[122]

The investigation of the murder of Poole and subsequent court testimony in the trials of Legion members also contributed to the group's downfall. Public opinion of the Black Legion plummeted in the wake of negative national media attention associated with the trials. Members of the group whose loyalty was based on fear of reprisals were able to leave, and others left due to concerns about getting caught up in a wave of criminal prosecutions. By 1938 the group appears to have disbanded, as Effinger had moved on to form a somewhat less radical group he dubbed the "Patriotic Legion of America." Effinger produced a membership card for the Lima News in 1938, and the form indicated that new members must attest to being "a loyal, patriotic, white Gentile person of temperate habits" dedicated to the "maintenance of the white race" and "pure Christian Americanism."[123]

Unfortunately for Effinger, the group does not seem to have attracted much of a following in subsequent years. However, ideals of white supremacy hardly vanished in Ohio, and they simply reverted to less-structured forms of expression. In the next section we examine how the ideology of white supremacy affected life for Black Ohioans in less overt ways during the twentieth century. However, these covert forms of white supremacy that Black Ohioans faced ran parallel with overt racism; in no sense was this a progressive shift from overt to covert racism.[124]

Ohio and "Everyday" White Supremacy

White supremacy often took subtler forms than the highly public actions of racist groups like the Ku Klux Klan and the Black Legion. Ideologies of white superiority influenced official and unofficial policies and actions in many spheres of twentieth-century life for Ohioans. This "everyday" racism manifested itself in such phenomena as lack of access to public accommodations, racially restrictive real estate covenants, housing discrimination, and segregated public schools in Ohio (see Figure 1.7). Much of the history remains hidden in the present day, concealed behind a shared mythology of Ohio as a racial utopia somehow free from the racism of the South. As we

FIGURE 1.7. Sign on restaurant in 1938: Lancaster, Ohio. Library of Congress, Prints & Photographs Division, FSA/OWI Collection. LC-DIG-fsa-8a17588.

will see, in some ways the negative effects of the ideologies of white supremacy equaled or even surpassed those in the South.

In the sphere of public accommodations in Ohio, racial segregation continued to be a significant challenge for Black residents of the state into the 1960s and beyond. Legal equality—with the passage of the Ohio Civil Rights Act of 1959 and the US Civil Rights Act of 1964—became the law of the land, yet the persistent influence of the ideologies of white supremacy have ensured that social inequality remains a very real specter in the twenty-first century for many racial, ethnic, and religious minorities in Ohio. Andrew Freeman, executive secretary of the Columbus Urban League, summed up the situation for Black residents of the state capital in a 1960 radio interview: "Negroes wishing service in Columbus establishments serving food and drink know that there is a 50–50 chance that they will be refused service in all areas except downtown."[125]

Many Ohio businesses routinely segregated public facilities, maintaining white supremacy in the form of whites-only sections. A 1909 incident in Cincinnati exemplifies the ways in which inequality was rigidly enforced. A man named George Green, described by the *Cincinnati Enquirer* as "a colored chauffeur employed by Casper

Rowe, Vice-President of the Market National Bank," attempted to use a pair of tickets to the Walnut Street Theater. The tickets were for seats on the main floor, an area reserved for white patrons, but theater employees would not admit Green. They offered to refund the purchase price or allow him to sit in the balcony section. Ultimately Green was charged with disorderly conduct, though his employer fortunately paid his bail and he was released that night.[126]

The *Enquirer* article on the incident, however, provides some insights into the reasons why the dispute resulted in police action. The reporter noted that when Green was told he could not be seated on the main floor, he "became abusive and threatening, and several other negroes who were in the crowd seemed willing to assist him." This section of the account resembles the "Angry Black Man" stereotype that continues to be studied by social scientists in the twenty-first century;[127] the white observers' perception was that a raised voice by Green was "abusive and threatening," while other Black males nearby "seemed willing to assist him" in carrying out his supposed threats. Even more interesting is the reason that Cincinnati police decided to arrest Green: the man "continued to talk in a loud voice, frightening many of the ladies and children who were nearby."[128] George Green's "crime" appears to have not been an action or behavior on his part but the perception by whites that his "loud voice" represented a threat.

Another example of the struggles faced by Black Ohioans against "everyday" white supremacy can be found in a series of 1943 incidents at a film theater in Xenia. On numerous occasions over a span of several weeks, African Americans were denied entry to the Xenia Theater. Employees had been directed by the theater manager, James Hibbart, to refuse to sell tickets to Black patrons. To verify the claims, the county prosecutor directed the sheriff to accompany "Calvin Thomas, Xenia negro patron," to the box office. The manager acknowledged the refusal and was arrested by the sheriff.[129]

Another racially charged controversy involved the public swimming facility in Oxford. A private benefactor had donated land to the city of Oxford in 1934 for the purpose of constructing a municipal swimming pool. The donor, however, stipulated that the donation was contingent on city officials permitting only "the white or Caucasian race" to use the pool. Between 1935 and 1949 numerous Black residents attempted to use the pool but were turned away each time. It was not until the NAACP filed suit in 1949 that Oxford finally lifted its ban on Black residents using the pool.[130]

One participant at a 1957 interfaith panel on race relations in Elyria discussed the challenges faced by African Americans with segregated public places in northern Ohio. Part of the difficulty, she observed, was that African Americans "are continually in a state of confusion as to which public places will cater to us and which ones will refuse service." Most public places would serve groups of people with a mix of races, but when Blacks were alone or in groups without the presence of whites, they were much more likely to be refused service in the Cleveland area.[131]

Even celebrity status might not guarantee equal access to public accommodations in parts of Ohio during the modern civil rights era. Such was the case for Marques Haynes and the Harlem Magicians, a touring basketball team who were rivals of the Harlem Globetrotters. The Magicians played a sold-out show in New Philadelphia in 1960 but were denied service at the Hotel Reeves bar after their performance.[132]

Segregated facilities were more common in Ohio than present-day Ohioans might realize. Cincinnati's Coney Island amusement park, on the banks of the Ohio River, enforced segregated rules for park-goers. Black patrons were completely barred from the park until 1955, but a change in policy that year did not extend to mixed-race groups of people.[133] In addition, this was really only partial desegregation: Blacks could not use the Sunlite pool—still the largest recirculating swimming pool in the world—or the Moonlite Gardens area of the park. Edward L. Schott, president of Coney Island, Inc., argued that Cincinnati officials and civil right activists were trying "to put us on the stand and ask us how we do or will run the park." Schott claimed that the ban on Blacks using the pool and Gardens facilities was due to unspecified "disorder in the past," and he acknowledged that he did not like Black teenagers attending concerts at the Garden because of the "trouble potential in the teenage gathering."[134]

Schott also accused a Black council representative of participating in protests against the park's segregation policy as simply "trying to stir up trouble" at the park.[135] Even the editorial page staff of the *Cincinnati Enquirer* sided with the segregationist policy in a 1956 editorial: "it can hardly be argued that admission to an amusement park is one of the basic rights of an American citizen." The editors seemed to believe that civil disobedience was bad for both business and the city's image, arguing that "it is hoped that further controversy will be limited to rational argument in the courts" instead of "petty incidents at the Coney Island gate."[136]

Some of these "petty incidents" at Coney Island were documented by the media, especially by Black journalists. William C. Brown of the *Ohio Sentinel* attempted to photograph an admissions-booth attendant who refused to sell swimming pool tickets to a pair of young Black girls on an outing with the rest of their class on a day when the park featured sponsorship by the Catholic diocese of Cincinnati. White Catholic children purchased pool tickets without trouble, but attendants refused to sell tickets to the Black girls. As Brown prepared his camera, an undercover security officer at the park told him: "If you take pictures, I will arrest you and destroy your camera." A Cincinnati police officer told Brown and an NAACP representative that he could not permit the young girls to enter the pool area because "I feel their lives will be in danger." A Hamilton County sheriff's deputy intervened, but told the group that there was "no use in trying, they will not be admitted."[137]

Segregation at the park did not officially end until a series of protests led by the Congress of Racial Equality (CORE) and the NAACP in May 1961. Dozens of picketers were jailed for acts of civil disobedience to protest park segregation.[138] Schott and park management finally capitulated after the picketing raised public awareness, and the cause for desegregation was also enhanced after "high officials had secretly endorsed the NAACP-CORE position."[139]

Retail transactions as simple as getting a haircut could be problematic in parts of Ohio, as barbershops and salons might have unwritten policies that they would only serve white clientele. Such was the case with Gegner's Barbershop in Yellow Springs. The city is also known for Antioch College, and students from the college spent years challenging the racist policies of the owner, Lewis Gegner. By the early 1960s the controversy began to attract attention, with crowds of protesters leading a judge to limit picketers to five at a time. In March 1964 a riot occurred, and over 100 people were arrested for violating the picketing injunction (see Figure 1.8). Gegner finally gave up and sold his barbershop rather than cut the hair of a Black customer.

FIGURE 1.8. Police dispersing crowd outside Gegner's Barber Shop, 1964. Used with permission, Antiochiana, Antioch College. Photograph by Axel Bahnsen.

The families of Black military personnel from Ohio also faced discrimination in state services and accommodations, especially at the former Ohio Soldiers' and Sailors' Orphans' Home in Xenia. Despite protests from groups as diverse as the NAACP, the American Legion, and the Colored Women's Federation of Ohio, children of Black military personnel who died in the nation's wars were segregated from white children. Facility superintendent Floyd Hartpence "did not feel that any segregation existed," but when pressed for comment, the board of trustees argued that children's cottages at the Home were "kept separated because this is 'the normal way of life' for Negro children." Segregated cottages at the home did not end until 1956.[140]

Black Ohioans faced discrimination and segregation in many health care settings around the state. Of particular concern were hospitals, as Black doctors were sometimes barred from practicing at hospitals in the state, while segregated floors or wards could be found in many Ohio hospitals as late as the 1950s. Dr. Robert M. Manuel addressed these issues in a forum among Black residents of Columbus in 1950 who were debating whether it would be more effective to have a city-owned hospital or a Black-owned hospital to address this form of persistent white supremacy in access to health care. He recounted having heard on "too many occasions: 'Sorry, Doctor, we have no colored beds,'" and that he had been told this "regardless of the condition of the patient." At the same forum, Rev. H. Beecher Hicks, minister of the Mt. Olivet Baptist Church, questioned why White Cross Hospital "in its advertisements for personnel 'white only' is stipulated."[141]

Few issues related to white supremacy in Ohio were as contentious as segregation in housing. Many cities in Ohio contained neighborhoods with racially restrictive covenants, which were agreements between buyers and sellers of property not to sell, rent, or lease property to minority groups. These agreements typically identified African Americans as the prohibited racial classification, but in some parts of the US, groups such as Jews, Chinese, Japanese, or Mexicans were also identified, and some agreements simply specified any non-Caucasians. These covenants began to appear in the late nineteenth century, and they were widely found in real estate documents by the early twentieth century in the US.[142] Though a decision in the 1948 the Supreme Court case *Shelley v. Kraemer* outlawed the legal enforcement of restrictive covenants, the court's decision "did not preclude informal or extra-legal means of enforcing covenants."[143] In fact, some real estate developers continued to insert these clauses into deeds even after the *Shelley* decision based on "the belief that purchasers would be willing to pay more for lots in exclusive subdivisions which purported to be 'protected' by racial covenants."[144]

The problem of racially restrictive covenants was especially pronounced in the many suburbs of Cleveland that began to appear in the early twentieth century. These racially restrictive practices (which were enforceable under contract law until the *Shelley* decision) in the deeds or covenants of homeowners, real estate transactions, and zoning in the suburbs of Cleveland, "prohibited the entry of what was considered undesirable ethnic, minority, and lower-income groups."[145] These practices not only stifled Cleveland's population growth, as more affluent whites departed for suburbs, but also increased de facto segregation in the region. This out-migration of whites, coupled with prohibitions on home ownership for African Americans in many suburbs, resulted in Cleveland becoming one of the most segregated cities in the US.

The Community Relations Board of the city of Cleveland agreed that the municipality was "one of the most segregated communities in the nation" in a 1964 meeting regarding housing and public schools. Ellsworth H. Harpole, executive director of the board, argued that artificial barriers in the area created "a ghetto situation in housing for minority groups." Harpole blamed "the lending institutions and the board of realtors" for the de facto segregation in the Cleveland area. In addition, Harpole indicated to Cleveland city council subcommittees that fair-housing complaints in Cleveland dated back to at least 1945, and that "Negroes and Puerto Ricans" were the principal groups facing housing discrimination in the city.[146]

Despite the *Brown v. Board of Education* decision by the US Supreme Court in 1953, some Ohio school districts continued to practice segregation in the years after the landmark court case. The city of Hillsboro was an especially noteworthy example of segregation, as the school district created gerrymandered "zones" that almost perfectly reflected segregated residential patterns in the district.[147] Black children were denied admission to a nearby elementary school and forced to attend a distant "all-Negro" school. At the same time, white students whose families resided in the "Negro" district were not required to attend the Black school.[148] The school board initially denied that segregated schools existed, and then changed its approach and admitted segregation, but requested time to build additional schools to correct the problem. A lawsuit filed by the NAACP gained traction in the courts, eventually resulting in a district court ruling that Hillsboro Public Schools must desegregate its system immediately.

On a side note, one of the Black parents leading the protest of the racially segregated nature of schools in the Hillsboro system was the target of harassment by unknown persons. Several months after the NAACP lawsuit began working its way through the federal court system, a wooden cross was planted and ignited at the home of Eber Blakely. The woman told the reporters that she wished that "people who burned the cross wouldn't do it again, because my husband has a violent temper and he will shoot first and ask questions later."[149] Presumably this statement was meant to give pause to any potential future cross-burners; however, ultimately the Blakely family and the rest of the protesters prevailed in getting Hillsboro schools desegregated.

Segregated school systems were not limited to isolated small towns like Hillsboro. Many facilities in Columbus Public Schools (now Columbus City Schools) were segregated. Desegregation would not begin in earnest until after the 1977 *Penick v. Columbus Board of Education* decision. The US Supreme Court found that a school boundary system developed by the district reinforced segregation, resulting in Black students attending mostly Black schools and white students attending mostly white schools.

This gerrymandered system of maintaining segregation in Columbus Public Schools appears to have been intentional. As late as the 1950s there were numerous schools that were entirely white and those that were entirely Black. Moreover, segregation was not limited to school enrollment; as late as 1954 the Columbus school district had yet to hire a full-time high school teacher who was Black. In a contentious school board meeting in 1954, district superintendent Novice G. Fawcett indicated that employment of Black teachers by the district was "being studied" and that any decision on hiring Black high school teachers would need to be evaluated "in light of its acceptability to the community."[150] Fawcett's reluctance to hire Black teachers for fear of alienating members of "the community" does not appear to have negatively affected his professional career, though: in 1956 he was named the eighth president of The Ohio State University, a post he held until 1972.[151]

No city in Ohio has struggled more with white resistance to desegregation than Cleveland. On one level this might seem surprising given the city's large Black population, its generally progressive politics, and its close proximity to centers of abolitionism in the nineteenth century. However, the gradual relocation of affluent whites from Cleveland to its suburbs (an option largely unavailable to African Americans) meant that Cleveland was increasingly becoming a city of segregated neighborhoods.

Black movement to the Cleveland area escalated during the Second Great Migration, roughly 1940 to 1970. Black population growth in Cleveland between 1950 and 1965 nearly doubled, rising from 147,847 to 279,352, while its overall population shrank to 810,858 from its 1950 level of 914,808. In 1950 Black residents of Cleveland made up just 16.2 percent of the city's population, but by 1965 they represented 34.4 percent of the total. Moreover, virtually all African Americans in Cleveland in this period lived in the highly segregated Black East Side neighborhoods.[152] Enrollment in Cleveland's public school system increased by more than 50 percent in this period, and much of this growth occurred in Black neighborhoods.

By the late 1950s Black parents noted many issues with the quality of education their children received in Cleveland's public school system. Some of these related to classroom instruction, such as poorly trained teachers and a shortage of remedial teachers. Other concerns revolved around inferior school buildings, a lack of vocational courses, and insufficient social services. At the same time, all-white schools on the city's West Side enjoyed experienced teachers, newer buildings, and a significantly lower student-teacher ratio. However, the issue of overcrowded schools was the chief source of aggravation for Black parents.[153]

The school board attempted several measures to address massive overcrowding in Black schools, but ultimately each measure adopted in Cleveland's public schools simply reinforced existing segregation. The first major reform, the so-called relay system, carved the school day for Black elementary schools into morning and afternoon sessions. Half the Black students attended the morning session, and the other half attended in the afternoon. Black parents were understandably outraged that their children were now receiving reduced instruction at a time when there empty classrooms in white schools. Observers at the time noted that this scheme resulted in "the loss of two months of achievement for every nine months of double session classes" for Black children in Cleveland's public schools.[154]

The school board appeared to give in to the demands of African Americans in Cleveland, announcing in spring 1962 that they would bus Black students to white schools in the 1962–63 school year to reduce overcrowding in Black schools. However, what the school board actually imposed was an even more odious system of segregation: once Black students arrived at white schools, they would be completely isolated from white students in the building. Black students had to remain in their classrooms the entire day and were not allowed to use the gymnasium, see the school nurse, or attend assemblies. They were permitted one restroom break per day at a designated time; in the words of one parent, Black children in the white schools were treated "'like a containerized shipment of cattle.'"[155]

The issue of school segregation became a primary focus of a new activist group known as the United Freedom Movement (UFM), a coalition of civil rights organizations formed to coordinate civil rights activity in the Cleveland area. The UFM believed it could no longer trust that the school board was negotiating in good faith; one UFM leader noted that "we have bent over backwards to accommodate the Board, but now we apparently have to take stronger action."[156] The group organized picketing campaigns, sit-ins, and even a one-day mass boycott of schools by Black students. The united front for desegregated schools in Cleveland began to nudge the board closer to greater integration, but these changes also brought to the surface the underlying ideologies of white supremacy.

There were numerous counterprotests by white parents, and the number of attacks on Black picketers sharply rose. However, most notorious in this era was a protest-turned-riot in Cleveland's Little Italy, where a mob of angry whites estimated at 1,400 people attacked a handful of Black protesters near Memorial Elementary School. Using "bricks, guns, knives, and clubs," members of the mob beat Black protesters and reporters, smashed vehicles, and far outnumbered the small detachment of police assigned to crowd control.[157]

The school board once again tried to appease white parents, developing a "solution" that involved the construction of three new elementary schools in Black neighborhoods. The UFM attempted to block this plan, filing lawsuits and staging additional public protests, but desegregation became mired in legal actions. A breakthrough did not emerge until the 1976 decision in the *Reed v. Rhodes* case in federal court, and an integration plan for Cleveland's public schools did not begin until the 1978–79 school year.

"Everyday" racism thus existed in many facets of the lives of Black Ohioans, permeating spheres such as public accommodations, housing, and education. Yet the evolution of the ideology of white supremacy into these more covert forms did not mean an end to overt racism in Ohio. In the next sections we will see that overt white supremacy was alive, well, and growing in the decades after the Second World War.

Civil Rights–Era Ohio and the Re-emergence of the Klan in Ohio

The emergence of the modern civil rights movement in the 1940s—particularly after the Second World War—coincided with a significant growth in organized white supremacist groups in the US. This trend was not isolated to violent Klan groups in the Southern states, and Ohio in particular proved to be an important center of white supremacist organizations. In particular, major cities in Ohio experienced considerable growth in white supremacist activity by the beginning of the 1960s.

As the 1940s began, the Ku Klux Klan attempted to shift the tone of its messages to fit the changes brought about by the arrival of the Second World War. The group identified Nazism and fascism as "Anti-American 'Isms'" that were "new names for the old world schemes to destroy Liberty-Freedom-Individualism." The Klan, according to a surviving propaganda flyer saved by an officer of Ohio's Wood County chapter, wanted to lead the US "back to the Constitution and the Republic it Guarantees."[158] Yet, in Northern states in particular, some Klan chapters had been making alliances with American fascist sympathizers in the 1930s, as illustrated by a high-profile open-air meeting between the Klan and the German-American Bund that drew over 700 participants in New Jersey in 1940.[159]

Unfortunately for the national Klan organization, the group faced investigations by state and federal authorities. These inquiries were sparked in part by the efforts of a Georgia man, Stetson Kennedy, who infiltrated the Klan after assuming the name of a deceased uncle who was once a member. Kennedy at one point retrieved evidence from the trash can of the national Grand Dragon, which provided information later used by the Internal Revenue Service to push for the collection of $685,000 in back taxes from the national Klan organization.[160]

The leadership of the National Knights of the Ku Klux Klan organization decided in an April 1944 meeting "to suspend the constitutional laws of the Knights of the Ku Klux Klan, Inc., to revoke all charter Klans and to order disbandment of all provisional Klans."[161] The national Grand Dragon, Samuel Smith, publicly asserted that the group was defunct. However, the state of Georgia soon began an investigation of the group's activities in the aftermath of the Second World War.

Undercover investigations of the Klan, directed by Georgia's attorney general, revealed a "tireless Klan campaign to organize police officers, cab and truck drivers so that the organization could seize control of government agencies" related to public security.[162] Georgia officials argued that the Association of Georgia Klans was simply a front for the continued operation of the National Knights of the Ku Klux Klan, and the state also argued that the Georgia Klan operated as a for-profit entity that continued to receive revenues from initiation fees and monthly dues remitted by chapters across the country. The state of Georgia ultimately revoked the Klan's charter, ending the legal basis for the group to function as a corporate entity. Of course, individual Klan chapters continued their activities on a regional and local level, and the efforts to "de-hood" the Klan as a national entity simply resulted in fragmented affiliations of competing Klan groups. In one sense, the destruction of the national Klan may have led to an increase in violence perpetrated by individual Klan chapters, since the lack of a national structure meant the elimination of an overarching authority that might put pressure on local chapters that engaged in particularly egregious actions. It is also more than coincidental that the demise of the national Klan is associated with the emergence of neo-Nazi groups like the Columbians, whose sales pitch to prospective members was alarmingly direct: "Number one: Do you hate niggers? Number two: Do you hate Jews? Number three: Have you got three dollars?"[163]

Ohio mirrored this national pattern of the fragmentation of white supremacist groups in the decades after the Second World War. In addition to remnant and then resurgent Klan organizations, there emerged numerous formal organizations promoting racist, fascist, or neo-Nazi ideologies. There were also informal, less-structured groups opposed to ending segregation in Ohio (especially in public schools and public accommodations) that emerged in the civil rights era.

A Black family in Athens was the target of a Klan cross-burning in 1949. A mother was home alone with her children when a carload of men "set fire to the cross and then screamed and yelled and ordered us to leave the neighborhood."[164] For their "safety," county sheriff George Bateman moved the family to a relative's house in Belpre, Ohio.[165] Some local reporting blamed "rowdies" for the terror incident, but watchdog groups like the Anti-Nazi League believed the incident was evidence that "the Ku Klux Klan is becoming increasingly active in Ohio." James H. Sheldon, chairman of the League, told reporters that his operatives had infiltrated the Klan, and they noted the presence of cars with Ohio license plates at major national meetings. Sheldon reported that Klan leaders were eyeing "Akron, Springfield, and Cleveland, and several cities along the banks of the Ohio River" for recruitment drives. Sheldon identified Robert Sheakley of Akron as the leader of the Klan in Ohio, while a man named Adam Lerch was the "top man for the Klan in Cleveland."[166]

Another example of activity by organized white supremacists can be found in 1956 in Columbus, as a group of whites coordinated their efforts to oppose a Black family who moved into an all-white neighborhood. Chanting "get out" to Mrs. George Lawson, who lived with her husband and small children in the home, the crowd of 100 people burned a cross on her lawn.[167] Lawson's husband was out of town, so the frightened mother of two young girls huddled inside until the angry mob dispersed.

The Lawsons had previously been offered $4,000 above the market value of the home to entice them to move out of the neighborhood, but they refused to leave their new house.[168] Mrs. Lawson indicated that the couple had hoped to "break down the barriers so that colored people could get a decent place to live," but in light of the events, she was not sure they continued to have the necessary courage to remain in the neighborhood. Adding insult, a threatening note scrawled on the family's newspaper the next morning read "You wouldn't take the profit. Now we're going to burn you out!"[169]

Cross-burnings in the 1950s and 1960s were all too common in Ohio, and some perpetrators sought out high-profile individuals to target with the hate messages associated with a fiery cross. Such was the case with Dayton resident David D. Albritton, Republican candidate for the Ohio House in 1960. On the night of May 2, 1960, Albritton's neighbor telephoned him to tell him of the burning cross, which was a little less than four feet in height and doused with gasoline.[170]

Incidentally, Albritton's life story was something that otherwise bordered on the heroic, even epic. He grew up the child of Alabama sharecroppers before the family moved to Ohio to seek a better life. He attended East Technical High School in Cleveland, and then he became a standout track star for The Ohio State University. Albritton was the recipient of a silver medal in the 1936 Berlin Olympics in the high jump and, along with Jesse Owens and other Black American athletes, was snubbed by Adolf Hitler in the medals ceremonies. Hitler refused to shake the hands of the Black American medal winners. Albritton later taught high school, opened an insurance business, and served six terms in the Ohio state legislature. Yet a small-minded bigot was threatened by this successful Black man, and chose to channel his racist rage into a failed act of domestic terrorism. "Failed," that is, because Albritton won that first election to the Ohio House in November 1960, just a few months after a white supremacist tried to frighten him away from politics.[171]

Formal, identifiable Klan activity in Ohio began to grow by the end of the 1950s in Ohio. The largest of the Klan groups to emerge in the post-dissolution era was known as the United Klans of America. With headquarters in Alabama, and led by Imperial Wizard Robert Shelton, the UKA reached a peak enrollment of perhaps 30,000 members in the 1960s. At least 40 Klaverns operated in Alabama between 1964 and 1966, and at least 556 Klaverns operated across the US in that three-year window.[172] This faction was also the most violent of Klan associations, most notoriously responsible for the 16th Street Baptist Church bombing in Birmingham, Alabama, in 1963 that resulted in the deaths of four young girls. UKA members also committed numerous floggings, murders, and lynchings. UKA members, for example, were involved in the killing of civil rights worker Viola Liuzzo in 1965.[173]

By the mid-1960s the UKA had emerged as a substantial white supremacist organization in Ohio. In 1967, for example, the UKA staged one of the largest Klan gatherings in Ohio since the Klan's heyday in the decade of the 1920s. The event occurred just outside the city of Cambridge, about 80 miles east of Columbus. As far as Klan meetings are concerned in the postwar era, this was a fairly well-attended affair, with 70 robed Klansmen present, and the local newspaper reported that "not more than 15 were counted from Cambridge."[174]

Speakers at the 1967 Klan event in Cambridge developed several recurrent themes. Visiting Grand Dragon William B. Chaney of Indiana argued that "the white race has been in retreat since 1933, the days of FDR." Chaney also urged the crowd to recognize that "now is the time the white man must make his stand." Cambridge district Klan leader Carl Marsh spoke from the back of a pickup truck "decorated with American, Confederate, and Klan flags." Marsh claimed that local turnout was lower than expected because "some are afraid of reprisals" against attendees of the Klan event. The UKA's Grand Dragon for the state of Ohio, Lowell G. Ballard, warned the media that "if any reporters are here looking for trouble, they have come to the right place." He also argued that the turmoil in cities like Detroit and Los Angeles would soon spread to small-town Ohio: "Cambridge hasn't had any riots yet, but your day is coming. I feel sorry for you."[175]

Anti-Klan protesters made several appearances at the Cambridge event. One Klan member acting as a security guard claimed that "two Negroes and a white man" punched him and beat him with a railroad flare. Protesters stationed on a hill overlooking the Klan gathering also tossed Molotov cocktails at the Klan group, but the incendiary devices "contained little gasoline and sheriff's deputies quickly stamped out a small grass fire."[176] As with virtually all periods of Ohio history in which ideologies of white supremacy were promulgated, in this case too there was significant local resistance to public expression of racist beliefs. By 1967 at least four active UKA klaverns were operating in Ohio. These were located in the cities of Hamilton, Cleveland, Columbus, and Newark.[177]

The second-largest Klan faction that emerged after the Second World War was a group known as the National Knights of the Ku Klux Klan (NKKK). The group was founded in 1963 by Atlanta lawyer James Venable, a longtime member of various incarnations of the Klan. Under Venable's leadership in the 1960s, the NKKK may have reached 9,000 members, though most of these were in Georgia. At times the NKKK has been referred to as "the Georgia Klan," with the UKA being known as "the Alabama Klan," but these nicknames belie the national reach that each Klan faction attained. Venable seemed to believe that "Ohio presented opportunities for expansion of his organization," and since "most parts of the South had been effectively organized by Shelton's UKA" [United Klans of America], he expended much of his organizational efforts to date on the state.[178]

The NKKK also developed a women's auxiliary Klan organization that was led by Eloise Witte of Cincinnati. Witte held the title of Empress of the National Knights of the Ku Klux Klan for the State of Ohio, a title that she claimed was a "commission given me by Mr. [James] Venable." In testimony before a congressional subcommittee, Witte indicated that she reviewed applications for the Klan and provided counsel to the various chapters. In the two years prior to her 1966 testimony, Witte claimed that "at least 15 Klan groups have passed through my house."

The original Ohio nonprofit charter for the Ku Klux Klan that dated to the 1920s had been revoked by the state government in August 1963 after no one stepped up to claim it. However, by October 1964 three Ohioans filed for nonprofit status on behalf of what was termed the National Knights of the Ku Klux Klan of Ohio, Inc. These individuals were Flynn R. Harvey of Columbus, William K. Smith of Groveport, and Lawrence Mink of Cincinnati.[179] Also listed as a trustee for the corporation was Bobby J. Stephens, also of Grove

City, who later became an undercover police operative.[180] Unfortunately for the Klansmen, Ohio Secretary of State Ted W. Brown revoked the new nonprofit charter several weeks later. The group vowed to file suit to get the charter restored, but it never followed up on its threats of legal action.

The spring and summer of 1965 seems to have been the peak period of activity in Ohio for the NKKK, at least in terms of public rallies. On the weekend of May 28–30, the group held a rally near Lebanon, Ohio, in the southwestern section of the state. On the weekend of August 20–21, the NKKK staged a rally near Brunswick, Ohio, and on the weekend of September 18–19, a rally in the vicinity of Lodi, Ohio.[181] Both Brunswick and Lodi are in the Cleveland metropolitan area. Two 1966 rallies were staged near Oregonia, Ohio, on the farm of NKKK organizer Parkie A. Scott.[182]

Scott's work as an Ohio NKKK organizer carried over into Indiana. He led a rally in November 1965 in the town of Dillsboro, just west of the Ohio-Indiana border. Scott's rally announcement indicated that the event was designed for "every white, Christian American" and that "no alcoholic beverage, Communists, Niggers, or Beatniks" would be permitted on the rally grounds.[183] Unfortunately for Parkie Scott and his fellow Klansmen, local authorities filed a motion asking for an injunction against the planned Klan rally, which was granted by the Seventh Judicial Circuit Court of Indiana. Scott, Venable, and other Klan members showed up at the rally site, but they simply read a prepared statement about how they would respect the injunction while their appeals were heard (the threatened Klan motions were never actually filed).[184]

A rally at Scott's Oregonia farm in July 1966 resulted in the arrest of the Klan organizer. Warren County sheriff Byron Kennard attempted to arrest two Klan members at the rally with outstanding warrants, but Scott blocked the road to his farm with his pickup truck. Scott was charged with interfering with a police officer, and he was sentenced to 30 days in jail plus a $500 fine in December 1967.[185] Immediately following the trial, handbills were mailed to the jurors in Scott's case, with a threatening statement: "you are being watched!" The handbills were also hand-delivered to homes on the streets where jurors lived.[186]

One of the most high-profile Klan events Scott organized was a protest against a visit by President Lyndon B. Johnson to Dayton in 1966. Scott claimed that Johnson traveled to Dayton so that he could "criticize officials for not turning the city over to the Negroes." He predicted that racial strife would soon engulf Columbus and Cincinnati, with "burning and rioting" being the direct result of Johnson's visit.[187]

Leading the Klan recruitment drive in Ohio for the NKKK was Klan Grand Emperor William J. Morris, who traveled to Ohio from his home in Buchanan, Georgia. Unbeknownst to the Klan, however, Klan member Bobby J. Stephens was working as a double agent on behalf of law enforcement. In testimony before the House Subcommittee on Un-American Activities, Stephens claimed that members of the Ohio NKKK units were involved in the planning of several terrorist plots.[188]

It is difficult to determine the extent to which Ohio Klan members had progressed on the various terror plots, and in some cases the reliability of Bobby Stephens (or his sources) might be questioned. Still, these plots were revealed under oath to a House subcommittee, so it would be reckless to dismiss them completely out of hand, simply because they were documented by an individual who was a true-believer-turned-informant. Stephens, who lived in Grove City, Ohio, in the mid-1960s, was also listed as an officer on state incorporation documents, so at the very least he was in a position of trust within the Ohio Klan community.

Members of the Ohio NKKK chapters were implicated by Stephens in a number of assassination plots. Some of the targeted individuals were high-profile political figures, such as President Lyndon B. Johnson and Vice President Hubert H. Humphrey, while their interest in killing Dr. Martin Luther King Jr. had both political and racial motives. Klan member Danny Wagner wrote a letter in which he indicated that his plan was to attack Dr. King at a speaking event at Antioch College in Yellow Springs, Ohio, the alma mater of Coretta Scott King. Wagner intended to shoot Dr. King while simultaneously "10 other men would blast the crowd."[189] Also on the alleged list of targets were "several fellow Klansmen they had taken a dislike to," such as NKKK leader William Morris and the husband of Cincinnati women's auxiliary Klan leader Eloise Witte.[190] The Cincinnati Klan leader was considered "too passive" by the more aggressive plot leaders, according to testimony by a police official.[191] Witte's husband became a target when he threatened to have her committed to a mental institution unless she ended all her work with the Klan and the National States Rights Party (NSRP), another right-wing white supremacist group.[192] However, Stephens admitted under questioning that he thought the plotters of these assassinations were "living in a dream world."[193]

Closer to operational fruition were plots involving homemade bombs, and the targets of the NKKK's terror attacks included the Columbus office of the NAACP, a "Black Muslim mosque, and the sewer system in the Negro section of Columbus," according to Stephens. Ohio Klan members Danny Wagner and Chuck Gilliam traveled to Georgia to procure dynamite and managed to transport it back to Ohio, but a tip from Stephens to local police thwarted this threat.[194] In one case, 4 1/2 sticks of dynamite were seized from a Klansman's vehicle after a training session near Carrollton, Ohio, where "some Klansmen had practiced setting off some charges of dynamite."[195] In another case, police recovered near Darbydale, Ohio, "a fused and capped bomb made of four half-pound sticks of 60 percent dynamite" from a Klan hideout known by the ominous name of the "Coon Hunters Club."[196] In both cases, though, existing laws regarding the transport of dynamite across state lines were difficult to enforce, as they relied on proving intent to commit violence. Congress would address the issue of transportation of explosives with the Organized Crime Control Act of 1970, which transferred many explosives regulations to the Bureau of Alcohol, Tobacco and Firearms and provided stricter guidelines and penalties regarding illegal transportation of explosives.[197]

Yet another plot conceived by Ohio Klan members during the 1960s involved a personal attack on a Columbus-area opponent of the Ku Klux Klan. Stephens testified that the Columbus leader of CORE was to be the target of a kidnapping plot, whereby he would be "blindfolded and taken out into the country, beaten, and left lying by a burning cross" to send a message of intimidation to the group and its leaders. This plot, too, was broken up through tips provided by an undercover operative.[198]

The strength of the NKKK in Ohio appears to have begun to diminish in the second half of 1965. Miffed at an apparent slight by the national NKKK leadership over an announced rally that lacked local backing, Columbus-based Flynn Harvey's Klan faction split from the NKKK and joined forces with the UKA in August 1965. It is unclear how many NKKK members joined Harvey, but the newly UKA-affiliated group set its sights on the Cleveland-Akron corridor for recruitment events. An August rally in that region targeted northern Ohio, as Harvey indicated that the Klan had "its greatest strength in Cuyahoga County." Harvey also noted that the focus of the rally speakers would be anti-Klan legislation under consideration by the Ohio legislature.[199] However, testimony before the House subcommittee suggested that Harvey "fell into disfavor with the membership" of the NKKK in Ohio; organizational charges against him ranged from "mismanagement of funds to drunkenness and ineffective leadership."[200]

Still, Klan members associated with the NKKK continued to plan violent acts of terror at least into 1968. One plot involved a former Chicago police officer who had been fired in 1967 for his Klan activities. Relocating to Akron, he apparently made connections with local NKKK groups while briefly living in Stone Mountain, Georgia. On August 22, 1968, Akron police arrested the former law enforcement officer Donald R. Heath along with an 18-year-old accomplice, David John Harris Jr. The pair were in possession of "a pistol, 75 rounds of ammunition, a lead-filled nightstick, a five-gallon can of gasoline, rags, and an assortment of plumbing fixtures." Also found in the car was a removable Ku Klux Klan sign that contained suction cups for easy placement and removal. When questioned by police, Heath replied that "there'll be a lot less policemen by tonight," and added ominously that "you won't know what is going to happen until it's too late."[201] Interestingly, despite his menacing statements and the questionable materials in his vehicle, Heath received a suspended sentence and a small fine after pleading guilty to a misdemeanor.[202]

Reflecting in part the high level of Klan activity in Ohio in the 1960s, a major Supreme Court decision addressed the constitutionality of Ohio's efforts to crack down on the Ku Klux Klan in the 1960s. At a rally on June 28, 1964, Klan leader Clarence Brandenburg gave a speech that state officials interpreted as a call to violence. In August 1964 Brandenburg was charged with two counts of violating the Ohio Criminal Syndicalism Statute.[203] The law criminalized speech that advocated "crime, sabotage, violence, or unlawful methods of terrorism as a means of accomplishing industrial or political reform."[204] Brandenburg was fined $1,000 and sentenced to one to ten years in prison. In 1969 the US Supreme Court overturned the conviction, finding that the Ohio law violated Brandenburg's right to free speech, and that the Ohio Criminal Syndicalism Statute ignored whether "imminent lawless action" would occur as a result of Brandenburg's speech.[205] The *Brandenburg v. Ohio* decision continues to be the standard for assessing government attempts to criminalize controversial speech, and in particular white supremacist groups rely on *Brandenburg* to defend against attempts to shut down rallies and other forms of expression.

Another white supremacist group that shared similarities with the Klan emerged in Ohio during the 1960s and was known as the National Association for the Advancement of White People. The NAAWP name has been used by a variety of white supremacist entities since the modern civil rights movement gained momentum during and after the Second World War. The frequency with which the NAAWP moniker has been invoked should not be surprising, given the symbolism associated with subverting the name of the NAACP, traditionally the leading civil rights organization defending constitutional protections for African Americans. However, it is worth noting that one of the earliest incarnations of a NAAWP group was the organization that developed in Ohio.

A Cincinnati-based NAAWP emerged by 1963, led by a man named William F. Miller (see Figure 1.9). The group's mission, according to Miller, was to "promote, aid, sustain and defend our American form of government; to keep the general public aware of the elements which seek to impair and destroy their government; and to promote the social, educational, and general welfare of the Caucasian race." Though only 15 people showed up for a public meeting in Cincinnati in July 1963, Miller claimed at that time that the group had over 300 members.[206] By August 1963 the group began to engage in public activities, including pickets of local schools over efforts to integrate some classrooms.[207] The group also became involved in protests against desegregation in Cleveland in 1964,[208] and the NAAWP were out in number among the protesters picketing an event in which Dr. Martin Luther King Jr. was the keynote speaker in July 1965 at the Cleveland Arena.[209] Internal NAAWP documents indicate that a man named John Barbie was president of the Cleveland chapter of the NAAWP, while Virgil P. Lacy was the head of the Dayton unit as of October 1964.[210]

Miller was among the arrested supporters of segregationist white barbershop owner Lewis Gegner.[211] The NAAWP placed a cardboard wreath outside the barbershop with the inscription "Another Communist Victory," in reference to court rulings finding that Gegner violated state public accommodation laws by refusing to cut the hair of Black patrons. Miller also marched around with an upside-down

FIGURE 1.9. William F. Miller of NAAWP, 1964. Used with permission from Burk Uzzle.

American flag to further illustrate his displeasure.[212] Miller and two other NAAWP members were charged with violating an injunction limiting the number of picketers outside Gegner's barbershop.[213] Joining Miller in the brief visit to jail were NAAWP members Flynn Harvey and Robert Leavey, both of Columbus.[214] Harvey and Leavey would also play important roles later in the decade in the National Knights of the Ku Klux Klan chapter in Ohio.

Life magazine profiled the NAAWP's Miller in February 1964. According to Miller, the group's motivations were to counter the efforts of perceived enemies from within: "The Negroes are out to take over the government. The Communists are behind it. The Jews are behind it." For white Americans the prospects were grim, according to Miller, who argued that "there's nothing but a bullet waiting for us in the back of our heads."[215] While claiming to be a moderate, Miller admitted that "I'm willing to resort to violence to protect what I believe in," since the "civil righters and do-gooders are out to destroy" white Americans.[216]

The NAAWP charged annual dues of three dollars per year. By early 1964 Miller claimed that the NAAWP had established chapters in five states with a total membership of 2,500 people. In addition, the group began to publish a newspaper called *The American People,* a publication that found readers around the US. The NAAWP seemed to be developing an organizational model that combined higher-profile activism with major media coverage, potentially challenging the Klan for national leadership among white supremacist groups.

Unfortunately for Miller, his tenure as NAAWP president was somewhat brief. An altercation with *American People* editor Walter Huff resulted in Miller's claiming that Huff pointed a pistol at the NAAWP leader (Huff was later acquitted of the charge). The group decided to replace Miller due to "poor administration by causing the national office of the corporation to become heavily indebted." Of particular concern to NAAWP dissidents was that Miller allegedly failed to properly get approval for his $500 monthly salary, and that he allegedly siphoned cash payments to the group by having NAAWP mail sent to his home.[217] It also did not help Miller in his fight to remain president that he made the error of "having employed a Negro lawyer and making statements to the news media that he felt he was very fortunate to get so talented an attorney."[218]

Leadership of the NAAWP seems to have devolved to Robert W. Annable of Parma Heights, who changed the group's name to North American Alliance of White People (while keeping the same acronym). Annable was quite active in the 1960s and early 1970s in several white supremacist organizations, including his role as the chairman of the benignly named National Christian Conservative Society (NCCS), and was also involved in the 1968 George Wallace presidential campaign in Ohio. Annable had a curious relationship with the Ku Klux Klan; in HUAC testimony by an informant, documents identified him as a grand titan for the "Provisional Realm of Ohio" for the UKA, but Annable denied Klan membership when called before the committee to testify.[219] However, he spoke highly of the Klan in his HUAC testimony: "The ideals of the Klan are of the highest type . . . these are people who have only the best interests of the Nation, the white race, at heart."[220] Yet, a reporter for the Ohio Press Service, Wally Guenther, went undercover and joined the Klan, and he recounted that Annable claimed that the NAAWP was just another Klan group, and that he was in the process of converting the NAAWP into a UKA chapter.[221]

In his role as NCCS president, Annable invited Dallas County, Alabama, sheriff Jim Clark to speak in Cleveland in 1966.[222] Clark was the notoriously racist architect of what became known as Bloody Sunday in 1965, an event that resulted in over 60 protesters being hospitalized after being attacked on the Edmund Pettus Bridge in Selma. After public outcry, Clark's appearance was canceled due to purported conflicts with his schedule.[223]

Annable told a *Wall Street Journal* reporter in 1967 that Blacks were "culturally and intellectually inferior" and that his organizations planned rallies to organize white citizens that year.[224] Annable further elaborated on his views regarding African Americans in a 1967 interview with a reporter from the *Akron Beacon Journal*:

> They've only been out of the jungle about a hundred years. You can't wipe it out just by sending them to school. The politicians up here [in Ohio] just don't understand the colored people. In Alabama, they don't expect them to act like white people.[225]

One of the principal goals for Annable and the NAAWP was the recall of Carl Stokes, elected in November 1967 as the first Black mayor of Cleveland. Under an umbrella group of white organizations known as the United Citizens Council of America, Annable's NAAWP and affiliated groups began circulating recall petitions for what complainants called a plan to elect Stokes "solely because of his race."[226] Annable named the recall group the "Citizens for Law Enforcement Committee," saying the recall effort was necessary "to protect police from 'left-wing do-gooders and liberals.'"[227] The petition drive failed, though Annable also similarly mounted a failed recall campaign against Louis Stokes, brother of Carl Stokes, who was first elected as a congressional representative from Cleveland in 1968. Annable next filed suit, claiming that Louis Stokes was illegally elected to Congress due to "alleged racial gerrymandering" of his district,[228] but the Ohio Supreme Court dismissed the NAAWP motion in 1970.[229]

In his role as president of the United Citizens Council of Ohio, Annable filed a complaint against Westinghouse Electric Corporation in 1969 with the Ohio Civil Rights Commission. Annable believed that Westinghouse discriminated against white applicants at its Columbus facility. In addition to the complaint, the UCC called for a boycott of Westinghouse products. At the same time, the UCC filed a complaint with the Ohio Civil Rights Commission that Governor James Rhodes discriminated against white Ohioans by appointing three African Americans to the five-seat Ohio Civil Rights Commission.[230]

Annable identified himself in 1969 as vice chairman of the American Independent Party (AIP), the same political party that George Wallace conducted his 1968 presidential campaign. Support for Wallace in Ohio was higher than any midwestern state, and one of the highest totals the segregationist tallied in any non-South state. Annable announced in April 1969 a three-plank party platform: opposition to gun control legislation, opposition to communism, and "favoring plans for 'repatriation' of American Negroes." Annable and an aide, Louis Molnar of Cleveland, told reporters that repatriation to the AIP referred to plans by unnamed "'responsible' Negro organizations to homestead overseas areas such as Liberia."[231]

Annable threw his hat into the ring for the race for governor of Ohio in 1970 as an AIP candidate. He faced a primary challenge from Edwin G. Lawton, who outperformed Annable by a 2-to-1 margin, though it should be noted that the combined 5,333 votes accumulated by both AIP candidates represented less than one half of one percent of all votes cast in the March 1970 primary. Lawton fared somewhat better in the general election, pulling a little less than 2 percent of the vote. Annable, however, was penalized with a five-year ban on filing for public office in Ohio for his failure to report campaign expenses as required by law.[232]

Civil Rights–Era Ohio and the Growth of Neo-Nazi Groups

Tapping into white anger at desegregation efforts allowed a number of neo-Nazis to gain footholds in Ohio in the 1960s, and one new organization had an undeniably fascist ideology. Founded by George Lincoln Rockwell in 1958, the American Nazi Party (ANP) found significant reception in Ohio, particularly among working-class whites. Rockwell, who estimated national ANP enrollment at between 600 and 700 in 1964, indicated that his group attracted "a lot of hoodlums and tough guys." To recruit this type of member, Rockwell said that he kept his approach blunt and simple: "if you put on a uniform and say, 'See them niggers? We're gonna kill them niggers' . . . they understand that. You reach their hearts."[233] Yet Rockwell did not hold delusions about his party's chances to grow:

> I will not have a mass organization until there is an economic catastrophe. Not until the people are poor. You can't make a revolutionary out of a guy with two cars and an electric lawn mower and a fur toilet seat.[234]

Rockwell included Ohio in a brief 1964 speaking tour of the Midwest, lecturing to a packed house in the 650-seat auditorium at Antioch College in Yellow Springs on October 14, 1964. Rockwell had been invited to speak by Antioch's Community Government. For most of Rockwell's speech, there was silence in the auditorium. When he opened up the floor for questions, Antioch students silently left their seats and exited Kelly Hall. Many students wore Stars of David in a silent tribute to victims of the Holocaust (Rockwell was an early Holocaust denier).[235]

The effectiveness of the silence tactic used by Antioch College students in confronting fascism and racial hatred was not lost on Rockwell and his followers. He was asked by a reporter several weeks later whether he had ever had a negative experience with a college audience. His answer was unequivocal: "Antioch College in Yellow Springs, Ohio." He noted that "Communists had organized a silence corps . . . that was just like talking in a graveyard." Even when Rockwell attacked the audience, calling them "yellow" and "cowards" for their silence, the audience "sat there quietly and took it all."[236] A reporter at the Antioch event, however, observed that Rockwell was somewhat unnerved by the silent treatment, lashing out at the audience and calling Antioch "the vilest college in America."[237]

Rockwell brought his traveling show to Ohio University in Athens on April 14, 1965, invited by Bush Hall, a men's residence hall on campus.[238] There had been considerable resistance to the event in the weeks prior to Rockwell's talk. Officials at OU denied requests by students and faculty members, as well as by Jacob Mirviss, director of the Hillel Foundation, to cancel's Rockwell's visit, but administrators claimed that OU students deserved "an open and free campus." University officials managed to get "Jewish and other anti-Rockwell students [to] pledge[ ] not to picket or to throw eggs at the Nazi."[239] One report indicated that OU students used the same tactic adopted at Antioch; the audience at Athens "sat in stony silence" during Rockwell's speech, with the exception of some derisive laughter when the Nazi Party leader announced that he would campaign for governor of the state of Virginia.[240] Rockwell, taking offense at the jeering, described OU students as "kids who are full of garbage," while predicting that "there will be complete economic collapse by 1969."[241] One reporter covering the event said that Rockwell spent most of his time lambasting Jews, with the Nazi leader claiming that "under every pile of degeneracy poke, I find the Jew at the base of it."[242] Vernon Alden, then president of Ohio University, defended the invitation to bring Rockwell to the Athens campus, arguing that "freedom of inquiry and discussion is essential to educational development."[243]

Yet, at least one observer believed that Rockwell had scored some points with the 2,800 students in his Athens audience in 1965:

> [Rockwell] is a great public speaker. He lowered his level to that of his audience to facilitate a maximum flow of ideas . . . In short, the intellectual level of Rockwell's performance was lowered to childishness and absurdity. Yet the audience responded favorably, giving him positive feedback. It is both surprising and disappointing that the students of Ohio University fell game to such a performance. But Rockwell had us completely "psyched" when he addressed us as "boys and girls."[244]

Rockwell continued to find Ohio college campuses an effective platform for publicity, if not necessarily for recruitment. The Nazi leader spoke to 2,700 students at Memorial Hall on the campus of BGSU on March 31, 1967. In a press conference before the event, Rockwell indicated that he would run for president in 1972 "if I am not dead or in jail."[245] Despite calls for silence, students occasionally laughed at Rockwell's jokes and applauded at the conclusion of the speech. Rockwell told the audience that he felt "sorry for the black man. He is not mentally or psychologically fit to function in our white society." Expressing views similar to present-day Holocaust deniers, Rockwell argued that he "did not believe that what we hear about Hitler's persecution is true" and that he possessed "evidence that it [the Holocaust] didn't happen."[246] Rockwell claimed that there were "50 or 60" ANP members in Ohio, and that there was a "large group [of Nazis] in Cleveland."[247]

Rockwell was invited to speak at BGSU by Phi Alpha Theta, the history honor society. Phi Alpha Theta chapter president Louis Berry indicated that his group decided to invite Rockwell because "it is the duty of all men to know the ideas behind the emotions."[248] PAT faculty advisor Michael Moore defended the BGSU group's invitation to Rockwell, arguing that it would be better to observe his oratorical style and demagoguery "under relatively controlled circumstances where there is opportunity for some sober thinking about the forces that produce and nourish him." However, Moore said, BGSU students needed to "maintain their good sense" and not heckle or attack Rockwell.[249] *B-G News* student columnist Fred Zackel criticized those who called for a boycott of Rockwell's speech, such as chemistry professor Emanuel Solon, and instead proposed a more welcoming, albeit reserved, approach toward the Nazis:

> [This] leads one to wonder about the breadth of his understanding and appreciation. Maybe Dr. Solon is the one who needs to be reminded about Hitler and Nazism . . . Phi Alpha Theta should be congratulated . . . [Solon] also feels that this confrontation will increase the power and influence of these American Nazis. I say differently. Let them speak. Let them have a chance to state their cause and their beliefs. Let's find out about them.[250]

However, opposition in Bowling Green to the Nazi leader's speech was significant and took several different forms. One interfaith group held a memorial service in honor of "Jewish and non-Jewish victims of Nazi oppression." A BGSU professor opened his home to students as an alternative to the Rockwell speech. A group of professors, including professor Solon, urged students to stay away from Rockwell's talk. Someone set off a firecracker during the speech, briefly startling audience members, though a cynical member of the *B-G News* editorial staff suggested that it might have been set off by "one of the four henchmen" who accompanied Rockwell to BGSU.[251]

It is difficult to verify the number of active members and chapters that Rockwell's American Nazi Party developed in Ohio during the 1960s. One of the challenges is the same in documenting any group deemed subversive: internal records are often hidden from scrutiny, and such documents frequently get destroyed if the group becomes inactive. The difficulty in getting a good sense of ANP strength is compounded by the fact that Rockwell was assassinated by a party member in August 1967; this turn of events temporarily disrupted all party activity. In addition, Rockwell had changed the name of the group in January 1967 to "National Socialist White People's Party" (NSWPP), further complicating present-day efforts to estimate Nazi activity in Ohio in the 1960s. Cleveland seems to have been an active center of Nazi activity in the mid-to-late 1960s, and the NSWPP recognized the importance of Cleveland by holding a national "congress" in Cleveland in 1973. The group, under the leadership of new *fuhrer* Matthew Koehl, opened a regional office in 1969 in Cuyahoga Falls that doubled as a bookstore.[252] Party leaders opened another regional office in Cincinnati in 1971, choosing the Queen City as a base because "it is truly the crossroads of America."[253] Another NSWPP unit numbering as many as 20 people was discovered by police at a meeting in Clarksville in 1971 after they witnessed a suspicious man entering a building carrying concealed weapons.[254] An Akron-area NSWPP organizer in 1969 named Thomas E. Watson attempted to recruit local police officers and sheriff's deputies through the direct mailing of anti-Black flyers.[255] Moreover, the people that the NSWPP were recruiting in Ohio in the late 1960s and early 1970s seemed prone to violence and criminal behavior.

The manager of the NSWPP bookstore and regional headquarters in Cuyahoga Falls, Charles R. Lawrence (see Figure 1.10), was arrested and charged with selling a firearm to a 14-year-old boy in January 1970.[256] The boy was working in the store with Lawrence, and for a $15 "donation" to the NSWPP, Lawrence sold him a .32 caliber revolver, along with a holster and some ammunition. Lawrence was found guilty and sentenced to up to 18 months in prison and a $1,500 fine.[257]

While waiting for his appeals to be resolved in the firearms case, Lawrence was arrested in 1971 on charges related to the placing of a bomb on the front porch of *Akron Beacon Journal* publisher Ben Maldenberg. Police also charged Lawrence with possession of a sophisticated explosive device reportedly intended to be deployed at a Catholic church in Pittsburgh. The Pittsburgh bomb contained ten sticks of dynamite, blasting caps, a 28-inch fuse, and a timing device.[258] Lawrence was found not guilty by reason of insanity and served three years at the Lima State Hospital for the Criminally Insane.[259]

FIGURE 1.10. 1970 photograph of Charles R. Lawrence in *Akron Beacon Journal*. © USA TODAY NETWORK.

Another NSWPP leader was arrested on weapons-related charges after police found a photograph of a man in a Nazi uniform posing with an illegal firearm. Police raided the home of Frank Zoretich of Cleveland in December 1968, seizing machine guns and "obscene pictures." Police also found Nazi paraphernalia, eight pistols, several thousand rounds of ammunition, and five daggers.[260] Zoretich pleaded guilty to the charge of illegal possession of a Thompson machine gun and was sentenced to two years of probation, although after he appealed, police eventually were forced to return all items not part of the criminal case.[261]

An offshoot of the 1968 presidential campaign of George Wallace transformed over a period of several years into one of the most formidable national neo-Nazi movements. The "Youth for Wallace" organization rebranded itself after the election as the National Youth

Alliance (NYA). Founded by Willis Carto of the Liberty Lobby (a noted Holocaust denier who grew up in Mansfield, Ohio), the NYA's original goals were geared toward attracting college students: "the opposing of the use of drugs on college campuses; the neutralization of Black Power; the preserving of Western civilization; and the expulsion of communists from college campuses."[262] Sociologist Seymour Martin Lipset offered the following summary of the group's racial views in 1971:

> They proudly announce their belief in racial inequality by wearing buttons with the mathematical symbol of inequality [≠]. They denounce the Jews, Negroes, American Indians, and all other nonwhite races as inferior. They call for teaching the superiority of the white race in "white studies" courses.[263]

The group initially exhibited a thinly veiled racist philosophy, more of a white nationalist philosophy, but an organizational coup in March 1969 left the NYA firmly in the hands of neo-Nazi ideologues like William Luther Pierce, who joined the NYA in December 1970 after severing his ties with the NSWPP in August of that year. The NYA would eventually transform into the National Alliance by 1974, and by the end of the twentieth century, the National Alliance boasted thousands of members and a well-financed organization.

Ohio was a major focus for the nascent NYA. By December 1970 NYA official Louis T. Byers announced that 62 campus chapters had been launched, including a chapter at Kent State University.[264] National NYA organizer Robert Lloyd spent three days in Cleveland in spring 1971 in "conferences with local activists" to size up the city's potential as a regional NYA center.[265] Detailed documentary evidence has survived regarding the NYA chapters at BGSU and the University of Cincinnati (UC).

The NYA successfully developed a chapter at UC by 1971. The NYA at UC organized to start a "'white students' revolt' against forced missing of races," and the group also hoped to "promote a 'white lifestyle' among young persons." Led by undergraduate Ken Hoop, the UC chapter of the NYA had recruited a "handful" of members and "20 or 25 supporters" by March 1971. NYA national organizer Patrick Tifer, on the UC campus to evaluate the group's initial progress, gave the group pamphlets to distribute that denounced Blacks, welfare, and forced busing.[266] In a second appearance at UC in May 1971, Tifer was more explicit in his white supremacist views, especially in his anti-Semitism. Tifer "scoffed" at the idea that Jews were a religious group but not a distinct race: "You can't always tell a Baptist, and you can't always tell a Catholic, but you can always tell a Jew." At this second UC event, Tifer was joined by NYA organizer Ken Hoop as well as John Baker, an American Nazi Party member.[267]

Hoop's connections to the NYA and fascist ideology were not a passing youthful whim. While still in high school, Hoop was suspended for objecting to a Black History Month program and passing out flyers for a group called "Nationalist Underground Movement." Hoop's flyer called for "racial purity" and an end to "filth, lawlessness, subversives, needless race-mixing, and anarchy."[268] Describing himself as a "national socialist," Hoop occasionally wrote columns for the UC *News Record,* the student newspaper, and his editorials and letters clearly explicated his far-right ideology. In a 1971 letter to the paper's editor, Hoop attacked a conservative columnist in the *News Record,* denouncing the columnist for being afraid to praise "Western White civilization" and the columnist's unwillingness to address "the general shortcomings of the black race." Hoop also attacked the columnist for failing to take on the "Communist plan to forcefully integrate, mix, amalgamate and finally destroy the white race and Western Culture."[269] In a 1974 *News Record* column, Hoop described civil rights Freedom Riders as "Northern majority students were sent south by pseudo-academician elders to assist in furthering minority interest." Hoop complained about how his tuition money was "bestowed lavishly upon black minority groups such as the UBA and the UC Gay Society." The multicultural US, according to Hoop, had degenerated into a "bordello-nation of cultural impotence and spiritual sterility."[270] Into the twenty-first century Hoop continues to write for periodicals with ties to anti-Semitic and neo-Nazi groups, such as the *Barnes Review*[271] and the *American Free Press,* where he was identified as Midwest editor along with noted Ohio Klan leader Van D. Loman as of 2017.[272]

In the struggle for control of the NYA, Pierce and his neo-Nazi associates renamed their splinter group Youth Action in 1971. Named vice chairman of the national Youth Action organization was Ken Hoop, who also served as acting chairman in 1972 when elected chairman Luke Herda was called up for active duty in the army. Interviewed by a reporter in the UC *News Record,* Hoop outlined the new organization's principal goals. The group was more explicit in its white supremacy but included antiwar and environmental themes in an effort to broaden its appeal among young people:

1. To defend the white race and culture;
2. To mobilize against the needless slaughter of American youth in foreign wars;
3. To save American youth from the deadly peril of drugs;
4. To combat leftist violence and black terror in America;
5. To create a healthy environment;
6. To end America's financial enslavement by international bankers;
7. To mobilize American youth as a new political force.[273]

Another NYA chapter emerged at BGSU in northwestern Ohio by January 1969. In response to a week-long Black culture event on campus, members of the group began passing out and hanging flyers around the residence halls titled "The Leftist Conspiracy Has Gone Too Far!" The NYA flyer suggested that BGSU students not forget "the chapter of black culture that includes rioting and looting."[274] The flyer urged readers to join the NYA in an effort to attack "SDS, Black Power Racists, Black Culture Week, sexual immorality on campus, and the spread of drugs." The NYA authors of the flyer demanded that BGSU "initiate courses in patriotism rather than Marxism," and it exhorted readers to "clean up the scum on campus."[275] Ostensibly it was NYA activists who disrupted a panel discussion of a film during Black Culture Week to demand discussion of "the other side of black culture," which they identified as "looting and burning" while denouncing the term "Afro-American" as "un-American."[276]

The BGSU campus in the late 1960s was overwhelmingly white, with just 120 Black students in the 1968–69 academic year.[277] The campus exhibited de facto segregation within Greek life, and there were issues with "landlords refusing to rent to Black students."[278] The Black Student Union did not get approved as a university group until February 19, 1969.[279] Even then, white students lodged formal protests against the two seats allotted to the BSU on the Student Council, unseating the newly seated Black representatives and holding up effective representation by the BSU until the 1969–70 academic year.[280] A frequent complaint of Black BGSU students in the 1960s was the lack of formal space dedicated to Black social and academic endeavors, and one Black student writing to the *BG News* complained that the only space for Black students to meet was at tables in the Rathskeller, a campus food service facility.

Yet, even the prospect of Black students gathering at the Rathskeller was too much for some white students to accept. One white student wrote to the *BG News* complaining that providing space to Black students was unnecessary because the Rathskeller was "obviously the Negro hang-out on campus." After all, the author continued, "the juke-box features their music and the dark dance floor is ideal for their rhythm." The student said that he spoke from experience about the Rathskeller, as he "had been in the Rathskeller and felt the problem." He complained that there was "prejudice in the room, prejudice that is the vilest form of hate." He concluded by urging the university to "not look for another place to satisfy the Negro" and to instead build new student facilities "for all of us."[281]

Another white student complained in the *BG News* that "unless you are a member of a darkly colored racial group, you don't have 'soul.'" Somewhat sarcastically, he suggested that proponents of soul might have to express 'soul' by "wearing the teeth of an African short-haired orangutan along with a gold ring through the left earlobe." He denounced the idea of "soul" as a cultural phenomenon: "if 'soul' comes from the problems your great-grandfathers had, that doesn't make much sense . . . how many of you 'soul' people were alive in 1855?"[282] The writer then discussed how "soul-less" whites were successful as a race:

> Assuming that the popular conception of light colored people not having "soul" is true, how has this hurt our development as a race? Unless the rest of your people have this empty feeling that I have, the lack of "soul" has not hurt us too badly. We have rockets and the wheel. We usually have a warm place to sleep. In fact, we have produced a few good paintings and a symphony or two. Pretty good for a bunch of "soul-less" people.[283]

It was in this period of conflict and animosity that the NYA emerged on the BGSU campus. The group engaged in outreach to far-right students dissatisfied with alternatives such as the Young Americans for Freedom (YAF). One scholar who specialized in student activism at BGSU characterized the BG chapter of the NYA as a group who "believed the Young Americans for Freedom were not conservative enough."[284] Group member and lieutenant commander of the BGSU-NYA Ronald Doughty said that the YAF was "liberal-oriented and contributes to the leftist cause."[285] The YAF, it should be noted, supported the nomination of Barry Goldwater in 1964 and all the presidential campaigns by Ronald Reagan, so it certainly possessed conservative credentials. What appealed to the members of the BGSU-NYA was the idea that the National Youth Alliance might work outside the political structures to combat what they viewed as dangers to the American republic and mainstream white culture. Doughty and Roger J. Pinta, co-founders of Bowling Green's NYA chapter, were noted for hanging posters with inflammatory slogans such as "Shoot Looters," "Fight the Left and Save America," and "Those Who Will Not Fight in the Streets for America Today Will Most Surely Die on the Streets of America Tomorrow!"[286]

Initially the BGSU chapter of the NYA engaged in grassroots efforts to build a name for itself on campus. This took the form of activities such as passing out flyers, writing editorial letters and columns for the student newspaper, and disrupting meetings sponsored by leftist and Black groups on campus. Interestingly, the BGSU-NYA claimed for itself "'the right to forcibly remove' any leftist groups disrupting campus activity." Doughty argued that the NYA—in the event of the takeover of a campus building by the SDS or the Black Student Union—was entitled to use "whatever action is appropriate to insure that law and order are restored."[287]

There were political struggles within the BGSU-NYA that emerged fairly early and likely contributed to its struggles to gain traction. One NYA member publicly denounced Pinta and Doughty in a March 11, 1969, letter to the editor of the *BG News*. Martin J. Molloy wrote that he was "sick and tired of being associated with two supposed members of NYA [Doughty and Pinta]." Molloy wrote that he had taken "personal action to remove Mr. Doughty and Mr. Pinta from NYA, for there is no room for such individuals."[288] The specifics of the "personal action" were not provided in the letter, and they seem to have been ineffective, since Pinta and Doughty continued to claim to speak for BGSU-NYA for several more months.

Doughty's views on race were extreme, and in many ways they were in alignment with Klan and neo-Nazi ideology of the era. In one editorial for the *BG News*, Doughty wrote that segregation should be permitted because "it prohibits the enslavement of the Negro and the extermination of the whites." He argued that segregation was "harmony" and claimed that "consent of the governed" had been "replaced by bayoneted troops on the campuses of Little Rock and Mississippi." Integration, Doughty argued, was not "freedom of choice, freedom of decision, or freedom of independence" but rather "pure and overt tyranny."[289]

A controversy at BGSU emerged in early March 1969 that was likely instigated by a member (or members) of the National Youth Alliance. During a dispute over the seating of two Black Student Union reps to Student Council, a racist flyer made the rounds. The flyer's author encouraged BGSU fraternities to "unite" and to "Stop The Niggers" by opposing the recognition of BSU on Student Council. The flyer claimed that "now is the time to save our university from leftist radicals and the BSU (Black Subversive Union)."[290] The flyer also made bigoted comments about Jewish fraternity Zeta Beta Tau, derogatorily attacking "Jew Houses."[291] While the perpetrator(s) was not caught, the language used in the flyer is quite similar to previous NYA flyers and posters, and it seems evident that the author intended to stoke a smoldering racial conflict with the goal of escalating tensions on campus. This would be wholly consistent with NYA goals and prior actions.

The national coup d'état by neo-Nazis to take control of the NYA seems to have influenced the decision by Pinta and Doughty to dissolve the BGSU chapter of the National Youth Alliance. However, it is difficult to say with any certainty the degree to which the BGSU-NYA members simply wanted to shed the "neo-Nazi" label they were acquiring. Doughty composed an editorial for the *BG News* in late April 1969 explaining the process behind the local chapter's discovery of the supposed "rightist conspiracy" and the steps they took to dissociate themselves. Pinta wrote a letter to the editor explaining that the former NYA members were joining a movement called COUNTERTHRUST, which seemingly espoused the identical NYA platform, minus the association with Willis Carto and William Luther Pierce:

> COUNTERTHRUST stands for a patriotic America. We will continue the fight against SDS, Black Panthers, White Panthers, drugs, sexual immorality, and the Free University. Yet, the shock of being engulfed in a rightist conspiracy has also caused us to lead a fight against Nazism.[292]

Given the many decades of de facto segregation in Ohio's major cities (especially the Cleveland, Cincinnati, Columbus, and Dayton metropolitan areas, which have consistently ranked among the top 30 most segregated cities in the US), it should not be a surprise that the pro-segregationist, quasi-Nazi NSRP would find Ohio a productive state for recruiting new members. In addition, Ohio NSRP chapters were highly active, and there was considerable cross-fertilization between NSRP groups in Ohio and other white supremacist organizations in the 1960s. In short: the NSRP proved to be the most durable, active, and dangerous white supremacist group in Ohio from the late 1950s through the early 1970s.

The NSRP was founded in Knoxville, Tennessee, in 1958 by Edward R. Fields and Jesse Benjamin "J. B." Stoner. The group's ideology revolved around racism, anti-Semitism, and in particular opposition to desegregation. The NSRP's flag used the same lightning bolt symbol that an earlier fascist group (the Columbians) used. Members of the NSRP were associated with several violent terror attacks, most notoriously the 1958 bombing of the Bethel Baptist Church in Birmingham, Alabama, as well as the 1958 bombing of the Hebrew Benevolent Congregation Temple in Atlanta. Stoner himself served over three years in prison for his role in the Bethel Baptist bombing, and federal authorities considered him a suspect in other terror attacks.[293]

Significant activity by the NSRP in Ohio dates back to at least 1958, and party correspondence from October 1958 indicated that "Ohio is making very rapid progress and will open an H.Q. soon."[294] An Ohio secretary for the NSRP was named in the February 1959 party newsletter, one Dorsey Dubbs of Dayton.[295] FBI spot surveillance of national NSRP meetings in 1960 indicated that several cars with Ohio license plates attended meetings in Chattanooga, though the names of the individuals remain redacted in the reports.[296]

As evidence of the early importance of Ohio to the NSRP, the group's first national political convention was held in Dayton in 1960, originally scheduled to be held at a local Odd Fellows Hall at the corner of Labelle and East 5th Street.[297] The event was moved at the last minute to a "secluded lodge" in Miamisburg. The change in venue was due to an "all-out assault" against the NSRP made by the "A.D.L., the NAACP, and the local media," which caused the Odd Fellows to cave to public pressure, according to an NSRP newsletter.[298]

Fields indicated that "185 persons from 28 states" attended the 1960 NSRP nominating convention. In the first of 36 campaign planks, the NSRP called for "the creation of a wholesome White Folk Community." Its second plank demanded "complete separation of all non-Whites and dissatisfied racial minorities from our White Folk Community."[299] About 200 protesters, mostly from regional colleges, marched around the convention site in opposition to the NSRP.[300] Delegates selected Governor Orval E. Faubus of Arkansas for president and Admiral John G. Crommelin of Alabama for vice president.[301]

A recruitment poster distributed by the NSRP in Ohio highlights the major concerns of the party while reflecting the significant influence of fascist movements on the group. The "BUILD A WHITE AMERICA" section contains an idealized illustration of a white man and a white woman with the NSRP flag in the background, an image that bears more than a little similarity to Nazi propaganda posters of the 1930s. In addition to racist and segregationist ideology, the flyer also displays a significant degree of anti-Semitism. The flyer's creator argued that Jews were engaging in a "determined effort" to "destroy the National States' Rights Party," and that joining the NSRP was the best way to subvert the imagined Jewish attempts to dominate whites.[302] In addition, the frequent anti-Semitic tirades found in the issues of the party newsletter the *Thunderbolt* are also reminiscent of Nazi propaganda, focusing on a supposed Jewish-Bolshevik global domination conspiracy theory and often containing crude caricatures of monsterlike Jewish persons. This affinity for Nazi propaganda went much deeper than aesthetics, however, as an FBI informant provided information that the NSRP and the American Nazi Party began talks regarding a merger of the two groups in early 1967. The informant hoped to broker a meeting between George Lincoln Rockwell and J. B. Stoner, though the assassination of George Lincoln Rockwell later that year ended any possibility of a merger.[303]

After the 1960 election, the NSRP in Ohio focused on grassroots efforts to build the number of dues-paying members, and reports of NSRP activity in the period from 1961 to 1963 can be found from all parts of the state. The *Dayton Daily News* reported distribution of an NSRP periodical titled the *Thunderbolt* in Wilmington, Ohio, in June 1962. Local officials were concerned because a local ordinance required "solicitors or anyone going door-to-door to make themselves known to the police department and state their business," according to Wilmington police chief Stanley E. Irwin.[304]

One NSRP member employed as a minister attempted to use his church as a base for NSRP activity. Reverend Frederick Harold "F. H." Johnson, who in 1961 was also the Ohio NSRP chairman, began to preach pro-segregation views and promote the NSRP at the Church of the Covenants in Dayton. In a letter to the editor of the *Dayton Daily Herald,* Johnson outlined his views on race:

> Historically in America, segregation has been the accepted mode of life, and those who violated it were rightfully looked down upon as pariahs . . . I believe that integration is bad for any race, and I believe that it is contrary to the fact that God is the creator of all men and has set the horizon of their times and the limits of their habitation.[305]

A majority of church members resisted the NSRP "invasion," and at one point in a service there were competing attempts to pass the collection plate between pro-NSRP and anti-NSRP factions, resulting in three Dayton police cruisers being deployed to break up the dispute. The anti-NRP faction filed suit on November 20, 1961, preventing the pro-NSRP faction from having administrative control over church affairs.[306] Rev. Johnson submitted his resignation on December 5, but the pro-NSRP faction filed a cross-petition the same day.[307] In the short term, pro-NSRP and anti-NSRP factions used the church on alternating Sundays.[308] In 1965 a Common Pleas court issued a decision laying the ground rules for a court-supervised church election.[309] However, the pro-NSRP faction appealed that decision.[310] The court cases would not be resolved until 1969, with the anti-NSRP faction eventually winning, though the victory was short-lived, as the financial strain exacted by the court battle left the church insolvent.

It appears that the FBI began making use of confidential informants by at least the year 1964 to gain information about the NSRP in Ohio. The group had been on the FBI's radar since its inception at the national level, and activities in states like Georgia and Alabama had been monitored since at least 1960. An informant reported to handlers that the Columbus NSRP chapter's active membership was "very low in number" as of late March 1964. However, the FBI learned from an informant that the Dayton chapter had at least 25 active members as of May 1964, and that the Cincinnati chapter appeared quite active.[311] An older mailing list from 1964 acquired by an FBI informant in 1967 contained over 200 names of Ohio NSRP–affiliated persons listed with some combination of the following codes: M (member), S (*Thunderbolt* subscriber), F (financial supporter), and L (whether the person would be willing to distribute literature).[312] Listed below are the Ohio cities for which the NSRP had at least three affiliated persons on the 1964 mailing list:

TABLE 1.1. City of residence for Ohio NSRP members

CITY	NSRP AFFILIATES
Dayton	33
Cleveland	23
Middletown	18
Cincinnati	11
Columbus	9
Toledo	7
Akron	7
Youngstown	3
Sandusky	3
Xenia	3
Lexington	3
Cambridge	3
Mansfield	3
Miamisburg	3
Lima	3
Trenton	3
Findlay	3

Candidates sponsored by the NSRP managed to gain some electoral traction in Ohio against the established major parties, despite a fairly limited budget. One example can be found in the 1964 Ohio state legislature campaign of William H Ingram Jr., who sought the Democratic nomination for state representative in a district encompassing parts of Dayton. While Ingram came in last place for the party nomination, the 8,047 ballots cast for him by Dayton-area voters were about 40 percent of those received by the eventual nominee. Irving Thacker, who was the state political coordinator for the NSRP, noted that Ingram's showing came despite the fact that he was "not well known and received little publicity."[313] Many candidates backed by the NSRP for state offices in Ohio that year ran under the banner of one of the two major parties due to the NSRP's difficulties in maneuvering the logistics of state electoral requirements.

Co-founder Edward R. Fields brought his fiery brand of NSRP racism to Dayton in July 1964. He spoke to a group of about 100 people at a hall located at 820 Linden Avenue. Fields argued that "Negroes haven't gone beyond the ape stage" and that they had yet to "earn the right to associate with white people." He described African Americans as "a black plague, animalistic, cannibalistic, inferior and immoral," and added that they "represent the ultimate destruction of the white race." Fields believed that desegregation was widely opposed by white America, and thus that opposing it represented a winning political strategy for the NSRP. Fields also discussed a conversation he supposedly had with a local restaurant owner: "I asked a restaurant owner if he would serve a nigger. He told me he wouldn't serve any nigger, and that he would tell that nigger to go to the Federal court for service."[314]

Incensed by the passage of the Civil Rights Act of 1964, NSRP members in Ohio began a campaign to picket the homes of the 23 Ohio representatives who voted for the landmark legislation. One of these demonstrations took place in August 1964 at the Piqua home of Rep. William M. McCulloch, an Ohio Republican noted for his support of civil rights initiatives. Picketers carried signs reading "McCulloch—you anti-white?" and "What about rights for whites?"[315]

J. B. Stoner, who became the vice presidential candidate of the NSRP in the 1964 elections, visited Cincinnati in August 1964. Speaking to a group of supporters and media representatives, Stoner railed against the federal government, arguing that "Cincinnati is under siege from the FBI," and adding that the late president John F. Kennedy was a "spoiled brat and a moron." The NSRP sought "good, white, loyal, Christian Americans" for its membership, according to Stoner. Addressing some conflict in the room over the presence of a *Cincinnati Enquirer* reporter, Stoner asked NSRP members to "refrain from attacking this newsman. Let's not hit him on the head. You know, I've spoke at places where this was done."[316] Stoner scheduled three stops in Ohio during the month of August 1964 during his presidential campaign, visiting the cities of Dayton, Cincinnati, and Medina.[317]

Likely reflecting the importance of Ohio to the NSRP—and to bolster the showing of the party in the 1964 elections—another party speaker made stops in the Buckeye State in October 1964. California NSRP leader Connie Lynch, a founding member of the group and a minister in the racist religious sect known as the Church of Jesus Christ–Christian (a forerunner of the notorious Aryan Nations), spoke to reporters after a party meeting in Dayton. He believed that the country was on the verge of "the ultimate awakening of the 140 million white people of America to the nigger problem." Lynch argued that the "solution" would be "sending them back to Africa, even if it takes a bloody race war to do it."[318]

A visit by Rev. Dr. Martin Luther King Jr. to the fieldhouse at the University of Dayton brought out NSRP picketers on November 30, 1964. William Ingram, spokesperson for the group, said that there would have been more than 15 picketers were it not for a national NSRP convention and the weather, which approached zero degrees Fahrenheit. However, the weather did not stop 6,500 supporters of Dr. King from filling the fieldhouse; incidentally, Dr. King had recently been awarded the Nobel Peace Prize for his activism. Picketers carried signs reading "Martin Luther King Fronts for Commies," Go Home, Martin Luther Coon," and "Communist *Daily Worker* Praises Rev. King." Ingram told reporters that Dr. King "was not a man of God . . . because he preached integration," claiming that the book of Genesis commanded segregation between races.[319]

In large measure due to the activism of—and civil disturbances caused by—the NSRP, the Cincinnati city council voted in 1965 to ban the sale or distribution of racially inflammatory or religiously bigoted materials under what became known as the "scurrilous pamphlet" law. Violations of the law could bring prison sentences of up to six months and a fine of up to $500 per violation.[320] City officials amended the ordinance in 1966, outlawing the "exhibition or display or bigoted, scurrilous material." Safety director Robert Lockridge asked the city council to amend the ordinance after NSRP members began to hang signs in their Hamilton Avenue headquarters railing against "'Nigras' and Jews."[321]

The first application and test of the "scurrilous pamphlet" law came a week after the ordinance was passed, as police raided the NSRP headquarters. Officers seized four boxes of what was deemed "scurrilous literature": two boxes of the NSRP *Thunderbolt* newspaper and two boxes of "miscellaneous printed materials." Police also seized copies of Klan literature, and then arrested group leader Jerrold Oliver Black.[322] Black was convicted and fined, but an appeals court overturned his conviction in 1966, arguing that the scurrilous material ordinance violated both state and federal constitutions.[323]

A *Dayton Journal Herald* reporter visited Ingram and fellow NSRP official R. D. Eldridge at the group's regional office in Dayton in November 1965. The year had been difficult for the NSRP: Lyndon Johnson had won the 1964 presidential election, the Voting Rights Act of 1965 had passed by a wide margin, and the House Un-American Activities Committee had included the NSRP in a probe looking for ties to the Ku Klux Klan. In addition, several Ohio men with NSRP ties (including Eldridge) had been arrested in Indiana for "racketeering in hate"[324] due to their efforts to distribute NSRP and Klan literature; also arrested were Dayton residents and NSRP members Rev. Dallas Bellar and Joe "Junior" Hignite.[325] Yet the true believers of NSRP racism kept plugging away, talking as they stuffed envelopes with NSRP materials and application forms. The platform of the NSRP had begun to evolve by this time, reflecting political changes. At this point the NSRP was hawkish on the war in Vietnam, urging that Vietnam be completely turned over to the American military. The group had begun circulating petitions calling for blood banks to identify whether donated blood originated in a white or nonwhite person. Finally, the group claimed success in defeating the bid of Don Crawford to become the first Black mayor of Dayton, though Ingram did not provide details on the NSRP's role in Crawford's defeat.[326]

In part of a 1966 series titled "I Joined the Far Right," a pair of *Dayton Daily News* reporters joined a variety of white supremacist and far-right-wing extremist groups, including the NSRP. The reporters—Bob Keveney and Doug Walker—penned first-person accounts of their time with white supremacist groups in Ohio, offering readers inside glimpses at the ideology and culture of the various incarnations of white supremacy in Ohio. Bob Keveney drew the NSRP assignment, and his reporting tended to highlight humorous incidents involving the group instead of focusing on the group's message and potential for violence. Keveney wrote about an NSRP picketing of the Montgomery County board of education offices regarding the cancelation of a Christmas play after a parent complained about references in the play to the Christ child. Keveney wrote that "the picket line might have engendered a great deal of sympathy for the party's campaign against non-Christians, but the leadership displayed its ignorance by demonstrating in front of the wrong office." The NSRP had accidentally targeted the county board of education, which had nothing to do with the cancelation of the play, instead of the offices of Dayton City Schools.[327]

Dayton continued to be a major hub of NSRP activity in 1966, holding the party's national convention that year at the Greater Beneficial Union Hall at 820 Linden Avenue. National leader Connie Lynch told *Dayton Daily News* reporters that the NSRP's "solution" to racial strife was to "resettle the Negroes in Africa." Lynch added that if urban unrest continued, whites would no longer sit idly by; "If that happens, there won't be much trouble getting what's left back to Africa, they'll be buried right here." R. D. Eldridge, who had been elevated to national organizer for the NSRP, claimed that 500 party members had registered, and that representatives would be present from all states, and even some from Canada.[328] Eldridge claimed that four days before the convention's start, 484 hotel reservations had been made, though he did not provide documentation for this total.[329] Contemporary observers, however, suggest that the number was somewhat lower, and that most license plates of attendees were from the South and Midwest, especially Ohio, Indiana, Kentucky, Florida, and Georgia. Eldridge added that in the ten days after the national convention, six rallies were planned in Ohio: Cleveland, Columbus, Springfield, Middletown, Cincinnati, and Dayton.[330]

An FBI informant within the Dayton chapter of the NSRP reported in January 1967 that a Cleveland unit of the group had been established in late 1966. The group's first meeting was on November 20, 1966, at the National Bohemian Hall. The informant indicated that the group met on the first and third Sundays of each month, and that a man named Charles O. Farris had been named chairman of the Cleveland NSRP chapter.[331] A second informant reported that an active NSRP chapter was also operational in the city of Middletown.[332]

A report prepared by the FBI on the NSRP warned of the group's "propensity for acquiring firearms by leaders and members alike." To illustrate this point, the FBI report discussed a cache of firearms and survival equipment discovered on a farm in Kentucky owned by the leader of the Dayton chapter of the NSRP, Dallas Hale. The cache was lined with polyethylene sheeting, and plastic piping had been added in the hole to ensure adequate drainage. In addition to survival gear, the buried cache included three .30 caliber carbine rifles, one .410 shotgun, five carbine cartridge clips, seven boxes of .30 caliber ammunition, one box of shotgun shells, and two boxes of .45 caliber ammunition.[333]

An incident involving members of the Dayton NSRP chapter demonstrates that FBI concerns about violence involving the NSRP had merit. A weekend rally in 1968 in Berea, Kentucky, turned deadly in the small Appalachian town after a gun battle broke out between NSRP members and several carloads of local Black citizens. The NSRP seems to have chosen the rally location based on its proximity to Berea College, which NSRP spokesman Edward Fields denounced for "the communistic degeneracy which has taken over Berea College."[334] The NSRP rally, held in a used-car lot on the edge of town, included a PA system, allowing the group's speakers to broadcast messages and insults into the range of nearby Black homes. Connie Lynch was the keynote speaker at the event, and the FBI singled Lynch out for "abusive anti-black oratory"[335] that angered local Black residents. At the rally's end on September 1, 1968, a group of up to eight Black citizens approached the NSRP and demanded that the group cease its racial taunts and take down Confederate flags.[336] According to the FBI, the Black Berea residents "were fired upon by the whites . . . and the blacks promptly returned fire."[337] NSRP member Elza Vernon Rucker, formerly of Dayton, was killed in the gun battle, as was Black Berea resident George "Leno" Boggs. Several other men were injured in the melee.[338]

Of the 14 men charged in the killings, six were Black Berea citizens and eight were NSRP members. Of the NSRP suspects, five were from Dayton, Ohio: Charles S. Eldridge, R. D. Eldridge, Dudley A. Hughes, Dallas Hale, and Kenneth W. Hale. A sixth suspect, Peter L. Xavier, was a longtime Dayton resident who had moved to Savannah. Charles Eldridge, incidentally, was a Montgomery County sheriff's deputy, while Dallas Hale was the owner of the aforementioned seized cache of weapons. Ultimately, though, the inability of the prosecutor and law enforcement officials to determine who fired the deadly shots led to reduced sentences for all 14 suspects; fines, probation, and suspended sentences (with credit for time served) were issued in various combinations to the defendants.[339]

The national convention of the NSRP in June 1969 was held in Jacksonville, Florida, and was well attended by Ohioans. Approximately two dozen residents of the Buckeye State made the trip south, representing one-sixth of the 150 members present for the convention. R. D. Eldridge began by reminding audience members that the NSRP was "determined to take our country back and put it in the hands of white, Christian Americans." Eldridge briefly outlined "repatriation" policy that the NSRP was developing, an ethnic cleansing program to remove Black Americans from the US:

> We must drive them [Black Americans] from our lands. They have acted like beasts, they are acting like beasts . . . We don't owe them one cent. Only thing we owe them is a trip on a boat back to Africa. Some people say, "oh, you'll not be able to do that," but we are gonna do it . . . We're National States' Rights Party people, and we accomplish a job we set out to do, and we're gonna do it.[340]

The FBI, in a 1970 assessment of the NSRP, outlined the dangers posed by the group. Focusing its recruitment efforts on "racists and bigots," the NSRP "condemns all law enforcement agencies, advocates violence to maintain its avowed aim of segregation, and urges its members to obtain arms and ammunition." According to the FBI report, the NSRP "constitutes a threat to this Nation's internal security."[341] In particular, the Ohio chapters of the NSRP more than lived up to the FBI's fears about the dangers posed by the group.

Dayton-area NSRP mainstay R. D. Eldridge continued his work with the group well into the 1970s. He was a featured speaker at the NSRP national convention held in Newport, Kentucky on June 20–21, 1970. According to an FBI informant at the event, Eldridge told approximately 300 convention delegates that "blood in the white man's veins was running hotter" than it had been in previous months. According to Eldridge, only "skunks" believed in integration. Moreover, Eldridge claimed, "the niggers were in a state of confusion, and while they are that way, we should set forth to take back our nation."[342] Another informant indicated that Eldridge claimed that he was once a Methodist minister in Tennessee until "communists got control of his denomination, at which time he left his ministry." The second source reported that Eldridge made numerous references to "niggers" and "black apes" in his speech, which outlined his opposition to integration and "race mongrelization." Eldridge claimed that "it was now necessary to use violence to fight for the white race in order to stop the menace."[343]

Unfortunately for R. D. Eldridge, his time in the NSRP came to an abrupt end in March 1972. An FBI informant told handlers that Eldridge was "forced to resign" from the party after J. B. Stoner "discovered that he [Eldridge] was embezzling party funds."[344] Another informant reported that Eldridge announced at a local NSRP meeting on March 12, 1972, that he was resigning because "the NSRP was taking too much time away from his family," adding that he was working 48-hour weeks on his full-time job. However, the informant was told by local NSRP officials that Stoner told Eldridge to resign after learning of alleged embezzlement of party funds, saying he would not push for criminal charges if Eldridge resigned.[345]

The Dayton-area NSRP members began to drift away from the group almost immediately, either leaving the white supremacist movement entirely or joining other Ohio-based groups, such as the newly formed neo-Nazi outfit known as the American White Nationalist Party (AWNP), which was based in Columbus. The party went on the decline the same year with the death of national leader Connie Lynch, and then lost additional crucial leadership when J. B. Stoner went to prison in 1980 for his role in a 1958 church bombing. By 1987 the NSRP ceased to exist, with members drifting away or joining other white supremacist and neo-Nazi groups.

•

White supremacy has taken many forms in the history of the state of Ohio. As the decade of the 1960s ended, white supremacist groups in Ohio that emerged during the civil rights movement began to lose members and influence. Simultaneously, the collective memory of white Ohioans regarding the growth of Ohio-based white supremacist groups like the NAAWP, NSRP, and the Klan began to fade. Yet, any decline in white supremacist activity by formal hate groups did not mean white supremacist ideologies disappeared.

While racial discrimination, religious bigotry, and ethnic conflict have in some ways decreased from earlier eras—especially those periods featuring extreme violence against persons of color—the ideologies of white supremacy have not disappeared, and by many measures white supremacist activity has sharply increased in recent decades. By the 1970s new white supremacist movements began to emerge, and the arrival of the internet has proved to be a useful tool for white supremacists, white nationalists, and neo-Nazi groups to recruit new members and spread the ideologies of hatred against racial, ethnic, religious, and sexual minorities. In the next sections of this book we explore the evolution since the 1970s of these ideologies in greater depth, and we also examine more recent history of white supremacist activity in Ohio.

NOW

Present-Day Hate Groups in Ohio

BOB FITRAKIS

Why does it seem that ever since the August 2017 torch-lit neo-Nazi march and rally in Charlottesville so many racist roads lead to Ohio?[1]

Central Ohio's Andrew Anglin heavily promoted the Charlottesville "Unity on the Right" event on his white supremacist website, *The Daily Stormer.* A 20-year-old from Maumee, Ohio, James Alex Fields Jr., rammed his car into counterprotesters at the hate rally, killing Heather Heyer and injuring several others.[2] Anglin's website gained such international notoriety when he called Heyer a "fat, childless, 32-year-old slut" that it was banned and shut down temporarily after the incident.[3]

"The neo-Nazis, white identifiers, and old-line pro-Confederates" named in a Charlottesville civil suit were introduced to their attorney by Cincinnati's James Condit Jr. During a run for Congress in Ohio, Condit gave interviews on YouTube raving about the "Criminal Zionist World Order."[4]

White nationalist leader Richard Spencer coined the term *alt-right* in 2008 to appeal to those who believe that white identity is under attack. It was a clever branding ploy to mask the alt-right's roots in the all-too-familiar fascism and white supremacy that had fueled the US Civil War and World War II. In the battle of ideas, terming a group's perspective as *alt-right* was a technique to counter multiculturalism on college campuses. It was a way to galvanize discontent against people of color, women, and the LGBTQIA+ community as a result of the gains made by the mass civil rights movements of the 1960s and '70s.[5]

Out of the ashes of the crushing defeat of German Nazism and Italian Fascism at the end of World War II, the world saw a dramatic increase in left-wing authoritarianism with the proliferation of communist doctrines. Communist regimes characteristically have brutally repressed freedom of speech, especially right-wing hate speech. A significant re-emergence of hate activities in the former Soviet Bloc countries, especially East Germany, followed the destruction of the Berlin Wall beginning in 1990. This symbolic collapse of communism coupled with the emergence of communication technologies to proliferate hate led to a resurgence of hate activities at the international, national, and state levels.[6]

Historically, the international suppression of hate groups and their activities lessened around the same time that personal computers became cost-effective and email became routine. Hate websites flourished. Prior to using computers to disseminate hate messages and recruit new members, white supremacist groups made widespread use of videos and audiocassettes. New technologies made it easier for individuals to create websites and more efficient for hate groups to recruit, publish, and disseminate their message on the internet.[7]

Through the internet and video technology, hate groups in Europe forged links with resurgent white supremacist groups in the US, particularly in Ohio. In the nascent era of high-tech hate, Ohio had much to offer: nine large urban centers, many in the northeast in the midst of industrial decline; plenty of farmland; and numerous Appalachian, economically hard-pressed, overwhelmingly white counties in the south. With its own long-standing history of white supremacy, Ohio presented a perfect battleground state to test the ideas of anti-Semitism, nativism, racism, ethnocentrism, and homophobia.

The struggle for Ohio should be put into historical perspective. The Ohio State University and central Ohio have a curious history related to eugenics and Nazi scientists. As the *Wall Street Journal* noted, "Long before cloned sheep, egg donors and sperm banks, a group of wealthy Northeastern conservatives embarked on an experiment with the help of the U.S. Army Air Corps to find a way to improve the human race . . . The Pioneer Fund, alarmed by the declining U.S. birth rate and rising immigration, was at the forefront of the eugenics movement."[8]

In 1940 the Pioneer Fund agreed to pay the all-white Air Corps members to breed children. Two of the 12 children were Ward and Darby Warburton, twin brothers born on August 18, 1940, at a hospital near Dayton, Ohio, according to the *Wall Street Journal.* Their father was stationed at a nearby airfield. William Pierce, a former physics professor and the leader of the National Alliance, frequently referred to scientists sponsored by the Pioneer Fund in his calls for race war in the US.

Founded in 1937, the Pioneer Fund is a nonprofit foundation with the stated purpose of studying "the problems of heredity and eugenics in the human race." Pierce's National Vanguard publication, citing race scientists, claimed, "It is the Negro's deficiency . . . which kept him in a state of savagery in his African environment and is now undermining the civilization of a racially mixed America."[9]

Still earlier in Ohio history, the state had the distinction of hiring away H. H. Goddard from the Vineland Training School for the Feeble Minded in New Jersey in 1918. Steven J. Gould, in his book *The Mismeasure of Man,* called Goddard "the most unsubtle hereditarian of all . . . [who] used his unilinear scale of mental deficiency to identify intelligence as a single entity, and [who] assumed that everything important about it was inborn and inherited in family lines."[10] So impressed were Ohio public officials with Goddard's work that they hired him to head the Ohio Bureau of Juvenile Research. Sharing Ohio officials' views, according to Stefan Kuhl in *The Nazi Connection: Eugenics, American Racism and German National Socialism,* were Nazi Party members. Kuhl points out that Goddard's pseudoscientific writings were central to the Nazi propaganda campaign to exterminate Jews and create a master race.

Madge Thurlow Macklin, an avid supporter in the 1930s of the controversial eugenics movement, spread the gospel of improving the human race through controlled breeding throughout North America. She co-founded the Canadian Eugenics Society in 1930, served on its executive committee between 1932 and 1934, and acted as its director in 1935. Macklin claimed that doctors ought to "determine who are physically and mentally qualified to be parents of the next generation." She advocated compulsory sterilization for the "unfit," such as schizophrenics. In 1945, as World War II ended, she was terminated from her appointment in medical genetics at Ontario University.[11]

What university would hire such a professor tied to Nazi science? In 1946 Macklin moved to Columbus and began lecturing in medical genetics at The Ohio State University, where she remained until her retirement in 1959. At the same time that Macklin moved to Columbus, US intelligence teams were busy rounding up Nazi scientists to bring to the US to work at places like Wright Patterson Air Force Base in Dayton. This is the infamous Operation Paperclip. These scientists were most visibly linked to the US space program and secretly worked on a variety of CIA projects, including mind-control experiments like the MK-Ultra project at The Ohio State University.[12]

Immediately following World War II, Wesley Swift sought to resurrect racism and Nazism in America by cloaking it in the garb of religion.[13] In 1946 he founded the Church of Jesus Christ–Christian in California. In 1970 the Reverend Richard Butler took control of the church and moved it to Hayden Lake, Idaho. In April 1973 he renamed it Aryan Nations.[14] White supremacists in the US in the 1990s had branched out from Hayden Lake, Idaho, to places throughout the Midwest, including a site in New Vienna, Ohio.

In May 1998 a neo-Nazi organization, the National Alliance, was openly recruiting in The Ohio State University area, with a post office box in nearby suburban Hilliard. That same month, south-side Columbus white supremacist gang members were convicted of armed robberies to finance their dream of a neo-Nazi revolution.

Unlike the more isolated American neo-Nazism of George Lincoln Rockwell's American Nazi Party of the late '50s (later renamed the National Socialist White People's Party), Butler's Aryan Nations actively sought alliances with older, indigenous white supremacist groups such as the Ku Klux Klan (KKK), and anti-federal-government patriot groups such as the Posse Comitatus.

In May 1978 neo-Nazi William Luther Pierce, under the pseudonym Andrew Macdonald, published the seminal novel *The Turner Diaries* (see Figure 2.1), the so-called blueprint for fomenting racial civil war and ultimately a white supremacist revolution. Federal prosecutors charged that *The Turner Diaries* was Timothy McVeigh's favorite book. The book's first chapter details a fuel-and-fertilizer-truck bombing of a federal building, and perhaps provided inspiration for the Oklahoma tragedy.[15]

The openness of the white supremacist movement in the late 1970s took them from a defeated underground clandestine organization to the steps of many state capitol buildings, including repeated visits to Columbus, Ohio. Moreover, the reborn white supremacist organi-

FIGURE 2.1. Cover of the book *The Turner Diaries*

zations turned noticeably more violent and aggressive. On June 2, 1983, Gordon Kahl, a leader of the racist Posse Comitatus, sought in the slaying of two US Marshals in North Dakota, died in a shootout with law enforcement officers in Smithville, Arkansas. A local sheriff was also killed.

Inspired by *The Turner Diaries,* Robert J. Matthews, an Aryan Nations member, created The Order in September 1983. The Order is perhaps the most violent neo-Nazi organization in American history. On June 18, 1984, Order members killed Denver radio personality Alan Berg outside his home.[16] The Order embarked on a robbery spree that made national news when it became the largest armed robbery in North American history.[17] This mountain of money found its way into neo-Nazi and white supremacist groups across the continent. The robberies, aided by an Aryan Nations printing press that counterfeited money, financed the explosive growth of high-tech hate in North America. On December 8, 1984, Matthews was killed in a shootout with the FBI, and Order members were subsequently arrested across the country. The trial, which led to their convictions, exposed Order members' religious philosophy as Christian Identity.

Beginning in the late 1970s and early 1980s, amid the farm crisis in the prairie states, the Christian Identity Church movement blossomed. A pseudo-theological justification for white supremacy and anti-Semitism, its basic tenet is that white Anglo-Saxons are the true and only descendants of the ten lost tribes of Israel. As God's "chosen people," they feel they must prepare for the final battle or Armageddon, which will take place in America. The Christian Identity religion serves as an umbrella theology and ideology for most of the white supremacist groups in America today. The religion preaches that Jews are the spawn of Satan, and that Blacks are "pre-Adamic" creations without souls, who are referred to as mud people.[18]

The Klan–Nazi merger under the guise of white supremacist Christian Identity theology is pivotal to understanding racial violence in Ohio. In 1996 Cheyne and Chevie Kehoe, members of the Christian Identity Church, made international news following a shootout with Ohio state troopers in Wilmington, Ohio. At his arraignment, Cheyne Kehoe told the court that "the reason I acted in the manner I did was due to the actions of men like Randy Weaver, Gordon Kahl, and Bob Matthews . . ."—all white supremacists. Media reports claimed they were visiting the newly established Aryan Nations compound in New Vienna, Ohio, just south of Wilmington.[19]

Currently in the US the internet is afforded constitutional protection and guaranteed First Amendment rights. Essentially, anyone can say anything on the internet, at least up to the standards of *Brandenburg v. Ohio* (1969), which draws the line at advocating "crime, sabotage, violence, or unlawful methods of terrorism," and hate speech can be sent electronically to and from sites all over the globe. The constitutional questions involving the First Amendment include the right of association and freedom of speech and of the press. The presence of Christian Identity religious doctrines further complicates the problem by affording additional First Amendment protections and considerations under freedom of religion.

The coalescence of several developments led to the phenomenon of "high-tech hate" to recruit new members and put them into motion in Ohio. For example, in the late 1990s the Aryan Republican Army, modeled on The Order, reportedly funneled large sums of money to neo-Nazi and white supremacist organizations to create a whole new generation of high-tech hate websites.[20] Their leader, Peter Langan, was operating out of a safe house on the south side of Columbus.

In 1998 the Associated Press (AP) reported that there were approximately 500 hate groups in the US, many with websites. The AP noted that year that there were 161 active hate websites. In 1995 there was only one.[21]

Hate groups can reach more and different people with current technology. Whether through the use of social media, podcasting, live streaming, or texting, hate groups can draw together the desperate, alienated, and isolated. Recruits no longer have to show up at rallies and can remain anonymous and invisible to the larger society. The electronic revolution has spawned a violent and racist voice in the middle of the "global village."

Racist battles in Ohio are simply the continuance of a long-simmering feud between the forces of equality and white supremacy. While the arc of the struggle has been toward human rights and dignity for all, the opposing combatants persist in their desperate fight to retain their traditional white supremacist values. Cues from the White House and racially coded white supremacist messages have renewed and invigorated even more racist behavior.

Candidate Donald J. Trump's comments disparaging Mexicans and Muslims ushered the way for xenophobic white nationalists' alt-right beliefs to enter mainstream political discourse. Stephen Bannon, Trump's chief campaign strategist, described his website Breitbart News as "the platform for the alt-right."[22] Following Trump's inauguration, Richard Spencer explained in an interview that "Trump is a white nationalist, so to speak. He is alt-right whether he likes it or not."[23] At a Washington, DC, rally just after Trump's election, 300 white nationalists demonstrated and Spencer led them in a chant of "Hail, Trump! Hail our people! Hail victory!" Many in the audience gave a Sieg Heil salute.[24] In the ten days after Trump's triumph, the Southern Poverty Law Center (SPLC) documented almost 900 bias-related incidents across the country.[25]

1970s

The 1970s were plagued by public disorder centered around issues of race and ethnicity, particularly the forced integration of neighborhoods and schools.[26] In the 1971 case *Swann v. Charlotte-Mecklenburg Board of Education,* the Supreme Court held that the federal courts had the power to order busing of students to desegregate schools. White supremacists took advantage of the racist sentiments that forced busing engendered to step up recruiting in Ohio.

James McNamara moved back to Columbus in 1971 after attending the University of Miami in Oxford, Ohio. He was uniquely positioned to observe and participate in the battle for Ohio between grassroots antiracist activists and the long-standing forces of white supremacy. He began law school at The Ohio State University in 1971 as racist sentiments seemed to be on the run, having been shattered in part by the civil rights, Black Power, and antiwar movements.[27] As McNamara recalled, many of the Marxist-Leninist movements that split from the Students for a Democratic Society (SDS) were heavily engaged in organizing against the Klan and neo-Nazis. In 1973 the Progressive Labor Party (PLP), claiming to control the remnants of SDS, founded the International Committee Against Racism. They were active in The Ohio State University campus area, as McNamara graduated and passed the bar in 1974.[28]

The American White Nationalist Party (AWNP), headquartered in Columbus, sponsored an event at the Imperial House North on Morse Road on May 31, 1975. Twenty-two members of various ultra-right racist organizations, including five American Nazi Party men in full regalia, met for the AWNP's "White Nationalist Strategy and Organizational Conference."[29] "The right-wing speakers proclaim that they felt that the American public is ready to accept their politics," according to *Columbus Free Press* writer Jim Hiser. He reported that the gathering committed to having more public meetings over the summer of 1975 and a "recruiting drive" in Ohio and neighboring states.[30]

AWNP President John Gerhardt told the crowd that the problems of America were caused by "niggers and Jews." His solution: white nationalist patriots must go on the offensive. Also on the offensive that night were demonstrators at the hotel from the PLP, their Committee Against Racism, and a group calling itself the Northside Freedom Corps. Demonstrators, 35 strong, arrived at the main door of the Imperial House at 7:00 p.m. and formed a picket line. When asked why the hotel would let the AWNP use their space, the manager told the demonstrators that she was running a million-dollar business and would rent rooms to anyone who could afford it.[31]

Kit Meade of Cleveland told the manager that they were not demonstrating against the hotel but against the Nazis inside. The manager called the police, and Meade was later arrested, charged with criminal trespass. Dave Mann of Columbus was also arrested for interfering with Meade's arrest. The picketers retreated from the hotel grounds and marched along Morse Road chanting "Hitler rose, Hitler fell, racist Nazis go to hell!"[32]

This clash between neo-Nazis and antiracists was minor compared with what happened two years later on Independence Day in Columbus.

McNamara was present at the Fourth of July 1977 Ku Klux Klan anti-busing rally. Anti-Klan protesters marched down High Street to oppose a Klan rally at the Statehouse. Instead of 35 antiracist demonstrators, Lance Ryder of the *Columbus Free Press* estimated that "500 people from an exceptionally broad, ad hoc coalition put aside political differences to unite against the racist actions and beliefs of the KKK, which mustered out about 15 members & supporters."[33]

The article offered an in-depth historical analysis of the confrontation: "It's a favored and time-honored tradition among northern newspaper editors and writers to locate the Ku Klux Klan in the deep South. Sometime between the postbellum Confederacy and the Black civil rights movement of the late 1950s and '60s."[34] "The KKK is at home in Ohio. In the 1920s, along with Indiana and Pennsylvania, Ohio was a northern mainstay of the Klan, boasting thousands of members. In the early part of the 20th century, the KKK helped push Klansmen into the state assemblies in all three states, elected a Klan governor in Indiana, and rallied with 20,000 other white-robed members for a massive parade through Washington D.C.," the Ryder article observed.[35]

In response to reports that the Klan was actively organizing in southwestern areas around Columbus, central Ohio antiracist activists had recently founded the Coalition Against the Klan (CAK), Ryder noted. News reports on the coalition referring to them as socialists and communists, he charged, focused more on "red-baiting" than on the facts. He pointed out that the CAK had a much broader coalition, including Quakers, young Blacks, Christians, liberal Democrats, and even a few Republicans.[36] In his article, Ryder complained that mainstream media accounts of the Klan rally emphasized a brief clash on the Statehouse steps between Klan members and a small splinter group. This group had broken its agreement with other coalition members in confronting the KKK, according to Ryder.

Anti-Klan demonstrator David Mann said that it was Revolutionary Communist Party members who attacked the Klan with long wooden poles, sweeping them from the Statehouse steps.[37] Contrary to mainstream press reports, Ryder stated, "what was seen was that a few 'communists' and a few Klansmen fought it out for 60 seconds on the Statehouse steps." Ryder concluded that, more importantly, "on a 90-degree national holiday 500 people said 'No' to racism . . . in what was otherwise the most forthright and principled action ever taken around racism in Columbus by such diverse groups."[38]

Three anti-Klan protesters were arrested on felony charges: George Allison, George Preston, and Tom Welch. They were charged with inciting violence but acquitted after an eight-day trial. Perhaps the most shocking evidence that emerged during the trial was from a Franklin County Municipal Court employee who stated that "the police and the Klan had been working together." He said that he "overheard officers and KKKers planning testimony and examining photographs together in a courthouse men's room before the misdemeanor trial of Annette Beauchamp." Beauchamp, an anti-Klan protester, was found guilty of disturbing a lawful meeting.[39]

Neo-Nazis in the Chicago area waged a relentless campaign to march in the Jewish enclave of Skokie, where, in 1977, an estimated one in six residents were Holocaust survivors. On June 21, 1978, US District Court Judge George Leighton ruled on behalf of Nazi leader Frank Collin that they could rally in nearby Marquette Park instead of Skokie. McNamara and other Ohio anti-Klan activists traveled to Chicago to join the Marquette Park counterdemonstration.

The Klan was back in central Ohio for the next national holiday. A Labor Day 1977 confrontation escalated the violence between antiracist activists and the Klan, once again at the Ohio Statehouse. This time 25 Klan members encountered 800 anti-Klan protesters. Added to the mix was "a line of Highway Patrol officers in riot gear," part of a massive law enforcement presence. Also, "During the rally a line of Columbus riot police moved through the demonstration and took up a position behind the PLP line."[40] A group of white men in the crowd began attacking the anti-Klan protesters. The protesters, believing the attackers were with the Klan, fought back. A later trial revealed that the white guys were undercover agents of the Columbus Police Department's Special Weapons and Tactics Team (SWAT).

"A bloody brawl between police and PLP erupted, injuring 7 police and 3 PLP members." In the aftermath of the fight, "police swept through the area and arrested 10 persons on charges ranging from felonious assault and disturbing a lawful meeting to disorderly conduct," the *Columbus Free Press* noted.[41] Three counter-demonstrators, John Woods, Dave Mann, and Bill Gilbreth, were among those arrested who faced felony charges. Mann was charged with felonious assault against undercover SWAT team member Harlan Hill. Mann had struck Hill with a lead pipe.[42] Mann reported that initially "the only offensive action were some eggs thrown. Our contingent was attacked by some thuggish-looking roughnecks that turned out to be police. I had been assigned to a 'security' role—and was carrying a strip of lead solder. I simply reacted in self-defense."[43]

After extensive trials, all three were found not guilty. Mann was acquitted because the jury believed that the undercover police failed to identify themselves and were brutal in beating his friend John Woods. Mann told the jury, "I attempted to restrain the individual I perceived was preparing to beat the brains out of my friend John."[44] Gilbreth faced three felonious assault charges and was acquitted of all of them. Jurors later stated that "they concluded that police had beaten Gilbreth and other CAR [Committee Against Racism] picketers, that they filed phony charges against Gilbreth to justify their attack, and they lied on the stand to back up the phony charges."[45]

Gilbreth was hospitalized twice on Labor Day, once before being charged at police headquarters and again at the police station. Police beat him "a second time while fingerprinting him, tearing open the nine stitches keeping his head together after the first beating." After the beating at police headquarters, they charged Gilbreth with three additional misdemeanor counts of assault.[46] Fortunately for Gilbreth, several defense witnesses testified that he had been brutally beaten without provocation by Columbus police. Defense witness Russell McGinnis, a 17-year-old Hilliard High School senior, filmed the Klan rally for his Problems of Democracy class. His 8mm film captured the ferocious police beating of Gilbreth and guaranteed his acquittal.[47]

Defense attorneys Robert Handelman, Thomas McGuire, and McNamara convinced the jury that what had happened on Labor Day was a "police riot." Handelman told the jury, "I'm just thankful we were able to present the witnesses and photographic evidence that we have at this trial. Without that, you would have had to make your decision after hearing only the honest testimony of the defendants and the perjured testimony of the police."[48] Mann stated, "The Lawyers Guild did a wonderful job on our behalf."[49]

Again, the *Columbus Free Press*'s analysis of the event accused the mainstream media of being ahistorical. Reporter D. C. Andrews noted that Columbus media coverage "existed in a historical vacuum." The Klan's history of encouraging and committing burnings, lynchings, and bombings against Black citizens went unmentioned. The murders of children and civil rights workers was unmentioned. The philosophical links between the KKK and Nazism went unexplored.[50]

It was reported that a week after the Labor Day clash, a 20-foot cross was burned in the median strip of Interstate 71 near Cooke Road on the city's north side. The next night another cross was found burning in a grassy area at the I-270 / State Route interchange in Mifflin Township. A spokesperson for the Franklin County Sheriff's Department said that the cross-burnings were not being investigated because "there were no leads."[51] Andrews complained that "the police and the local news media say there's no activity of the KKK in Columbus," while "hate literature" was being circulated throughout the city.[52]

After being tested at the Capitol building in 1977, anti-Klan demonstrators confronted white supremacists two years later in both Parma and Middletown. "On June 24, anti-racist groups broke up a demonstration staged by the racist White Power Party in Parma, Ohio."[53]

"Until last month, the Ku Klux Klan's efforts to rebuild itself in Ohio by public rallies in Columbus and elsewhere had failed. Klan supporters consistently found themselves outnumbered, outshouted, and in some cases physically attacked by militant anti-Klan groups," read Jeff Coleman's lead on the front page of the August 7–September 10, 1979, issue of the *Columbus Free Press*. "These roles were reversed during a well-organized and relatively well-attended July 22nd Klan rally in Middletown, Ohio near Dayton."[54]

At the Middletown rally, rising racist star David Duke outlined his vision of uniting Klan and neo-Nazi members. Approximately 150 Warren County sheriffs and Middletown police officers initially fought to keep the overwhelming Klan contingent separated from the anti-Klan activists. At one point, 50 Klan supporters rushed past the police lines and attacked Black counterdemonstrators from the Republic of New Africa Movement.[55] Bill Wilkinson, head of the Imperial Empire of the Ku Klux Klan, was at the mic and was heard shouting "Look at the niggers run!" One Klan supporter was arrested for carrying brass knuckles. It was reported that about a half-dozen anti-Klan demonstrators were beaten.[56]

A *New York Times* article documented that the Invisible Empire had arrived in Middletown with an estimated 900 supporters. They reported that 100 antiracists who had planned to protest the rally left before it began. "We aren't suicidal," Cathy Pekel of the International Committee Against Racism (INCAR) told the *Times*.[57] Anti-Klan groups left the park before dark and the Klan later burned a cross before police cleared the area at 10:30 p.m.[58]

McNamara pointed out that a new tactic was used against the Klan in Middletown. Attorney Fred Gittes, a partner in McNamara's law firm, filed a lawsuit to ban the Klan from their traditional cross-burning, citing Environmental Protection Agency regulations. McNamara conceded that this was primarily a "publicity suit," but it brought awareness to anti-Klan activities. While the lawsuit failed to block the Klan's actions, McNamara stated that it was helpful in raising public consciousness.[59]

Alongside INCAR, a united front created by the highly disciplined PLP, there was a new antiracist grassroots force: Those United to Fight Fascism (TUFF). The group, formed in September 1979, was dedicated "to combat[ing] a growing fascist movement." In TUFF's analysis, rapidly expanding white supremacist tendencies in Ohio were tied to a bad economy. "Economic and social conditions exist now which are causing poor and working people to become increasingly frustrated and be in search of solutions for their problems," a TUFF spokesperson said.[60] "When we get to the point where members of minorities can be attacked in public without fear of reprisal, that's what fascism is." TUFF explained that fascists are "racist, sexist, anti-Semitic, anti-gay, anti-union, anti-alien, and anti-communist."[61]

TUFF's goal was to build a mass anti-white-supremacy organization from the bottom up, in contrast to the top-down model of INCAR and other Marxist-Leninist groups. McNamara explained how TUFF hoped to galvanize the grassroots in partnership with the PLP, the Revolutionary Communist Party (RCP), the Workers World Party (WWP), and the Communist Workers' Party (CWP). In McNamara's analysis, TUFF flourished in central Ohio while many of the Marxist-Leninist cadre groups did not, because they required application for admission and a loyalty pledge to the party line. McNamara said that TUFF was not explicitly "Left." It was plainly antifascist and sought the broadest possible coalition.[62]

TUFF's first public appearance involved sending 25 people from Columbus for a protest outside Nazi headquarters in Cleveland on September 16, 1979. TUFF took the streets back in Middletown on October 7 for an antiracist march along with the National Association for the Advancement of Colored People (NAACP) and the Southern Christian Leadership Conference (SCLC). The purpose of civil rights demonstrations was to counter the Klan's July march that had called for "forced black repatriation to Africa" and a "get tough policy with arrogant non-whites in the high schools."[63]

A blockbuster press conference on October 24 escalated racial tensions in Columbus when the Police Officers for Equal Rights (POER) charged that there were ties between the Fraternal Order of Police (FOP) and the Klan. The FOP claimed to represent 40 percent of Columbus's Black police officers. At the press conference, POER spokesperson Ollice Stubblefield charged that the FOP was sympathetic to the Ku Klux Klan. He noted that a FOP flyer targeting Democratic mayoral candidate Bill Boyland smeared "lawyers who filed a civil rights case for people opposed to the Ku Klux Klan." Stubblefield stated, "We do not understand why the FOP is attacking lawyers who believe in protecting the rights of people to oppose the Klan. The fact that the FOP picked this one case as an example shows they are concerned about protecting the Ku Klux Klan."[64]

Later that year, the CWP took the offensive against the Klan. They organized a "Death to the Klan" march in Klan territory in Greensboro, North Carolina, on November 3, 1979.[65] Well-armed Klan members and neo-Nazis showed up to counter the march. A shootout initiated by the Klan ensued. Four members of the CWP and a marcher were killed. Eleven other anti-Klan marchers were wounded along with a single Klansman.

A few weeks later, at the CWP's funeral march in Greensboro, they were unexpectedly joined by 70 members of TUFF organized out of the central Ohio area. As McNamara explained it, the CWP requested that no other groups join them with their own banners. McNamara, who still owns the TUFF banner, said, "We told them that we had no problem with this." After that, McNamara said, central Ohio developed a national reputation as fearless anti-Klan organizers.[66]

1980s

In the 1980s a new white supremacist movement with roots in Great Britain found its way to the American heartland. Members of TUFF and their allies began to notice that the new threat was not from small-town Ohio or Appalachian Klan; rather, it was neo-Nazi punks influenced by the far-right fascist National Front Party of England. Their growth, accentuated by the anti-authoritarian punk rock scene and spin-off hate music, sprouted local groups.

Out of the British cauldron of white nationalism, Nazis emerged in Cincinnati on May 10, 1980. Under the name of Hitler's old party, these new National Socialist members were met with overwhelming resistance by the local Anti-Klan Network. Seeking to avoid the previous violent clashes at the Ohio Statehouse, Cincinnati police seized the protesters' sticks and signs. The Nazi signs remained in full view and read "Hitler Lives" and "White Power."[67]

TUFF sent a contingent from Columbus. The group's spokesperson, Kate Schulte, explained why TUFF was there: "Since the Klan and Nazi murders of five anti-Klan demonstrators in Greensboro, North Carolina last November, people have realized that ignoring fascism is very dangerous in a time of economic crisis. People are beginning to see that the forces that trot out these racists we saw in Cincinnati are doing it to polarize people against each other instead of against the real causes of inflation and high employment."[68] Schulte announced that TUFF would be headed back to Middletown on June 14 in a planned counter action against the White Knights of the Ku Klux Klan. Richard Wills led the White Knights, a splinter group of the larger national Klan organization, the Invisible Empire of the Ku Klux Klan. Schulte worried that Middletown was "becoming a center of racist activity."[69]

Despite 250 anti-Klan demonstrators appearing in Middletown on June 14, there was no confrontation. The Middletown Anti-Klan Network decided not to directly confront the men in white robes but instead to march through neighborhoods urging residents to oppose the Klan.[70]

Reports of the Klan intimidating individuals proliferated in central Ohio. A Black woman told the police that she encountered the Klan on August 10 while looking to rent a house on Noe-Bixby Road on Columbus's east side with her husband and two small children. As they drove up to the house, a group of whites were sitting on the lawn next door. The woman claimed that a man in the group shouted loudly, "Looks like we're going to have some niggers around here." After looking at the house, the family was met by a man standing in the middle of street wearing a Ku Klux Klan hood and leading a large boxer on a chain. The family got in their car and quickly left.[71]

Three days later, in Lemon Township, Butler County, the home of a Black couple was riddled with nine bullets from a high-powered rifle at 10:30 p.m. Tom Kimbrough, his wife, Eva, and their young child were not injured. The attackers left Ku Klux Klan literature on the Kimbroughs' front lawn. Tom Kimbrough told the *Columbus Free Press* that he suspected the shooting was connected to his "membership in the Middletown Anti-Klan Network which had organized a counter-action at a Klan rally in Middletown last June." Kimbrough stated that the Butler County Sheriff's Department and the Lemon Township Police refused to investigate the shooting. TUFF responded by organizing a letter-writing campaign to the Lemon Township Chief of Police and the Butler County Sheriff.[72]

The Klan endorsed Ronald Reagan in 1980, which he rejected—but not before appearing in Philadelphia, Mississippi, and telling the raucous white crowd that he, too, believed in "states' rights."[73] Reagan was repeatedly criticized for opening his campaign at the Neshoba County Fair, the same county where young civil rights activists David Goodman, Michael Schwerner, and James Chaney were murdered by the Klan in 1964. A few days before the murders, the Klan had firebombed a Black church and beaten the terrified worshipers.[74]

Lee Atwater, political consultant for presidents Reagan and George H. W. Bush, admitted to manipulating the race issue with code words during the 1980 presidential campaign. "You start out in 1954 by saying, 'Nigger, nigger, nigger.' By 1968 you can't say nigger—that hurts you, backfires. So you say stuff like, uh, forced busing, states' rights, and all that stuff, and you're getting so abstract."[75]

TUFF organized an informational picket in Columbus at a fundraiser for Reagan on August 27, 1980. TUFF member Bob Hart asked Reagan supporters: "Did you know that racist groups like the Ku Klux Klan are backing Ronald Reagan?"[76] After all, it was one of the Grand Wizards, David Duke, who noted that the 1980 Republican platform "looked like it was written by a Klansman." TUFF also endorsed an attempt to create a statewide antifascist network, announcing that they would hold an All Ohio Conference Against

Racism and the Klan in Ohio in October 1980.[77] TUFF's conference was endorsed by both the Miami Valley and the Cincinnati Anti-Klan Networks.

The conference climaxed with a debate between National Lawyers Guild attorney McNamara, representing TUFF, and David Goldberger, an Ohio State University law professor who represented Nazis in the Skokie case. The debate was entitled "Fascism and the First Amendment."[78] McNamara stressed that fascism was a clear and present danger in the US. He cited over 30 incidents of white supremacist violence against Blacks since March 1980. He specifically mentioned a case in which four elderly Black women were gunned down by "a carload of self-professed Klan members in Chattanooga, Tennessee on April 17."[79]

Goldberger argued that historically the government has repressed the Left, not the Right, so that it made sense to fight for the rights of all people. He said the way the Left could ensure its right to free speech was "to loosen government power, not to give it more power by allowing it to stop Klan members and Nazis from speaking." He continued, "Free speech keeps the Klan and Nazis up front, in the open, observable."[80]

McNamara contended that there was a frightening comparison between present-day America and budding Nazism in 1930s Germany. "We need to decide when to stop it from happening, not to argue that it won't." Goldberger countered, "To compare the United States to Germany is ridiculous."[81] McNamara recalled the emergence of white-only male gangs in the Columbus suburb of Westerville and the Clintonville neighborhood. These new neofascists began to play in bands in The Ohio State University campus area, mostly at the Newport Music Hall and Bernie's Bagels and Deli.

In order to combat the new wave of white supremacy, Anti-Racist Action (ARA) was created. It began in Minneapolis, Minnesota, with members of a multiracial skinhead crew called the Minnesota Baldies. They were described as left-wing punk rock fans.[82]

In the late 1980s Klan activity shifted to southeast Ohio. In 1987 the Ku Klux Klan staged rallies in Jackson County and Belpre, Ohio, a city near Parkersburg, West Virginia. The *Athens News* offered this analysis: "In the late 1980s and early 1990s, a surprising number of these rallies were held, usually orchestrated by KKK members coming to southeast Ohio from outside the area. The rallies often had more protesters than actual supporters."[83]

FIGURE 2.2. William Donta Jr. from the *Athens News*. Credit: Paul Walsh/Flickr CC https://creativecommons.org/licenses/by-sa/2.0/.

In an infamous photo for the *Athens News*, William Donta Jr. posed in full, white-hooded Klan attire holding a rifle with a 30-round clip (see Figure 2.2). Donta kicked off the southeast Ohio KKK recruitment drive on September 1987 with a Klan gathering in Jackson County at his Oak Hill farm that drew 200 people, most of them protesters. Donta was driven by financial distress. He invited the Klan to his farm because of "damage done to his land by a coal company." Two and a half years later, Klan recruitment ran into problems when Donta was charged with murder for allegedly shooting his neighbor in a dispute over a chainsaw.[84]

Sixty or so Klan members and supporters attended a 1989 gathering that culminated in the burning of a 30-foot cross, sponsored by the Knights of the Ku Klux Klan Number 87 (Belpre, Ohio, chapter). The *Athens News* noted that young people in the skinhead movement were visibly present in supporting the Klan's view of white supremacy.[85] Notions of white racial purity abounded, as the paper reported: "Several apparent sympathizers wore T-shirts that said, 'Pure white and damn proud of it.'"[86]

Economic hardship appeared again as a theme at the Belpre rally. Rita Ray, a local farmer, had offered her land for a Klan rally. She told the *Athens News* that life had been hard on the farm: "This is supposed to be America, you know—life, liberty, and the pursuit of happiness." Tom Willard of Jackson County explained that he was joining the Klan because "I feel like I'm getting shafted all the time, at least now I feel like I'll have some kind of say-so."[87]

Imperial Wizard Pete Collins and the Grand Dragon James Glass directed the cross-burning. A SWAT team, attack dogs, and 30 law enforcement officers were present. The *News* reported that at 11:00 p.m. a car drove past and fired shots at Ray's farm.[88]

By 1989 TUFF had disappeared from central Ohio, and the Anti-Racist Action chapter began holding weekly meetings. In 1990 Ohio's ARA made its street debut to protest a yearly Klan rally in Oxford, home of Miami University. A debate ensued in the pages of the *Columbus Free Press* over ARA's actions. Virginia Richards of Columbus took issue with McNamara's account of the rally: "If indeed counter-protesting anti-racists threw rocks at anyone including Klan members they were validating a dangerous sentiment—that violence against those with whom we disagree is an appropriate response." Illustrator James Beoddy offered a different analysis: "The danger begins, and their First Amendment rights end, when they can no longer be arrested or identified or held accountable for their actions. Why should we treat them [Klan] like American citizens under their masks if we don't know who they are?"[89]

1990s

In the late 1990s, an inexcusable—and often ignored by the mainstream media—pattern of behavior emerged wherein so-called conservative Republicans gave aid and comfort to explicit racists and anti-Semites. After Ohio's 1990 gubernatorial election, investigative reporter Russ Bellant linked then-governor George Voinovich to money sources provided by Eastern and Central European former Nazis and fascists.[90] Nationally, two of President Bill Clinton's chief critics in Congress, Representative Robert Barr and Senator Trent Lott, contributed columns to a white supremacist organization, the Council of Conservative Citizens.[91]

A Klan Christmas cross appeared in Cincinnati's Fountain Square in 1992. The Klan claimed that they'd put up the cross to "put Christ back in Christmas." The cross was under 24-hour police protection and behind a barricade but was knocked down or damaged six times over the course of ten days by protesters. In all, ten people were arrested for attacking the cross. Cincinnati preacher and famed civil rights activist Reverend Fred Shuttlesworth said, "The Klan may have a legal right to put a cross here but not a spiritual right."[92]

On the morning of April 3, 1993, over 100 antiracist activists and hardcore anti-Klan fighters assembled at Whetstone Park in Columbus to join a caravan to protest a Ku Klux Klan rally in Coshocton. A small town east of Columbus, Coshocton is nestled in the rolling rural no-man's-land of east-central Ohio. McNamara passed out maps of Coshocton and some last-second advice: "Keep with friends, the Klan slime will attack if you stray."[93]

This confrontation would be with "the new Klan." The recent growth of the new Klan can be tied directly to the Reagan and Bush years. When George H. W. Bush ran for president, he sent the new Klan a valentine in the form of the infamous Willie Horton TV commercial, suggesting that his opponent Michael Dukakis was going easy on a Black male accused of raping a white woman.

Debate over strategy and tactics in dealing with the Klan inevitably came to the forefront in Coshocton. Reverend Cliff N. Biggers had invited the anti-Klan forces to a prayer service at Shiloh Baptist Church in Coshocton. An organization called the Coshocton Community Coalition, along with the Coshocton Peacemakers Project, welcomed "anti-Klan demonstrators." They requested that the group "voice your opposition to the Klan peacefully" and informed them that "peace activists from the Ready Response Team from Athens, Ohio," were there to train them as "nonviolent peacekeepers."[94]

The coalition also invited the activists to Coshocton Lake Park to express a positive message of interracial community spirit at a family picnic. They enticed them with "free hot dogs, soft drinks and activities for young people," including "clowns, games and fishing."[95] Most of the anti-Klan activists never made it to the picnic.

The Klan took a stand at Coshocton's courthouse grounds that afternoon. Seven Klansmen in white-and-black sheets with hoods faced a thousand anti-Klan demonstrators mobilized from around the state. The Coshocton Community Coalition exchanged flyers with the anti-Klan demonstrators. One read "The whole world is watching! We'll all be on tonight's news. If we attack the Klan, (verbally or physically) the Klan appears victim. Which group will then appear as the 'hate group'?"[96] The Klan was waving the Confederate battle flag and bearing a cross. Chris Conner, the Grand Wizard from Bowling Green, Kentucky, was decked out in his best white robe with green trimming. He began his speech by muttering into the mic condemnations of "faggots and queers." The crowd's first chant swelled from the direction of the Skinheads Against Racial Prejudice (SHARP): "You better watch out, we're going to fuck you up, the KKK, you know what's up." The next chant followed: "Hey, hey, ho, ho, fascist pigs have got to go."[97]

McNamara explained to the anti-Klan group the importance of protesting. "These people are dangerous, they come in contact with a lot of young people. There's a lot of young people here that came to hang out with the Klan, and they'll recruit their friends and become part of a movement. Anti-Klan activists provide an alternative voice at Klan rallies, giving kids a chance to listen to reason even as the Klan tries to fill their heads with hate."[98] McNamara further noted, "There's already a small group in Worthington High School and a small group at Westerville High School"—both schools are in relatively affluent Columbus suburbs—"[and] they're not very big. It only takes two or three of them to hurt people. I think the most effective thing here is to interfere with their ability to recruit new young members."[99]

The *Columbus Free Press* approached three young Coshocton males for an interview. One said, "I ain't allowed over here," meaning the area set aside for anti-Klan activists. But they referred the reporter to their mentor, a middle-aged Coshocton man, for comment. In his assessment, the counterdemonstrators were all "queers on welfare." He wondered, "Why are there so many Blacks here? They know they can't join." His young friends giggled.[100]

Students from Kenyon College showed up in force. Forsaking the chants, they let their banners voice their opinions: "Difference is Our Strength." "My Race is Human." "The Time for Hate is Over."[101]

As the Grand Dragon taunted the crowd with an Arsenio Hall "woo-woo!" and discussed the need for Blacks to put Crisco oil on their hair, the first signs of violence emerged. A SHARP member lobbed a large, economy-sized Coke bottle toward the Klan. It fell short, smashing into the skull of a frontline anti-Klan protester. As the Wizard advised everyone to "buy Coca-Cola," the frontline Klan fighters chanted, "Stop the attacks on the working class, kick the Klan in the ass." The chanting continued: "Anti-union, anti-gay, fascist pigs, go away!"[102]

One unidentified female Klan sympathizer, who would make her presence known later, loudly proclaimed, "You can't fuckin' hear nothin'." She seemed dismayed that she could not hear the words of the first Klanswoman to speak. Wearing a Confederate flag as a bandana, the Klanswoman screamed, "We need to stand together! White is right! What about white pride?!" Klansmen looked on with pride as she puffed on a cigarette throughout her tirade. A Coshocton woman, dressed similarly, repeatedly flipped the Klanswoman the bird and shouted "Bitch! Bitch!"[103]

The cops looked on. The growing line of county sheriffs stood pensively, but quickly leaped into action to make their first arrest as an anti-Klan protester leaned over the yellow police ribbon and refused to back up. As he was carted off to jail, he surely heard the chant "Let him go! Let him go!" And he no doubt heard "The cops and the Klan go hand in hand, the cops and the Klan go hand in hand."[104]

More antiracists shouted "Scum in sheets, get off our streets! You in blue, you can go too." The rhetoric was escalating, as was the video war. The Klan was videotaping the protesters. The protesters were videotaping the Klan. And the police were videotaping everyone, including themselves. The ever-growing horde of blue-and-black-clad law enforcement officers loomed large on the courthouse lawn. No one could miss the club-wielding, mounted police on large antiriot horses moving to protect the Klan.[105]

As the moment to march grew near, the protesters challenged, "C'mon, just try it, fuck with us, we'll start a riot." The frontline antifascist forces seemed sincere. Suddenly, the seven Klansmen bolted toward the street, protected by a regiment of 175 rural sheriff 's deputies and what seemed like a traditional 7th Cavalry unit. The counterprotesters moved just as quickly to engulf the parade. "Move, move, move! Go, go, go," the protesters advised one another. The distinctive baritone voice of a TV news reporter floated overhead: "The crowd is moving exuberantly."[106]

All seven of the Klan then controlled the street, and they were hellbent on holding it with the aid of the Coshocton Sheriff's Department. The first sounds of launched projectiles echoed amid cries of "Rock that bitch!" which quickly gave way to a singular chant, "Death, death, death to the Klan!" The police were determined to hold the street. Everyone was ordered to the sidewalk, even news crews. There were Confederate banners in the street, police attack dogs, and cops with clubs on horseback.

The police frantically chased a reported 16-year-old, whom they suspected of throwing rocks with "extreme malice." An officer on foot finally cornered her against the building with the help of a cop on horseback. They let her go after she chanted, "I didn't throw shit! I didn't throw shit!"

Another officer on foot confided, "I hate this job." Yet another on horseback seemed to better relish his sworn duty as he galloped his horse up on the sidewalk, panicking the protesters.

A woman lay in the street bleeding from a head wound as a cop stood over her with a club. The police would later officially report that she had been hit by a rock. That's not how the protesters saw it as they scattered before the thundering hooves. Meanwhile, back at the courthouse, someone lobbed a chunk of metal at the Klan, which missed its intended mark and shattered the glass door of the building. The female Klan supporter looked worried. The police swarmed into the crowd to arrest a female student from Antioch College alleged to be responsible for the shattered glass. They also arrested a camerawoman who attempted to videotape the arrest. "What law was I breaking?" she asked.

Finally, the Klan gave in as the police fought to control the courthouse turf. The Klan displayed their traditional bravery and requested protective custody from the police. An officer grabbed a megaphone and addressed the crowd, his words drowned out in wave after wave of counterdemonstrator chants. Another officer told the crowd to go home. Somebody responded, "It is not over until the Klan goes home!" Another added, "It's not over 'til the fascist bullshit's gone!"

Sighted at the rally was Coshocton's most notorious Klan member, Calvin Reese. As the cops ushered the Klan away, most of the crowd drifted toward their vehicles. A small hardcore group stayed on the courthouse lawn, dodging the riot horses and reminiscing about the day's anti-Klan activities.

In the rally's aftermath, about 50 anti-Klan protesters marched to the police station and demanded the release of their friends and comrades. The Coshocton sheriff would later describe them as "a riotous mob bent on a jailbreak." The protesters obviously did not know they were a mob, and nobody informed them of their plans to take over the Coshocton jail. The mounted police had other ideas. As the group approached the police with a friendly and simple question, "Which way is the police station?" the officers responded by charging their horses into them.

The police were determined to clear the park. No citizen could be on the courthouse property, and they had the horses to enforce it. They drove the scattered remnants of the anti-Klan forces to the edge of the street. A woman from Coshocton, as she backed up, explained why it was a strategic retreat: "Well, they hit a girl over here and sliced her head wide open. She was just standing there." A demonstrator demanded that the officers explain under what authority they were dispersing peaceful protesters. "If you want to take on the First Amendment, take it on!" the remnant antiracist activists cheered. The cop on horseback responded, professionally, "We're just trying to protect you, sir." But the protesters had the final word. Spontaneously, and in one voice, they shouted "Bullshit!"

On October 23, 1993, the Ku Klux Klan, like in 1977, stormed Ohio's capital. The KKK, due to massive counterdemonstrations, had no real supporters or potential recruits to talk to this time. Despite an intensive PR campaign by city officials and downtown business leaders, they could not keep counterdemonstrators away from the rally. Younger Generation X anti-Klan protesters displayed a new level of militancy and rage.

City officials created a counter event called Unity Day far from the Statehouse on The Ohio State University campus. The longstanding debate over how to deal with the Klan once again appeared in the pages of the October 1993 *Columbus Free Press*. Black activist Cornell McCleary argued that "when the Klan comes to Columbus, the citizens of this community should be anywhere but at the Klan rally."[107] Mike Dittmer, a gay rights activist, came out in strong support of the city-backed Unity Day: "Unity Day will be held downtown to remind that downtown belongs to all of us, not the Klan. The program is being coordinated by a gay-friendly committee within CCRC [Columbus Community Relations Commission]; openly gay attorney Elliot Fishman is serving on the initial planning committee."[108]

INCAR organizer Andy Allen argued, "From its beginning, the Ku Klux Klan has been a racist group that pushes racial segregation by any means necessary. It has used terrorism, murder, cross burnings, rallies, and even elections to promote segregation in schools, business, government, and neighborhoods, and it has shown a lot of flexibility in pursuit of its aims." Allen predicted that "those who oppose racism will go to the Statehouse steps on the afternoon of October 23rd to turn the Klan rally into the biggest anti-racist event the city has ever seen."[109]

Only an overwhelming police presence—an estimated 500 officers or more—and expensive and extreme security measures preserved the Klan's ability to speak. Marching counterdemonstrators were directed along official routes and subjected to metal detector searches before entering the fenced-in anti-Klan containment zone. On the other side of the newly erected fence a massive police phalanx protected the Klan as they propagandized behind yet another metal security fence.

There was consensus among mainstream media types that the public would never learn the exact taxpayer cost of protecting the Klan. Journalists joked about a betting pool, trying to predict how many budgets the costs would be buried in. They included overtime for 500 highly trained police officers, the new fences and scaffolding, the resulting round-the-clock construction, new high-tech police surveillance equipment, a communications command post in the high-rise across from the Statehouse, helicopters and undercover expenses for well over a month of both secret and blatant surveillance of anti-Klan organizational meetings, and the police junket to Indianapolis for training.

McNamara, attorney for the counterdemonstrators, called it "a million-dollar press conference for the Klan." The mainstream press seemed to settle on a $250,000 figure in their informal discussions.[110]

From their fortress enclave on the Statehouse steps, the two dozen thoroughly modern Klansmen—sans robes, with sunglasses replacing hoods, preaching "love" of white folks while singling out "queers" over "Negroes"—preened for the cameras, giving a Sieg Heil–type salute on cue.[111]

This was the new, high-tech, Euro-style Klan: GQ white supremacy. They're not interested in their granddaddy's white-trash Klan. But their followers missed the Klan show. Only six pro-Klan supporters briefly mingled with the estimated 2,000 anti-Klan demonstrators. One white supremacist couple, identifying themselves as Russ and Lisa, found themselves in police protective custody along with four visibly shaken neo-Nazi youth. Russ lost his prized Confederate bandana to overwhelming hostile forces promising him unity with their fists unless he gave it up. "I'm not pro-Klan, I just think states should be allowed to have their own flag if they want it," he explained. "I tell Black people, they've got their X, and I've got my X on the Confederate flag."[112]

Lisa was a little bolder. "I support the Klan, and I'm not scared." Russ looked pained as his bandana was set ablaze to the chant of

"Burn, baby, burn!" Russ, Lisa, and their four neo-Nazi cohorts were escorted out before they could hear the words of Klansman Thom Robb. No other pro-Klan individuals asserted their presence during the rally. "The Klan has no real following, that's the story," according to Bob Handelman, local attorney and longtime Klan foe. Indeed, Klan fever seemed extremely noncontagious in Columbus. McNamara declared the counterdemonstration a great success: "I don't think they recruited one new member today, and they may have lost a few. That's why we organize to confront them."[113]

Still, the Klan may have turned the sparsely attended rally into a recruitment drive. The Klan's banner contained no slogan, only its name and post office box, and was flashed on TV screens across the nation; a free how-to-contact the Klan ad for anybody too intimidated to travel to Ohio's capital.

If there were any obvious government failures during the Klan rally, it was the mayor's inability to keep large numbers of anti-Klan protesters away from the site. The repeated warnings that the police could not "guarantee" the public's safety at the rally were sneered at by Black activist Barry Edney: "Hell, they've never been worried about my safety before; it's the Klan's safety they can't guarantee."[114]

The *Columbus Dispatch* claimed that the Klan turnout was smaller than expected, but the daily paper ran photos of the counterdemonstrators alongside the officially sanctioned Unity Day crowds, documenting that the protesters at the Statehouse outnumbered the people at The Ohio State University by at least four to one.

The officially orchestrated Unity Day procession began according to script on The Ohio State University campus. Mark Welsh, of the Native American Indian Center, pondered, "Why doesn't that Community Relations Commission investigate that 300-foot statue of a racist headed for our city?" referring to the Russian-made Christopher Columbus statue sought after by city leaders.[115]

The mayor's first-time use of the so-called Community Relations Commission, an organization established in the wake of the Rodney King beating in Los Angeles and The Ohio State University wrestler Oleatha Waugh's brutalization by Columbus police, seemed not only disingenuous but surreal. During the weeks leading up to the Klan rally, members of the CRC invaded various anti-Klan organizational meetings and pleaded for young activists to attend Unity Day events. Police, both uniformed and plain-clothed, also attended the anti-Klan meetings, claiming that they were there to assist the organizers with their protesting needs. With Columbus's Republican Mayor Greg Lashutka denouncing the anti-Klan demonstrators and presiding over Unity Day, this struck the activists as odd. Anti-Klan activists repeatedly charged that Lashutka condoned the overtly racist electoral strategies of the Reagan years. They pointed out that the 1980 Republican platform was endorsed by the KKK and that Reagan had granted Bob Jones University tax-exempt status while the school practiced apartheid in the name of Jesus.

Handelman recalled that Lashutka was the point man for Supreme Court nominee Robert Bork in central Ohio. "He supported Bork for the Supreme Court, a man who argues the 'original intent' doctrine, a man who believes that states should be able to discriminate against Jews, Blacks and gays. Give me a break. Unity Day?"[116]

A local American Federation of State, County, and Municipal Employees (AFSCME) staffer pointed out that Lashutka was currently in the process of privatizing the city's sanitation department, historically the source of decent-paying jobs for minorities and inner-city residents: "He should be forced to explain at Unity Day how he is going to destroy civil service jobs and give sweetheart deals to his rich, white suburban friends."[117]

Not only did the counterdemonstrators come in large numbers to protest the Klan; they demonstrated a new spirit of militancy and, some of them, a frightening amount of pure rage. They attempted, despite the massive police presence, to tear down the security fence protecting the Klan. They were forced back with mace.

New groups like the National Women's Rights Organizing Committee and Love and Rage, an anarchist federation, displayed a fearless contempt for police authority. These groups, incubated in the low-income urban neighborhoods of New York, Detroit, and Cleveland during the devastating deindustrialization and urban blight of the Reagan-Bush years, were determined to overthrow the status quo. Their attitudes and tactics picked up a few adherents even in the staid all-American test market of Columbus.

Indigenous militant organizations, like Columbus's Ordinary People's Movement, were seen as voices of moderation, as these outside groups grew amid the poverty and despair of the central city. Barry Edney, spokesperson for Ordinary People, made it clear that he favored "confrontation, not violence" with the Klan. His organization, marching from the Near East Side, proved successful in organizing and policing their own members.

Still, when the Klan had finally retreated, and the counterdemonstrators had begun to disperse, there was a minuscule but menacing group of Black youth who wanted to fight not only the police but the white anti-Klan protesters as well. Steeped in rap and rage, distrusting all formal institutions, they sought to provoke violence.[118]

"Spend a million dollars defending the Klan and my car's broke down and I can't get a job. What have you ever done for me?" one asked a white passerby.[119]

Some threatened to "kick all white ass" as soon as the cops left. This was a small but growing sentiment in urban America. The multicultural united front carried the day at the Statehouse. But the forces of radicalism, anarchism, and pure nihilism festered. As the riots of South Central L.A. demonstrated, what did the urban underclass really have to lose if they tore down the system and started all over again?

McCleary abruptly changed his mind about how to deal with the KKK when the Klan announced that they were returning to Columbus to protest Martin Luther King Day in January 1994. As part of his new strategy, McCleary began publishing the addresses of Ohio's Klan leaders in the *Columbus Free Press*, including the names of five Klan leaders: Vincent Pinette, Van Darnell Loman, Joseph Gosciniak, William Donta, and Calvin Reese.

Pinette, a Cleveland resident, was a Grand Titan of the Klan who spoke at the October 23, 1993, Columbus Klan rally at the Ohio Statehouse where he hurled racist epithets (see Figure 2.3).[120] He focused on recruiting young white males and favored neo-Nazi-style Klan uniforms and insignias to indicate the merging of the white supremacist movement. Pinette came to public notice during the 1993 Christmas season after erecting a Klan cross on the grounds of the Ohio state capitol.

Loman, a former Grand Dragon of the Ohio Klan, had run for Congress in 1992 in Cincinnati's second congressional district. Gosciniak held the title of Imperial Wizard of the Klan for the Northwest Territory. He resided in Indiana near the Kentucky border.

Donta, a southern Ohio farmer, had gained notoriety for hosting several Klan rallies on his 428-acre farm. Travelers heading south on I-75 passing Oak Hill, Ohio, could see the large Confederate flag painted on the Donta family barn. Donta had ties to several Klan

FIGURE 2.3. Vincent Pinette and other Klan members on the stairs of the Ohio Statehouse. Credit: Allen Zak, *Columbus Free Press* photographer, 1993.

organizations: the Ohio Knights of the KKK, the US Knights of the KKK, and the Northwest Territory of the KKK. He was fond of telling the media that "the Klan's the best thing that ever happened to me."[121] Reese held the title of Giant Cyclops of the Klan and was known for his ravings against race-mixing. He lived in Coshocton.

Although McCleary did not have their addresses, he outed four additional Ohio Klan leaders involved in organizing the anti-MLK demonstration. They were Peter Collins from Hamilton, Ernie Edwards from Monroe, Ronald Lee from Cincinnati, and Robert E. Mahlerwein from Oxford.

McCleary was a licensed private investigator, founder of the Coalition of Concerned Black Citizens (CCBC), and a Republican. Coalition President Robert Short explained the rationale for their new approach to the Klan: "To allow the Klan to do this is to give the impression that we are a people who are less than what we are. In taking on the Klan head on, this is a move from the slave mentality or impression of being a 'boy,' needing to be looked out for by someone else, to one of maturity and taking care of ourselves by being a man."[122]

In the spring and summer of 1994, Pinette undertook an aggressive recruitment campaign throughout Ohio. He pledged to hold a Klan rally in each of Ohio's 88 counties. A Klan rally on March 9 in Painesville tested the Anti-Racist Action strategy of bringing overwhelming force to bear on the Klan whenever they appeared in public. The Klan huddled in a gazebo in a Painesville park while approximately 1,500 protesters pelted them with snowballs, mudballs, and chants. One Klan supporter and two counterdemonstrators were arrested. As a result, Grand Dragon Robert Armstrong said that he no longer favored public rallies. He said that the dozen Klan members who showed up in Painesville never had a chance to recruit. "We just got snowballs and mudballs thrown at us. I don't call that an achievement."[123]

In Dayton, Pinette's March 19 Klan rally was met with a "percussion protest." Counterdemonstrators with drums, milk jugs, and pots and pans attempted to drown out the Grand Titan.[124] That same day, the KKK also marched in nearby Springfield. The *Springfield News-Sun* reported that "fifteen members of the Knights of the Ku Klux Klan dressed in black and white with Nazi-like swastikas on their shoulders stood in front of the courthouse to deliver their message of white power." They were met by 300 counterprotesters, and the Klan was protected by "an immovable line of law enforcement officers." The *Springfield News-Sun* also noted that "a group of out-of-town Klan haters slowly trampled a plastic snow fence and moved within inches of Springfield police in the middle of Limestone Street. The inch-by-inch movement by the opposition came near the end of the rally in front of the Clark County Courthouse . . . but the silent officers, clad in helmets and carrying shields stood firm and the verbal confrontation never became physical."[125]

On April 9 the Klan returned to Coshocton seeking new supporters. Pinette moved on to Chillicothe on April 30. Bowling Green was next, on June 18. The Klan campaign hit its zenith on July 9, when Pinette addressed supporters in both Newark and Cambridge on the same day. Lisa Ryan stood near him in Klan regalia, a self-described proud "white patriot." She became widely known later that night as the Grand Titan's mistress. Ryan was the 30-year-old daughter of Obetz-area Klan leader Jim Ryan. She and Pinette met at the Martin Luther King Jr. holiday Klan rally in Columbus that year. Jim Ryan was the owner of Possum Holler Pizza in Obetz, a Klan meeting place easily recognized by a Klan cross sign on its door.[126]

At Ryan's Obetz home on the Saturday following the Newark and Cambridge rallies, several Klan members gathered, including Pinette and his wife, who spent the night. Pinette grew angry while watching video footage of the Klan rally, believing that his mistress had been flirting with another man. According to police records, Pinette beat Lisa for nearly two hours between 1:30 and 3:30 a.m. He used his fists and a leather belt with a red-and-black KKK buckle that became imprinted on Lisa's skin. Lisa's daughter fled the house and called 911. Police records indicate Lisa was unconscious from the beating and was transported to Grant Medical Center.[127]

The fallout from Pinette's attack on Lisa was immediate. Her father switched his allegiance from the Knights of the Ku Klux Klan to the Federated Knights of the KKK. Jim Ryan said, "We're supposed to be a Christian organization and he's committing adultery." Ryan also stated that "it's a paper Klan, the Knights, all they want is money." Columbus Klan leader Donnie Carr, who aided Pinette in erecting a Klan cross on the Ohio Statehouse lawn during Christmas 1993, announced that he was also leaving the Knights of the KKK.[128]

The married Pinette had four kids. At the crux of his speech during his Klan recruitment tour of Ohio was the concept of "lazy Negroes" who get government checks at the "expense of the white man." He would shout to his angry Ohio followers "We pay for them!" Court records indicated that Pinette cited a Social Security disability check as his only source of income.[129]

Pinette was charged with felonious assault, and his bail was set at $500,000 for his attack on Lisa Ryan. He was sentenced to serve four to 15 years. At the time of his arrest, Pinette's Knights had 200 Ohio members, according to Franklin County Deputy Sheriff Steve Martin. Two months earlier, Pinette had been arrested for breaking into his ex-girlfriend's mother's house in Cleveland. His Cleveland mistress had just broken up with him, and reports noted that the mother and daughter were defending themselves with baseball bats when police arrived.

By the end of 1994, according to Andrew Welsh-Huggins of the AP, Ohio recorded 32 Klan rallies and four other events involving white supremacist groups.[130] Ted Almay, the superintendent of the Bureau of Criminal Identification and Investigation, told Welsh-Huggins that Klan activity in Ohio peaked in 1994 as a result of Pinette's high-profile activities. When Pinette went to prison, Almay noted, Klan events died down.[131]

What died down were the public rallies. The Klan resorted to traditional terror tactics and racial intimidation. On October 6, 1994, a Cincinnati-area family woke in the middle of the night to find their house ablaze. Media accounts stated that "all the window seals and doors had been soaked with gasoline." Four young white males were arrested on attempted murder and other charges. The family was white but appeared to be targeted because they had invited a Black friend to their home. The police reported that during the arrest they confiscated KKK literature, Klan "threat cards," and Klan robes.[132] The next month, a Black Cincinnati resident went outside at 1:00 a.m. and found six men smashing his car windows and urinating on his vehicle. The men were reported to be KKK supporters and were indicted for rioting and ethnic intimidation.[133] A Cincinnati-area student, John Wallace, 21, was expelled from the Great Oaks Institute of Technology for wearing a Ku Klux Klan T-shirt. The UPI reported in October 1994 that he successfully sued the school, claiming that his First Amendment rights had been violated.[134]

Despite Pinette's absence, the Klan repeated its traditional Christmas Klan cross-raising for the fourth year in Cincinnati. The Klan, unannounced to the public, raised the cross at 3:00 a.m. in Fountain Square in downtown Cincinnati, protected by a large police contingent. Back in 1993 the cross had been guarded around the clock by neo-Nazi skinheads. The skinheads, in turn, were guarded by law enforcement.[135]

Over 200 ARA supporters turned out to protest the Klan cross in 1994. ARA handed out 2,000 of their iconic "Stop Racism" stickers. A clash broke out when dozens of mounted police dressed in full riot gear suddenly encircled the protesters. Police ordered them to leave the square, herding them slowly away from the cross and dispensing mace to disperse the crowd. Demonstrators ran in all directions, some stopping to topple the Klan cross. Police arrested six protesters, who were charged with felonies.[136]

ARA's rapid growth in central Ohio included the chapter hosting the first conference of the Midwest Anti-Fascist Network in 1994. Columbus's ARA chapter initiated the gathering with the goal of coordinating anti-neo-Nazi and anti-Klan activity throughout the region. "The keynote speaker was a survivor of the 'Greensboro massacre' of 1979," according to the ARA handbook.[137] Promoted as the founding conference of the new Antifascist Network, the event drew 221 attendees from states as far away as Alabama, Missouri, Minnesota, and New York, as well as from the city of Toronto, Canada.

While the Klan was busy passing out flyers predicting that "it's going to be a great year for the Knights of the Ku Klux Klan in the Ohio Realm . . . So let's stick together to bring about a white Christian revival in our great state," Midwest Antifascist forces met at North High School in Columbus. Workshops at the conference centered around confronting the Klan: Our Recent Experience at Klan/Nazi Protests; How Best to Organize When They're Coming to Town; and Legal Defense/Offense Techniques. ARA activists discussed how the Klan and other white supremacy groups were still actively recruiting at suburban and rural high schools.

Of particular concern at the gathering was the rising subculture of hate rock music. Antiracists from Minnesota and Detroit organized a panel titled "Confronting the Nazi Music Underground." The activists focused on the explicitly racist Resistance Records and the glossy music magazine *Resistance.* Slick ads for Resistance Records had appeared in popular tattoo magazines.

Klansman Calvin Reese offered a new approach to the Ohio Klan. In 1995 his group petitioned the state of Ohio to join the Adopt-a-Highway cleanup program. They offered to clean up a two-mile stretch of Route 31 in Union County, north of Marysville. Angela Septer, of West Mansfield, Ohio, signed the application but listed a mailing address in Groveport. Reese warned the state of Ohio that if the Klan was denied, a protest and legal battle would follow: "It's in the state's best interest to let it go through."[138]

The police adapted to the ARA movement by adopting new practices to contain and counter the antiracist activists. Marvetta Davis was one of hundreds of anti-Klan demonstrators to counter the KKK on June 18, 1995, in Bowling Green, Ohio. Davis, a Detroit resident, was arrested the next month in Dayton while protesting at another Klan rally. She was charged with inciting violence, a fourth-degree felony, for allegedly spitting on a Klan supporter at the Bowling Green rally. The police showed up in Dayton with photographs from the rally and a warrant for her arrest. Five other anti-Klan protesters were also arrested on charges stemming from the Bowling Green rally. Davis spent three days in jail, and her bail was set at $15,000. Clearly, ARA was then under heightened police surveillance.[139]

The second annual Midwest Anti-Fascist Network conference met in mid-October 1995, again at Columbus's North High School. Excitement centered around the keynote speaker, Floyd Cochran, former number-two man in the Aryan Nations. Cochran had a conversion experience after his comrades in hate told him that come the revolution, his son with a cleft palate would have to be killed because he was a defective white child. Cochran explained to the conference audience that he had abruptly left the Aryan Nations and given up everything: his "job, friends, and home." Cochran emphasized that "so much of the white supremacist organizing attempts to give angry or unpopular white kids a sense of belonging." He became an anti-racist activist after meeting with Loretta Ross, Leonard Zeskind, and other members of the Center for Democratic Renewal. Cochran now organizes rural white kids, exposing "the lies and tricks of the neo-Nazi recruiters."[140]

Perhaps Ohio's best-known racist in the 1990s was Cincinnati Reds baseball team owner Marge Schott. She frequently made the news during that decade. In 1992 the *New York Times* wrote: "Marge Schott, under fire in Cincinnati and in baseball after she admitted in a deposition to making racist and anti-Semitic remarks, made racial slurs in the presence of other baseball club owners, a former member of the Oakland Athletics' front-office staff said yesterday."[141]

But racism and anti-Semitism were not just centered in Cincinnati, where Schott was barred from direct involvement with the Reds during the 1996 through 1998 seasons. Anti-Semitism emerged as an issue in Ohio's state capitol as well. On May 8, 1996, Devon Rice, a messenger with the Legislative Service Commission, reported delivering forms to House Speaker Jo Ann Davidson's office. Rice claimed that he overheard Ohio House Sergeant-at-Arms Robert Foster loudly proclaim: "The Jews are just like the Democrats, all they do is whine." After Foster "repeated himself several times," Rice confronted the Statehouse official and said, "Could you do me a favor, next time you make anti-Semitic remarks, could you lower your voice so I don't have to hear you?"[142]

Rice says that Foster initially denied that his remarks were anti-Semitic and offered a half-hearted apology. Rice then dashed off a letter to Speaker Davidson, a Republican from Reynoldsburg, informing her of the incident: "As a citizen of Ohio, as a human being and as a 'Jew,' I felt compelled to inform the gentleman that I heard him, that I was offended, and that his behavior was intolerable." Foster was sitting at his desk in the reception area at the time the remarks were made. Rice wrote, "I personally do not care what the Sergeant-at-Arms says at home, at a bar, or on the golf course. However, this type of behavior clearly has no place within his official capacity as an employee of the Ohio House of Representatives. His behavior was, aside from being ignorant and offensive, unprofessional."[143]

Speaker Davidson seemed to concur. She ordered an immediate inquiry into the matter. Foster admitted that he had called two specific groups—the ACLU and the Jewish Defense League—"whiners just like the Democrats." Foster denied that he ever referred to "Jews" specifically. Nevertheless, Davidson concluded in a letter dated May 15, 1996, that Foster's conduct was "entirely inappropriate and should not be condoned in the House of Representatives." Davidson directed Carol S. Norris, the executive secretary of the Ohio House, to "verbally reprimand Mr. Foster for his 'inappropriate' comments."[144]

A copy of her letter to Rice was forwarded to the director of the Legislative Service Commission, Robert Shapiro. Within a week, Rice was given his six-month evaluation and told that his services would no longer be needed after the session ended. Instead of talking to Rice face-to-face, the evaluation from his immediate supervisor Eric Rodriguez and Office Manager Cathy Kamer was simply left on his desk. Rice claims that every time he was five minutes late was suddenly highlighted, although no one had ever spoken to him about tardiness before. And, curiously, a vague reference to having "gone above a supervisor on one occasion" appeared.[145]

Rice resigned after the evaluation rather than finish the session and requested an exit interview with Kamer and Shapiro. When he arrived at the appointed time, he found State Trooper Sergeant Moore waiting to escort him out of the building. "It's insane. The trooper threatened me with arrest," Rice said. Shapiro acknowledges that he saw Davidson's letter but refused to give Kamer's or Rodriguez's names when asked who evaluated Rice or whether they had seen Davidson's letter. "I'm not going to help you, you'll have to find out yourself," Shapiro told *Columbus Alive*.[146]

Not only was House Speaker Davidson confronted with an anti-Semitic controversy; information was leaked about House Speaker Pro Tempore William G. Batchelder, a Republican state representative from Medina. Investigative reporter Russ Bellant exposed Batchelder as a member of the little-known and highly secretive far-right Council for National Policy (CNP): "the CNP is attempting to create a concentration of power to rival and eventually eclipse traditional centers of power in the U.S."[147]

Newsweek reported that the CNP's first executive director, Louisiana State Representative Woody Jenkins, told council members, "I predict that one day before the end of this century, the Council will be so influential that no president, regardless of party or philosophy, will be able to ignore us or our concerns or shut us out of the highest levels of government."[148] The CNP emerged again during the Trump presidential campaign when the SPLC revealed that two of Trump's key advisors, Kellyanne Conway and Stephen Bannon, were CNP members. Michael Peroutka, a longtime member of the white supremacist League of the South and professed neo-Confederate, is also a member of the secretive organization.[149]

Chip Berlet of Political Research Associates pointed out that the CNP included "a former Ku Klux Klan leader and others who champion segregationist policies." Berlet conceded that these charges might seem "shocking" yet easily verifiable. He described the beliefs of the CNP members as "not only traditionally conservative, but also nativism, xenophobia, theories of racial superiority, sexism, homophobia, authoritarianism, militarism, reaction and in some cases, outright neo-fascism."[150] Bellant, author of *The Coors Connection* and *Old Nazis, The New Right, and the Republican Party,* monitors ultra-right political organizations. Bellant said the "membership of the Council comprises the elite of the radical right in America" and that "many Council members would prefer that their participation not be made public."[151]

During the Iran-Contra scandal, the *State Times* of Baton Rouge reported that Oliver North was a CNP member and quoted the CNP's Norman Blackwell as saying that "the policy [of CNP] is that we don't discuss who attends the meetings or what is said. The Council for National Policy is a tax-exempt 501(c)3 membership organization."[152]

Some of the more well-known board members of the CNP in the 1990s include the Reverend Jerry Falwell, the leader of the now-defunct Moral Majority; Phyllis Schlafly, a leading antifeminist; the Reverend Pat Robertson, right-wing TV evangelist; and Joseph Coors, whose family finances an interlocking network of ultra-conservative and far-right institutions. In 1983 the CNP bestowed their Thomas Jefferson Award on Senator Jesse Helms. The less-known members of the CNP, like Batchelder, perhaps give better insight into the organization's politics:

- Richard Shoff, a former Ku Klux Klan leader in Indiana.
- John McGoff, a supporter of the former apartheid South African government.
- David Noebel, author of *Rhythm, Riots and Revolution,* a '60s book that attempted to show that folk music was a Communist plot.
- R. J. Rushdoony, the theological leader of America's "Christian Reconstruction" movement that advocates that Christian fundamentalists take "dominion" over America, abolish democracy, and institute Old Testament law. He said "Homosexuals . . . adulterers, blasphemers, astrologers and others will be executed."
- Reed Larson, head of the anti-union National Right to Work Committee.
- Don Wildmon, TV censorship activist and accused anti-Semite.[153]

Bellant specializes in the difficult task of tracking the historical roots of far-right groups. In his last book he noted: "The Council's creation was inspired by business and political leaders who are also leaders of the John Birch Society." This, in Bellant's analysis, is an important factor since it places the CNP not within the boundaries of mainstream conservative thought or traditional Republican Party ideals but within the antidemocratic nativist tradition in American politics.[154]

The John Birch Society, founded in 1958, was initially identified by scholars as a racist and anti-Semitic organization. The Birch Society spent much of its time in the '60s organizing against Martin Luther King Jr. and the civil rights movement. They accused King and civil rights activists of being communist-controlled. The John Birch Society, for example, saw President Dwight Eisenhower as part of the international communist conspiracy.[155]

The Birch Society and the CNP have been intertwined since the council's inception in 1981, when Tim LaHaye, a Moral Majority leader, received backing from Texas billionaire Nelson Bunker

Hunt, a member of the Birch Society's National Council. LaHaye is perhaps best known for his best-selling *Left Behind* series of apocalyptic fiction. In 1982 Tom Ellis succeeded LaHaye as CNP president. Ellis was a director of the Pioneer Fund, the foundation that finances efforts to prove that Black Americans are genetically inferior to whites. Recipients of Pioneer Grants have included eugenicists William Shockley, Arthur Jensen, and Roger Pearson. Pearson is on record stating that "if a nation with a more advanced, more specialized, or in any way superior set of genes mingles with, instead of exterminating, an inferior tribe, then it commits racial suicide, and destroys the work of thousands of years of biological isolation and natural selection."[156] By 1984 both John Birch Society Chairman A. Clifford Baker and Executive Council member William Cies were CNP members.[157]

Mark Potok, former Senior Fellow of the Southern Poverty Law Center, wrote that "the CNP is an intensely secretive and shadowy group of what the *New York Times* once described as 'the most powerful conservatives in the country.' It is so tight-lipped that it tells people not to admit their membership or even name the group."[158]

According to the Southern Poverty Law Center, individuals can only join the CNP by invitation. The last time their membership was leaked externally was 1998. The Center made their 2014 membership directory public. Former Ohio Secretary of State J. Kenneth Blackwell, the state's first Black American to hold statewide office, was listed as a member in 2014.

On December 20, 1998, the *Columbus Dispatch* featured a story on Batchelder. The article, written by *Dispatch* Statehouse reporter Lee Leonard, described Batchelder as "a rock-ribbed conservative."[159] How Ohio's mainstream media covers the issue of white supremacy and neo-Nazi ties helps explain why there is a hidden legacy of racial conflict in the state. By consciously ignoring obvious connections to white supremacy groups by political figures or by mislabeling them as "rock-ribbed" conservatives, the media helps cover up perhaps the key issue in American politics: racism.

A follow-up op-ed by Leonard on Batchelder's retirement recognized him as the second-most powerful man in the Ohio House. In Leonard's analysis, "Batchelder longed to be Speaker of the Ohio House and might have been, except that he refused to exchange his conservative principles for today's go-along practical politics." Leonard's articles are vague on the specifics of Batchelder's vaulted "conservative instincts." Leonard ended his opinion piece by quoting Republican House Majority Leader Randall Gardner, who claimed, "There are few people who can't be replaced. Bill Batchelder is one of them."[160]

Leonard's article and op-ed piece failed to mention Batchelder's membership in the CNP. Due in part to this type of media coverage that avoids prominent politicians' ties to white supremacy, Batchelder returned to become the Speaker of the Ohio House from 2011 to 2014.[161] While the Birchers are regarded as extremists, both Bellant and Berlet warn that CNPers like Batchelder are accepted as mainstream Republican Party leaders despite the company they keep.

Every 30 years or so, the American left recreates itself. The communists and socialists of the 1930s "Red Decade" later became the decentralized, radical Students for a Democratic Society and New Left of the 1960s. In the '90s, participatory democracy no longer dominated the left, replaced by multiculturalism and direct action by groups like Anti-Racist Action in Ohio.

The program for the ARA's Third Annual Conference in 1996 screamed "Do Something!" It featured a photo of an activist taking a swing at a bloated, pot-bellied, robed, cone-headed Klansman. The conference was again held at the old North High School in Columbus. Grizzled veterans of the '60s and '70s antiwar and anti-imperialism movements mingled freely with the next New Left. Before the weekend was over, they had attended workshops on racism and fascism, marched together, and been maced while protesting police brutality. Welcome to antiracist activism, '90s style.

At the opening of the conference Friday night, the mostly straight-edge Generation X participants—wearing "Fuck Racism" T-shirts, the "Mean People Suck" slogan taken to its logical extreme—exuded an aura that made the Weathermen look like the Brady Bunch. But how much was posing and posturing? This new generation of antiracist militants has grown up knowing no victories. The civil rights movement, which in 1965 brought the end of legalized apartheid in America, was ancient history. The antiwar struggle was like the war stories that World War II GIs would tell their kids in the 1950s.

This new breed of activists had done battle in the cities, suburbs, and small towns of North America against the rising tide of neofascists. White supremacists were ushered in through the rhetoric of the Reagan and Bush eras and the infamous political wedge issues of immigrant and welfare-mother bashing, a tide unquelled by the hollow promises of President Clinton's law-and-order centrist policies. This was true not only for the Americans present but for the large Canadian contingent as well. The dozens of ARA members from Toronto were hardened by their ongoing battle with white supremacists in the Great White North. Toronto was the home of Ernest Zündel, a key player in the international Nazi movement. From his fortress at 206 Carlton, Zündel ran Samisdat Publishers, Ltd., one of the largest Nazi propaganda operations on the planet. His chief goal was to deny the Holocaust, producing such publications as "Did Six Million Really Die?" and *The Hitler We Loved and Why.*[162]

Canadian courts have dismissed Holocaust denial charges against Zündel, instead characterizing his work as concerning "ethnic conflict between Germans and Jews." Zündel's racist skinhead followers revered him as a hero and chanted "Six million more!" But when government action fails, the new breed of antifascist activist is willing to use other means: Zündel's property was recently firebombed.

Shedding light on the rise of the American religious right on the conference's opening night was Russ Bellant. His book *The Religious Right in Michigan Politics* was the first to investigate and document the origins and objectives of the popular group, the Promise Keepers (PK). Many are familiar with former University of Colorado football coach Bill McCartney's original 1990 vision: to fill a stadium with Christian men willing to reclaim authority from their wives, capitalizing on the gender bashing and male backlash against the women's movement so prominent on talk radio. As Bellant explained, the vast majority of men of various denominations who attend these PK rallies come with good and sincere intentions.

He pointed out how McCartney, while serving as assistant football coach at the University of Michigan at Ann Arbor, "encountered and was deeply influenced by the Word of God (WOG) Community." WOG, according to Bellant, practices a "shepherding/discipleship" form of worship that requires total submission to a person called "the head." He calls Promise Keepers' views fundamentally "antidemocratic" and potentially "totalitarian."[163]

"The use of sophisticated lighting and sound in a stadium setting, psychologically playing on people's emotions, breaking down the denominational differences and merging nationalism and religion really echoes the Nazi rallies of the Third Reich," Bellant argued. He demonstrated how virtually all top Christian right leaders—Pat Robertson of the Christian Coalition, D. James Kennedy of Coral Ridge Ministry, and Bill Bright of Campus Crusade for Christ—had signed on to the Promise Keepers. The family values rhetoric and homophobia are part of a larger cultural revolution that the PKs hope to bring about. Robertson, Kennedy, and Bright, along with James Dodson, author of the Promise Keepers manifesto *Seven Promises of a Promise Keeper,* are all members of the CNP. According to Bellant, the big bucks funding the CNP come from Jeff Coors and family members of Coors Brewing Company, Linda Bean of L. L. Bean, Richard DeVos Jr. of Amway, and Texas oilman Nelson Bunker Hunt. "While they appeal to black members, their real agenda is to destroy affirmative action, and they have links to white supremacist ideology," Bellant concluded.[164]

Activists attended ARA conference sessions like Leonard Peltier / Political Prisoners, Black-Jewish Relations, Lesbian and Gay Oppression, and the essential Surviving Radical Demos, to name a few. A small contingent of anarchists from the Love and Rage group unfurled a red-and-black flag. Banners were held with slogans reading "No Police Brutality" and "No Nazis, No Killer Cops, No Fascist USA, Anti-Racist Action." Appropriate slogans for the twenty-something generation whose educational benefits have been cut while government prison spending quadrupled.

Other marchers lit torches—lawful, but virtually unheard of in Columbus—creating an eerie and disturbing mood. These were not drunken frat boys reveling in a football victory frenzy. They crossed High Street, and more than a hundred people began marching south. Police squad cars with lights flashing immediately began to escort the marchers. The police persisted, despite the marchers' insistence that they knew their way to 12th Avenue. As a police helicopter began to hover overhead, there was an unfamiliar cry: "Aim high, pigs in the sky!"

Just before Blake Avenue, in front of Radio Shack and the 24-hour video store, there was a scuffle. Officer Julie Appenzeller, not wearing riot gear, was attempting to arrest a male marcher. He had his hands raised out to his sides, and she was screaming and pulling on his arm. Someone was pulling on his other arm, a literal tug-of-war. Someone in the crowd was yelling "Fuck the pigs!" It seems that one Jason Robert Maffettone, 27, of Hoboken, New Jersey, had stepped off the curb in Columbus known as "jaywalkers gulch." Startled and disbelieving male officers stood by Officer Appenzeller as the crowd shouted "No police brutality! Let him go!"

Columbus cops drew their black cans and began spraying the demonstrators. One ARA medic advised the maced demonstrators to "just ride it out."[165]

The crowd continued to march toward The Ohio State University campus flanked by 30 or so police officers in riot gear. Their main goal appeared to be avoiding getting maced again. Also present were reporters from the *Columbus Dispatch,* Channel 4, and Channel 10. Tensions mounted as the marchers, now swelled to nearly 300, found themselves pinned against a construction fence in the middle of The Ohio State University campus. Fearing that the Columbus police on High Street would attack, the marchers found an opening at the Wexner Center and snaked through the campus. Once on campus, the antiracist activists found sanctuary as one lone campus police car escorted them several blocks back toward High Street. No one feared a macing from the campus cops.

Finally, there was a key decision to make. As the activists stood at 12th Avenue on The Ohio State University campus side of High Street, they decided to brave the riot police and move back into the city. This time the police did not attack, the march ended without incident, and the activists re-emerged at 15th and High. Later that night the police reported that no mace had been used on the demonstrators. The *Dispatch* accurately reported the macing and wrote that the post-macing chant was "Police brutality, we're sick and fucking tired of it."[166]

The 1996 ARA conference in Columbus showed the mood of these young ARA activists as increasingly bitter. America was incubating a whole new generation of hardcore fascist-fighters. They're not the Promise Keepers, but they are the product of America's broken promises and dreams, particularly on race. Key battles were being waged in the Buckeye State.

Whether it was January around Martin Luther King Jr. Day or February during Black History Month, Columbus in the 1990s always expected a yearly visit from hate-mongering white supremacists. From subzero wind chills to Alberta Clippers, the weather never seemed to cooperate with the Klan and new Nazis.

In 1997 Harold "Ray" Redfeairn, leader of Ohio's wing of the white terrorist Aryan Nations organization, was busy trying to unite the state's white supremacist groups under the Christian Identity theology umbrella. Redfeairn used the so-called Church of the Good Shepherd in New Vienna, Ohio, to spew his theology of hate. About 40 white supremacists, including Redfeairn and Troy Murphy, an Imperial Wizard of an Indiana Klan group, rallied at the Statehouse on February 16, 1997. As usual, state, county, and local police provided tough and overzealous security for the white supremacists. At 12:30 p.m. counterdemonstrators began gathering at the corner of Broad and High.

Hundreds of Anti-Racist Action activists, primarily from the Midwest and the East Coast, swelled the ranks of the anti-Nazi protesters. The campus-area organization Food Not Bombs offered up vegetarian chili to the gathering throng. Barry Edney, of the Ordinary People's Movement, who had organized the most noticeable Black contingent, was whipping up the crowd.

Police officers used a familiar tactic to harass counterdemonstrators: crowd them together, make them pass through an X-ray gate, run metal detectors over them, and search and frisk them before they can exercise their First Amendment right to heckle the Klan.

Less than an hour into their rally, the Klan's vituperative diatribe was over. The rally posed the eternal post–World War II debate question: What do you do with a nascent Nazi movement? "We tried ignoring them in Germany in the 20s and 30s," argued McNamara. "This gives our organization an opportunity to educate people. We had a lot of energy out there. I was proud of the spirit of our activists. We stopped the Nazis from recruiting and we got to recruit, communicate with our fellow citizens, and leaflet a lot of neighborhoods in the name of interracial unity. I'd call that a success."[167]

Hate in the Buckeye State made national news in 1997. White supremacists Chevie and Cheyne Kehoe shot it out with state troopers in Wilmington, Ohio. The Aryan Nations, the American Nazi Party, Klansmen, racist skinheads, and Christian Identity hate preachers converged at the Statehouse. The FBI busted Aryan Republican Army leader Peter Langan, after a shootout in Columbus, here in the heart of it all.[168] In the early 1970s Aryan Nations founder Richard Butler established his 20-acre compound in rural Hayden Lake. In the 1990s it seemed that the dream of a racist white homeland had shifted to rural southern Ohio.

Floyd Cochran, former high-ranking Aryan Nation official turned antiracist activist, repeatedly warned that Ohio, especially the southeast region, was a prime target of white supremacists. "Just last fall I spoke in Athens, Ohio, before a feminist group and I warned them of the growing danger in Ohio. The organizer told me that I should quit frightening people, that she lives in Ohio and I don't know what I'm talking about," recalled Cochran.[169] Unfortunately, Cochran knew all too well the dangers of the Aryan Nations. He lived in Pennsylvania, close to Mark Thomas's farm outside Macungie. Thomas was indicted on January 30, 1997, as a co-conspirator in the Midwest Bank Bandit robberies. The Aryan Republican Army was a white supremacist gang of bank robbers in the early to mid-1990s.

Between January 1994 and January 1996, the Aryan Republican Army, under Commander Langan, committed as many as 22 bank robberies, primarily in the Midwest, to fund their activities. On January 15, 1996, the FBI arrested Richard Guthrie in Cincinnati, and three days later, the Bureau arrested Langan at an Aryan Nations safe house in Columbus. A search of the safe house, according to the *New York Times,* turned up 13 pipe bombs, "seven homemade grenades, a pistol hidden in a hollowed-out Bible, assault weapons, components for producing explosives, T-shirts and hats from the FBI, the Drug Enforcement Administration, and the Alcohol, Tobacco and Firearms Agency."[170] Newspapers, especially the *Columbus Dispatch,* referred to the group as the Midwest Bank Bandits, presumably to avoid the negative connotations of an armed neo-Nazi gang based in Ohio's capital.[171]

Thomas was a key link between white supremacist organizations. He served as national leader of the violent antigovernment Posse Comitatus, as Imperial Chaplain of the Invisible Empire Knights of the Ku Klux Klan, as a Christian Identity preacher, and, until his indictment, as the Aryan Nations' leader in Pennsylvania. During the 1990s Thomas attracted scores of skinheads and assorted white supremacists to rallies and weekly Bible studies at his Macungie compound. His tactics revolved around creating a united front of racists and anti-Semites.

The Kehoe brothers came from Colville, Washington, a short distance from Butler's Hayden Lake compound. They were thought to be in the area for the gathering of the racist tribes when they shot it out with state troopers in Wilmington during a traffic stop. New Vienna, just ten miles from Wilmington, was the new national home of the Aryan Nation.

Anthony "Tony" Wayne Gamble, Imperial Wizard of the Knight Riders of the KKK, testified back in June 1995 in a case concerning the tearing down of the Klan cross in Cincinnati. He revealed how his Ross, Ohio–based Klan members worked with Aryan Nations supporters at the Christian Identity House of the Good Shepherd's Church in New Vienna. This is where the Klan's Cincinnati Christmas cross was constructed in 1994.

In the 1990s the alliance between the Klan and neo-Nazis under the guise of white supremacist Christian Identity theology was pivotal to understanding racial violence in Ohio. Aryan Nations had declined dramatically after its peak in 1983–84, after its offshoot The Order killed a state trooper, who was an Aryan Nations member, as well as Jewish talk-show host Alan Berg. The Order, like the Aryan Republican Army, specialized in armed robberies to finance the racist revolution. In 1993 Aryan Nations was present in only three states. As Klanwatch reported in March 1995, Aryan Nations staged an alarming comeback in 1994.[172] Aided by money from the Aryan Republican Army, the Idaho-based group swept into 15 states, including Ohio, in 1994, and ended up in 30 states by 1995.

With the rise of the Aryan Nations in 1994, so rose militia and states' rights organizations in the aftermath of the 1992 Ruby Ridge, Idaho, shootout between the FBI and the white separatist Randy Weaver, and the destruction of the Waco, Texas, Branch Davidian complex in 1993. Ohio saw the dramatic rise of the Ohio Unorganized Militia. Michael Hill was a chaplain in the militia and an organizer of Ohio's One Supreme Court, a "common law" court that met regularly in Columbus. He was shot to death during a traffic stop on June 28, 1995, in Muskingum County.

The *Columbus Dispatch* reported that Michael Hill's widow, Arlene, held a memorial service for her slain husband on Sunday, June 30, 1995. It casually mentioned that Colorado preacher Pete Peters and North Carolinian Nord Davis "are scheduled to speak."[173] What it failed to mention was that Peters was one of America's more influential and active Christian Identity propagandists and theologians. His sermons were based on the militant Christian Identity and anti-Semitic beliefs that Jews pose a satanic threat to American civilization, that Blacks and other people of color are subhuman, and that homosexuals should be executed.[174]

In his book *Religion and the Racist Right,* Michael Barkun discusses Peters's Remnant Resolves—a statement of political principles concerning Identity believers. Peters held that God's law is "binding . . . on all men, regardless of their political persuasion or personal beliefs." Thus, "the role of civil authority is to administer God's law."[175] The logic of the belief is that secular humanist civil authorities, whether cops or judges, do not have to be obeyed. The implication is that God's law is known only to enlightened racists like Michael Hill, Pete Peters, Tony Gamble, Richard Butler, and Mark Thomas.

Nord Davis, the other speaker mentioned in the *Columbus Dispatch*, was a well-known North Carolina white supremacist who organized a trip to Jordan during the Gulf War to support Saddam Hussein. It is standard Christian Identity doctrine that Zionist Jews are spiraling history toward Armageddon. The presence of preeminent racists like Davis and Peters at Hill's memorial established distinct links between the Ohio Unorganized Militia and the white supremacist movement.

The antigovernment sentiments of the militia movement make it a prime recruiting ground for white supremacists. A May 1995 *Newsweek* article reported that federal investigators of the Oklahoma City bombing were "looking closely at a white supremacist group headed by Robert Millar in Elohim City, Oklahoma."[176] Following the Oklahoma City bombing, the militia movement came under intense government scrutiny. The media revealed that both suspects, Timothy McVeigh and Terry Nichols, had attended militia meetings in Michigan. Federal prosecutors charged that McVeigh's motivation was his intense hatred of the federal government for its destruction of the Branch Davidian complex. Moreover, media reports claimed that McVeigh's favorite book was the notorious *Turner Diaries*. The book, billed by the neo-Nazi National Alliance as a "handbook for white victory," is a primer on race war masquerading as a violent fantasy novel.[177]

Written in 1978 by William Luther Pierce, *The Turner Diaries* proved an inspiration to The Order. "Today has been the day of the rope—a grim and bloody day but an unavoidable one. . . . But the night is filled with silent horrors from tens of thousands of lampposts, power poles and trees throughout this vast metropolitan area, the grisly forms hang. . . . There are many thousands of hanging female corpses like that in the city tonight, all wearing identical placards around their necks. They are the white women who are married to or living with Blacks, with Jews, or with other non-white males," Pierce wrote.[178]

Pierce, like Thomas, lived near the community of Millpoint, West Virginia. The Church of the Creator (COTC), one of the most vicious American racist organizations, sold its property in North Carolina to Pierce in September 1992. The COTC operated openly on High Street on The Ohio State University campus area during the late 1980s and early '90s. Under the leadership of Joey Hager, neo-Nazi skinheads terrorized the campus community, culminating in the murder of a Black woman. Their cry was "RAHOWA!" (RAcial HOly WAr). That incident, along with intense pressure from anti-racist activists, caused the demise of the local organization.

The climate for racist recruiting was ripe in the 1990s. As Floyd Cochran likes to point out, David Duke's 1990 political agenda was then virtually mainstream Republicanism: destroy affirmative action because it is taking white guys' jobs away, keep those dirty Mexicans out of California, kick those promiscuous Black welfare mothers off public assistance, stop Big Government regulations, build more prisons, and gut education. In the economic transition from an urban-industrial to a high-tech, postindustrial suburban society, lawmakers decided to use ordinary people as the shock absorbers on the rough ride to the twenty-first century.

An industrial state like Ohio is an easy place to find displaced factory workers and small farmers desperately wanting someone to blame for their problems. These disgruntled white men were more than willing to listen to Rush Limbaugh or even the Klan, who basically offered the same scapegoats: Blacks, gays, Big Government conspiracies, liberals, feminists, and immigrants.[179]

A 1995 Klanwatch Intelligence Report listed the following hate groups as active in Ohio: the International Ku Klux Klan in Sandusky, Knight Riders in Ross, Knights of the KKK in Columbus, Northern Knights and Aryan Nations in Dayton, Aryan Racial Loyalist Party, White Christian Guard in Euclid, National Alliance in Parma, and the G. A. Kleve Propaganda Ministry in Maple Heights.[180]

McNamara had long argued that government officials were making a big mistake by pushing the "just ignore them" line regarding hate groups. Ex–Aryan Nations official Cochran agreed, advising ARA members to protest their presence so that it was harder for them to recruit. Anti-Racist Action, still headquartered in the north campus area in Columbus, had become the fastest-growing antiracist organization in the nation.

"It's true that the number of real, live American Nazis is small right now, but don't tell us to just ignore them. Don't tell us they're just a joke," said McNamara. "Tell it to the friends of Eric Freeman, the 11-year-old white kid killed by his older brothers David and Brian, under the inspiration of Mark Thomas. Tell it to the families who lost loved ones in the Oklahoma City bombing. Tell it to the cops that were just shot at by the Kehoe brothers. I hate to say 'we told you so,' but they're not a joke. They're for real and they kill."[181]

The Detroit-based Resistance Records held a music festival in Cleveland in 1995 attracting some 500 racists. ARA, composed mostly of college students, brought its message of racial harmony to challenge the hate spewed at the racist concerts. An alliance of ARA activists, Barry Edney's Ordinary People's Movement, and Cornell McCleary's Coalition of Concerned Black Citizens, in conjunction with the local NAACP, devised a novel tactic to combat racists. Their outing of Klan members in 1995, by taking busloads of people to the homes of known white supremacists, appeared to have shaken up the racists in Ohio. That action, despite being widely denounced by Columbus's power structure and the mainstream media, made a lasting impact on Klan leader Tony Gamble.

Under oath, Gamble said, "There's seven Ron Lees" in his KKK organization. "These people don't want their name to be shown on TV because if anti-protesters found out where they lived, they would bring busloads of people and picket up and down in front of their nice homes. They have good jobs. They don't want to lose their jobs."[182] McCleary announced publicly that the FBI had informed him that five of the nine men he had outed as Klan leaders had fled the state. Cheyne and Chevie Kehoe continued to make headlines in central Ohio. A *Columbus Dispatch* headline had the boys insisting that they were not "white supremacists."[183] A nationwide manhunt ended on June 16, 1997, when Cheyne turned himself in and squealed that his brother was hiding on a Utah farm. Cheyne faced numerous criminal charges, including a 16-count indictment in Ohio stemming from the shootout.

Cheyne read a highly publicized statement when he turned himself in that confirmed his admiration for white supremacist leaders: "The reason I acted in the manner I did was due to the actions of men like Randy Weaver, Gordon Kahl and Bob Matthews. The government and law enforcement agencies abused the individual rights of these men."[184]

Weaver, a virulent anti-Semite, believed that the US government was under the control of an international Jewish cabal. He frequently visited the Hayden Lake, Idaho, compound of the Aryan Nations. There he could discuss his racist conspiracy theories that ZOG, the Zionist Occupied Government, ran the US. Weaver became a far-right icon after he was injured and his wife and son were killed in a shootout with federal agents in August 1992 at Ruby Ridge, Idaho. During the siege, neo-Nazi skinheads and Aryan Nations members rallied to support Weaver. Aryan Nations Ambassador-at-Large Louis Beam co-founded a Weaver support group, Citizens United for Justice.

In 1994 under the slogan "No More Wacos, No More Weavers" the militia movement exploded nationwide. Its organizational roots are linked to 150 ultra-right-wing leaders who met in Estes Park, Colorado, on October 23, 1992, and gave birth to the militia strategy. The event was hosted by Christian Identity pastor Pete Peters. The Kehoes claimed Christian Identity as their religion. In 1983 Gordon Kahl was an active member of the Posse Comitatus, a loosely organized band of Christian Identity antigovernment activists. Kahl murdered two federal marshals in North Dakota and, like the Kehoe brothers, became a fugitive. Rather than surrender, Kahl died in a shootout with Arkansas law enforcement officers in which a local sheriff was also killed. Kahl is considered a martyr by the Posse Comitatus, Aryan Nations, and other white supremacists like the Kehoes.

Cheyne Kehoe confessed after his arrest that "I do have knowledge of my brother's involvement in the bombing of a federal building."[185] The FBI announced that it would probe any connections between convicted Oklahoma City federal building bomber Timothy McVeigh and Chevie Kehoe.[186] Chevie had ties to both the Aryan Nations in the Idaho panhandle and the white supremacist compound in Elohim City, Oklahoma. Telephone records prove that McVeigh called the Elohim compound on April 5, 1995, just two weeks before the bombing. Also, on October 12, 1993, McVeigh was ticketed within ten miles of Elohim City on County Route 220, the only access road into the compound.

McVeigh's highly publicized motive of avenging the Waco massacre eclipses the equally important significance of the April 19, 1995, date for white supremacists. A few hours after McVeigh and John Doe Number Two lit the fuse to the Ryder fertilizer-and-fuel truck bomb, racist cop-killer Richard Snell was executed in an Arkansas prison. His body was brought to Elohim City by the Reverend Robert Millar for a white supremacist martyr funeral.[187]

Antiracist activists and investigators have long been fascinated with the testimony of a former manager of the Shadows Motel outside Spokane, Washington. The manager told authorities that "days before the bombing, he [Chevie Kehoe] mentioned to me that there's going to be something happening on the 19th and it's going to wake people up." The manager described Chevie as "ecstatic" when a news flash reported the federal building bombing.[188]

Chevie was also indicted in December in Arkansas on seven counts of murder, racketeering, and conspiracy to bring about an Aryan Republic. Prosecutors claim that Chevie planned to create the racist republic through "a campaign of murder, robberies and kidnappings," according to the AP.[189] As part of that indictment, Chevie was specifically charged with "transporting stolen goods from the white supremacist community of Elohim City, Oklahoma, to Spokane in March 1995," a month before the federal building bombing.[190] Additionally, Chevie was charged with directing his Aryan Republic cohorts to murder gun dealer William Mueller, his wife, Nancy, and Nancy's eight-year-old daughter in 1996.

Following the conviction of Terry Nichols, the jury forewoman, Niki Deutchman, said, "I think a decision was made early on that McVeigh and Nichols were the ones they were looking for. The same resources were not used to try and find out who else might be responsible." The trial also made it clear that Nichols was not the individual seen with Tim McVeigh just prior to the explosions.[191]

Clinton County, Ohio, Assistant Prosecutor Rick Moyer's January 1998 comments to the *Columbus Dispatch* are worth remembering: "The white supremacist issue is for some other trial in some other time and place . . . all I am trying is a man who came into Wilmington and fired at two law enforcement officers."[192] An interesting and curious comment from a county prosecutor. The Kehoe brothers' shootout with state troopers coincided with Aryan Nations' first public rally at the Ohio Statehouse.

Neo-Nazi propaganda flourished in The Ohio State University campus area in the spring of 1998. Local Anti-Racist Action activists reported finding National Alliance flyers as far north as 18th Avenue and as far south as West 8th Avenue. The flyers would make Goebbels proud. They contained identical text with two different pictures. One displayed a young Aryan poster child doing her homework in a seemingly blissful suburban setting; the other featured a preschooler with a puppy on the lawn. The headlines blared: "She Needs The Truth" and asks "Where Will She Find It?" According to the National Alliance flyers, not "on television, with its racially mixed couples and multicultural propaganda," or "in her classroom, which has been converted into a neo-Communist brainwashing pen," or "on the streets, where she stands a greater than one in four chance of being raped, probably by a non-white." The National Alliance assured the reader: "We are here to make sure that more and more young people like her will have access."

The National Alliance organization sprang from the National Youth Alliance, during the 1968 hate-filled George Wallace for President campaign. Initially controlled by Willis Carto, the head honcho behind the anti-Semitic Liberty Lobby, the group became ardent admirers of Adolf Hitler. They sold and promoted Francis Parker Yockey's *Imperium,* a 600-page tome intended as the second *Mein Kampf.*

In 1970 former members of George Lincoln Rockwell's American Nazi Party split with Carto and renamed the organization the National Alliance.

Pierce professed that his calling in life was to "save white people from themselves."[193] He ran his neo-Nazi organization from an isolated, heavily wooded 400-acre compound in West Virginia. In 1998 National Alliance members were indicted in Florida as part of an alleged 12-state terror network with plans to plant bombs around Disneyland to distract the police so they could rob banks for their movement.

Another disturbing thing about the flyers is that a local post office box in Hilliard, Ohio, was given as the address. As the Alliance targeted Columbus, they already had a chapter in Cleveland, headed by Erich Gliebe, and one in Cincinnati, led by William Sinkhorn.[194]

White supremacists and neo-Nazis were often supported in the '90s by organizations calling themselves conservatives. One of the most infamous examples was Ohio State University student Matt Ball's guest column in the *Observer,* a right-wing newspaper distributed free in the campus area. The *Observer* described itself as "an independently run student newspaper published by the Buckeye Conservative Studies Foundation."[195] Above an ad for the College Republicans, a typical *Observer* article offered the lead "Newt!,

Newt!, Newt!, the crowd of young and old roared," under the headline "Newt Speaks at Notre Dame."

But the real politics of the editors were revealed by their choice of guest columnists. First, Andy Rufus ponders, if the recently tortured and slain Matthew Shepard "was not gay and had merely been robbed, would we have heard about it?" and wonders, "How long will it be until being a Clinton hater is a federal offense?"[196] While Rufus was merely sophomoric, Ball's *Observer* column was sinister. After pointing out that there are "17 organizations I found for Black/African students" and "nine organizations I found for Jewish students," Ball used the *Observer* as a recruiting tool to form a "European-American" student organization at The Ohio State University. That was an old tactic à la David Duke and his infamous National Association for the Advancement of White People.[197]

Ball was a frequent writer of letters to the editor of the Ohio State student paper, the *Lantern*. In a May 22, 1998, letter, Ball proudly admitted to posting the National Alliance flyers in the campus area. Ball wrote that "there is ample evidence to show that Jewish losses during World War II are nowhere close to 6 million." And, he pointed out, "CNN is no longer owned by a Gentile, neither is CBS, ABC, nor Disney. Don't let me forget Time Warner, the *New York Times*, the *Wall Street Journal* and the *U.S. News and World Report*. All are controlled by Jews."[198] Ball was so proud of his National Alliance membership that he was featured on the neo-Nazi group's web page. Anti-Racist Action activists posted flyers exposing Ball's neo-Nazi connections.

As McNamara recalled, from 1989 to 1998 the ARA was wildly successful in driving white supremacists from Ohio, the Midwest, and virtually the entire nation. Although ARA continued as a formal group through 2013, the last national conference occurred in 1998. McNamara responded as to why the conferences stopped: "We won. People quit coming to their rallies." He also pointed out that the ARA newspaper was regularly printing 150,000 copies.

The last national ARA conference held in Columbus on October 16–18, 1998, offered 27 workshops including Surviving Radical Demonstrations, Marxist View of Fascism and How to Defeat It, and Relationships between Different Tendencies in the Antifa Movement.[199] ARA literature at the conference claimed that there were "more than 120 groups" in the ARA network. The network was united by "four points of unity":

1. We go where they go. Whenever fascists are organizing or active in public, we're there. We don't believe in ignoring them or staying away from them. Never let the Nazis have the street.
2. Don't rely on the cops or the courts to do our work. This doesn't mean we don't ever go to court. But we must rely on ourselves to protect ourselves and to stop the fascists.
3. Non-sectarian defense of other antifascists. In ARA-Net, we have lots of groups and individuals. We don't agree about everything, and we have a right to differ openly. But in this movement an attack on one is an attack on us all. We stand behind each other.
4. ARA-Net intends to do the hard work necessary to build a broad, strong movement against racism, sexism, anti-Semitism, homophobia, discrimination against the disabled, the oldest and youngest of our people. We intend to win.[200]

ARA was rocked when two of its key activists were murdered in Las Vegas: Dan Shersty, 20, and Lin "Spit" Newborn, 25. On Friday, July 3, 1998, two young women came into Spit's tattoo shop. After one got a piercing they invited Newborn and Shersty to a party. Shersty was found dead by his car the next day after being beaten and shot. Spit was found 150 feet from the car, his body riddled with bullets. In August, Columbus Anti-Racist Action members joined hundreds of others from across the nation to march through Las Vegas's Spring Valley neighborhood, vowing "to take back the streets from white supremacist terrorists."[201]

A few months later, Las Vegas police charged local neo-Nazi John Edward Butler with the murders. Columbus ARA stated, "The murders of Spit and Dan were political assassinations committed by members of the modern U.S. fascist movement."[202]

Over the weekend of July 4, 1999, racist Benjamin Smith went on a shooting spree, wounding nine Orthodox Jews in the West Rogers Park neighborhood of Chicago. First he killed Black former Northwestern basketball coach Ricky Byrdsong, and then he killed a 26-year-old South Korean graduate student in Bloomington, Indiana. Smith was a member of the World Church of the Creator, a neo-Nazi terrorist organization, and deemed Creator of the Year in 1999. He went on his rampage only hours after Reverend Matt Hale, the church's anointed Pontifex Maximus, lost his appeal to obtain a license to practice law in Illinois because of his racist beliefs and total disdain for the US government and its laws.

Hale's church, based in East Peoria, Illinois, had a long-documented history of racist violence. It was also one of the fastest-growing racist organizations in the US, expanding from eight churches in early 1995 to 31 in 1999. Church of the Creator Reverend George Loeb murdered Black Harold Mansfield Jr. on May 17, 1991, in Florida. Another Church of the Creator Reverend, Joey Hager, was convicted after killing a Black woman in Columbus during that same period.

Smith, like Matt Ball, had been busy flyering a college campus with neo-Nazi literature, in this case the University of Indiana. Shortly after Smith's bloody spree, police seized white supremacist literature from the home of the Williams brothers, Benjamin Matthew and James Tyler, suspects in the murder of a gay couple in northern California and arson attacks on three Sacramento synagogues. The AP reported that police investigators are "examining whether the case is part of a wide hate-crime conspiracy and whether the brothers are linked to the World Church of the Creator."[203]

Church founder Ben Klassen in his 1987 tome *RAHOWA! The Planet Is All Ours*, told his congregation that they should prepare for "RAHOWA!: In the one word we sum up the total goal and program of not only the Church of the Creator, but of the total white race . . . We regard it as a holy war to the finish—a racial holy war. RAHOWA! is inevitable. It is the ultimate and only solution . . . No longer can the mud races and the white race live on the same planet and survive."[204] Aryan Nations member Buford Furrow Jr. followed Smith's path in August 1999 with his own shooting spree at a Jewish community center in California that wounded five people, including four kids, and that killed a Filipino American mail carrier.

From 1989 to 1991, 20 to 30 campus-based racist skinheads, or boneheads, openly operated in Columbus. The boneheads were members of the Church of the Creator. Smith's progenitors of neo-Nazi ideology in Columbus were local Creator leaders John Reid and Matthew Hayhow. John Backstrom, a local music promoter, was violently assaulted by Reid and nine other neo-Nazis in April 1990 in Columbus. Backstrom informed the police that he recognized all ten of his bonehead assailants, yet assault charges were only brought against Reid. Hayhow and Reid were sentenced in March 1993, with a third man, for robbing two Columbus banks in 1990.

In August 1992 Hager stabbed 19-year-old Black woman, Nichele Trice, to death in an altercation on 18th Avenue. In February 1993 Hager was sentenced to eight to 25 years in prison for voluntary manslaughter. Oddly, Hager's judge deemed his well-known involvement with the neo-Nazi Creators to be irrelevant and inadmissible at the trial. After the trial, *Columbus Alive* managed to examine Hager's personal papers and effects. This included his personal copy of *The White Man's Bible,* which lays out the five basic racist beliefs of the Creators: our race is our religion; the white race is nature's finest; racial loyalty is the greatest honor; racial treason is the worst crime; and what is good for the white race is good for nature.

The *Columbus Dispatch* ignored or downplayed Hager's neo-Nazi connections. Only the *Columbus Free Press* and the defunct weekly *Columbus Guardian* pointed out that Trice's killing was not even counted as a hate crime, despite its racist nature.[205]

In March 1993 another Central Ohio man with neo-Nazi ties, John W. Gerhardt, was sentenced to three to ten years for abduction. Gerhardt sought sanctuary at the Aryan Nations compound in Hayden Lake, Idaho, after attempting to kidnap a woman from a Bank One ATM machine in a Central Ohio suburb. He hid out with the Aryans in 1991 until his arrest in May 1992. Gerhardt and his brother Edward both attended Columbus's Mifflin High School and first attracted national attention when they founded the American White Nationalist Party in 1972.[206]

Gerhardt served time in the Orient Correctional Facility, where prison sources stated that he was an Aryan Nations minister. Prison sources also reported that he recently converted former Ohio Grand Titan of the Knights of the Ku Klux Klan Vince Pinette away from the Klan to the neo-Nazi movement.

The book *The Silent Brotherhood: The Chilling Inside Story of America's Violent, Anti-Government Militia Movement* by Kevin Flynn and Gary Gerhardt, depicts the rise and fall of The Order. It charts the connection between Robert Matthews, a neo-Nazi bank robber and murderer, and Columbus, "where he met a college history professor he knew through the National Alliance." The authors fail to name the professor, whose identity was redacted from government documents.[207]

When Aryan Nations staged a rally in Columbus in February 1997, a member of the racist Southside Greathouse armed robbery gang shot and critically wounded a Black newspaper carrier. This gang had gone on a 19-day crime spree in October 1997. An FBI agent told Judge James Graham that the shooting was both random and racially motivated.[208]

2000s

With the dawning of the new millennium came the resurrection of the original white supremacist ideology that carved out the state of Ohio from Native American territory. The neo-Nazi was fading away, and new young leadership emerged.

Central Ohio's WCMH-TV reported on the National Alliance's leafleting in the Columbus suburbs of Dublin and Grove City. Erich Gliebe of Cleveland told Channel 4 that the organization targeted the two communities because the areas were "most receptive to their messages," producer Karen Baker informed *Columbus Alive.*[209]

National Alliance leader William Pierce called Gliebe, a former amateur boxer, a "tireless recruiter and organizer, a man who has spent nearly every available minute working for the Alliance."[210] Gliebe's Cleveland organization is the single largest in the Alliance, boasting some 60 openly neo-Nazis and hosting an annual Euro-American Cultural Fest. A recent Intelligence Report from the SPLC named Gliebe one of the elite "dirty dozen" of white supremacist leaders in the US.[211]

Gliebe served as the National Alliance's Midwest spokesperson and regional coordinator. His cultural fest drew the likes of Pierce, head of the neo-Nazi White Aryan Resistance Tom Metzger, and editor of the white supremacist magazine the *Resister,* Steve Barry. Not far behind in the Alliance hierarchy was Hilliard's Matt Ball, also seen on Channel 4's January 16, 2000, news report.

The influence of the Idaho-based Aryan Nations was beginning to fade as the health of its founder, the ailing and aged Richard Butler, 81, declined. Meanwhile, Pierce and the National Alliance appeared to be growing stronger by the day. The Alliance was busy building bridges to other fascist and white supremacist groups. In summer 1999 the SPLC reported that Pierce and two "gussied-up skinheads" dined at the exclusive Washington, DC, University Club with former Reagan White House staffer and GOP strategist Todd Blodgett.[212] Blodgett, a protégé of the late Lee Atwater, is the son of wealthy Republican State Representative Gary Blodgett of Iowa.

In October 1998 Pierce went public with his ownership of Resistance Records, the largest catalog and inventory of "white power" music in the US. Prior to its demise, the record company was selling an estimated 50,000 white supremacist CDs every year. On April 26, 1999, Pierce and Blodgett incorporated Resistance LLC in the District of Columbia. The deal gave the National Alliance control over the now-defunct Resistance Records. Pierce projected that he would sell 70,000 units in the year 2000, at a $10 per unit profit margin, pumping $700,000 into his organization. Where did all that money go? Among other activities, the National Alliance was actively leafleting in Columbus suburbs like Bexley, Dublin, Hilliard, and The Ohio State University area. Pierce's objective was straightforward, as he said in a National Alliance newsletter: "As Resistance Records regains strength, that acquisition should add an increasing number of younger members in the 18 to 25 age [group] to our ranks."[213]

Resistance Records distributed bands such as The Midtown Bootboys, whose lyrics stated: "Stop the threat of AIDS today / Cripple, maim or kill a gay / We've got to take a stand today / We've got to wage a war on gays." Pierce had the anti-Semitic band Mudoven with lyrics: "You say you've seen the Holocaust / You ain't seen nothing yet / Six million lives will not compare / To what you're gonna get." The group Imitation One moved from the promise of genocide to specific tactics: "Slam you down into the ground you filthy slimy shit / Break your nose and your toes and split your fucking lip." Pierce and Resistance Records took advantage of a network of 26 US record labels and distributors that carried white power music. The bands ran the gamut of genres, from heavy metal to ska and folk. Two labels were based in Ohio: 88 Enterprises in Canton and Hate Rock in Chesapeake. "88," for the uninformed, is neo-Nazi code for the eighth letter of the alphabet twice—HH, or Heil Hitler.

The Alliance's strategy was to reach out to both young neo-Nazi shock troops and older, more mainstream racist organizations with Republican ties, like the Council of Conservative Citizens (CCC). Two reports from the SPLC, "Money, Music and the Doctor" and "Sharks in the Mainstream," documented Pierce's activities. The CCC was little more than the reincarnation of the racist White Citizens Councils of the '50s and '60s. The CCC and the National Alliance had many things in common, including attacking the Martin Luther King Jr. holiday, Black History Month, and affirmative action. The CCC refused to disclose the names of its members, but the SPLC collected the names of 175 of them and "found [that] a significant number of members have been linked to unabashedly racist groups including the Invisible Empire, Knights of the Ku Klux Klan, the Carolina Knights of the Ku Klux Klan, the National Association for the Advancement of White People, the America First Party and the neo-Nazi National Alliance."[214]

The CCC's leader, Gordon Lee Baum, attempted to recruit Vince Reed, the head of security for the Aryan Nations, to the CCC's national board in 1995. North Carolina Republican Senator Jesse Helms also endorsed the council, as did various Republican politicians, particularly in the South. Council leaders have claimed responsibility for the defeat of former South Carolina governor David Beasley, who angered the group by opposing the continued flying of the Confederate battle flag over the state's capitol.

The National Alliance would pass out information attacking the Martin Luther King Jr. holiday the day before the event, and less than two months before Ohio's 2000 presidential primary. The emergence of a highly emotional and polarizing political wedge issue, as Atwater liked to call them, came at an opportune time for George W. Bush's presidential campaign in Ohio. His father, President George H. W. Bush, was elected as an anti–civil rights "states' rights" representative from Texas in 1966, and his son defended the states' rights of South Carolina to fly the Confederate flag in his 2000 presidential campaign.

Floyd Cochran, former national spokesman for Aryan Nations, pointed out that the Midwest is potentially a much more fertile recruiting ground for white supremacist hate organizations. White supremacist David Duke, former Nazi and Klan leader, understood this when he proposed that southern Ohio become part of an all-white homeland, to be founded after the US was shattered. "Most of the white supremacists seek out mountains and hills in their belief that this is where God's chosen people should flee in preparation for the final days," Cochran explained. "Draw a line from the Alleghenies in Pennsylvania down through Appalachia and its foothills and you're going to pick up a lot of white Anglo-Saxon Protestant and white supremacist organizations."[215]

A brief comparison of hate groups in 2000 revealed that Idaho had nine hate groups compared with Ohio's 22, the seventh-largest total in the US. The state of Wyoming, Idaho's neighbor, has one hate group; the Columbus suburb of Hilliard alone has two. This concentration of hate was seen throughout the Midwest, but not the West, according to Southern Poverty Law Center data. Pennsylvania had 27 hate groups. Montana had five; Michigan 24. Oregon had ten versus Indiana's 17. Washington and Illinois were a wash at 17 each. Heading south, ten hate groups called Kentucky home, compared with Nevada's two. The data showed that there were 117 hate groups in the Midwest but 44 in the West.[216]

The Center for New Community concurred that Ohio entered the new millennium with the most hate groups in the Midwest. The Center counted 73 white supremacist groups in the Buckeye State. Devin Burghart, who authored the report, pointed out that white supremacist groups foster anti-immigrant sentiment, and in their flyers in Columbus, Jews were blamed for the September 11 attack. He stated that "Immigration is certainly an issue that's being pushed forward with a white-nationalist bent since September 11." Burghart noted that the World Church of the Creator added Cleveland and Akron chapters for a total of four in Ohio. Also, the traditional Nazi group—the National Socialist Movement, based on Hitler's teachings—had grown from one to three chapters in the state.[217]

Overall, McNamara and other ARA leaders noted that many of the new racist groups existed only in cyberspace. In the SPLC's assessment, the early years of the twenty-first century proved to be "a period of realignment and rebuilding for hate groups."[218] Gone were the continuous Klan and neo-Nazi rallies throughout Ohio.

One of the most violent neo-Nazi groups attempted to fill the vacuum in Ohio left by Pinette and the Klan's departure with a rally on April 21, 2001, in Newark (see Figure 2.4), the day after Adolf Hitler's birthday. This time it was the November 9th Society, a group that drew its name from Kristallnacht, the "Night of Broken Glass," when in 1938 Hitler's Nazi militia attacked Jewish-owned businesses throughout Germany, breaking windows and terrorizing Jewish families. These neo-Nazi storm troopers adopted the Sieg Heil salute, shaved heads, and the slogan "We must secure the existence of our people and a future for white children." The phrase is the mantra of the white supremacist movement known as the "14 words," coined by David Lane, a member of the terrorist group The Order.[219]

As rallies dissipated, Ohioans continued to experience more hate incidents. Police reports document numerous examples, like in

FIGURE 2.4. Photo taken at a Newark November 9th rally showing a woman holding a sign with the "14 words." Credit: Bob Fitrakis, *Columbus Free Press* editor, 2001.

October 2002, when Donald Fletcher of Canton allegedly assaulted a Black man with a sword and was later charged with a hate crime for ethnic intimidation.[220]

The SPLC summary of 2003 found substantial increases in certain sectors of the hate movement, notably hate websites, which rose from 443 in 2002 to 497 in 2003, a 12 percent increase. The only group that showed a decrease were the neo-Nazis. The SPLC attributed this in part to the death of William Pierce on July 22, 2002, which cost his group the National Alliance half its membership. The SPLC's ratings placed Ohio fifth among the 50 states with 33 active hate groups capable of mobilizing actual members for rallies.[221]

The November 9th Society's elaborate website announced their goal of "Taking National Socialism into the 21st Century." Their site describes in great detail on how to "organize a resistance movement." The society made its ties to Hitler clear: "Like the heroes and heroines of the Third Reich, you may choose to answer the call to *idealism and sacrifice.*" The November 9th Society embraced a particularly vicious strain of neo-Nazism linked to the Outlaw Hammerskins, and they idolized The Order. The site argues that freedom is sustained by three boxes—the ballot box, the jury box, and the ammo box—and urges members to "begin guerilla operations." The includes step-by-step instructions for creating a terrorist organization.[222]

Nationwide, the hate groups with the ability to mobilize the most people on the ground were the skinheads. In 2003 the number of skinhead chapters more than doubled. No longer in retreat, independent and regional skinhead crews rapidly increased. The growth was largest in the Ohio State Skinheads, the Hoosier State Skins, and the Keystone State Skinheads. The first Ohio State Skinheads meeting was in Central Ohio in 2003. They deemed the National Alliance their official political arm.[223] The independent skins were not affiliated with the long-standing and more centralized Hammerskin crews.[224]

Hammerskins came to national prominence in 1988 when members of the Confederate Hammerskins patrolled Robert E. Lee Park in Dallas, Texas, assaulting any nonwhites they encountered. In 1994 regional Hammerskin factions united under the common moniker Hammerskin Nation.[225]

During the summer of 2003, two major hate crimes occurred in Ohio. In July Larry Webb and Nathan Mefford were charged with aggravated assault felonies for screaming racial threats at a Black man in Xenia before stabbing him with a barbeque fork and hitting him with a frying pan. In Warren a more traditional white supremacist event involved someone burning a cross in front of a racially mixed apartment building.[226] In the last quarter of 2003, the only major hate incident reported in the media came from Cuyahoga Falls. There, William Fowler, 43, was charged with ethnic intimidation and criminal damaging for allegedly using racial slurs toward a coworker and burning a cross on his workstation.[227]

Ohio hate incidents made the news again in early 2004. Skinhead recruitment among high school- and college-age white males remained brisk. A 17-year-old high school senior and a 15-year-old sophomore in Bevis were charged with aggravated arson and inducing panic for scrawling racist graffiti at their school and threatening to "blow up" the building. In March the neo-Nazi National Alliance, despite their recent hemorrhaging of members, hit the streets to distribute literature in sections of Cincinnati.[228] At the end of 2004, racist rituals continued. In Middletown, Ohio, Michael Ray Miracle and Eric Fugate were both charged with aggravated menacing and ethnic intimidation in connection with a cross-burning at a Black family's residence.[229]

Members of the Ohio State Skinheads and Hoosier State Skins merged in 2004 to form the Vinlander Social Club. Vinlanders envisioned themselves as a warrior clan dedicated to drinking, fighting, and a racist form of Odinism. A form of ancient paganism, Odinism was a Norse religion practiced by the Vikings. Vinlanders did not require their members to renounce their membership in other skin crews.[230]

During the 2004 presidential election in Ohio, the religious right launched a crusade against gays. The key wedge was Issue One, which sought to make gay marriage constitutionally illegal in the state. Then–Ohio Secretary of State J. Kenneth Blackwell led the charge to pass Issue One. Karl Rove, George W. Bush's political advisor, had advocated for the issue on the ballot since new voters would be enticed to come out and vote for it, and would likely vote Republican as well. In a close election separated by only 118,000 votes, Issue One may have been the deciding factor in Bush's re-election.[231] Just before the general election in 2004, Martin Baxter beat a 39-year-old man to death in Waverly, Ohio, because Baxter believed he was gay. Baxter was sentenced to life in prison.[232]

A racist underground remained active in 2005. The white supremacist prison gang Aryan Brotherhood had 32 of its members arrested in Cleveland for gun, drug, and racketeering charges in June.[233] Debate over racial issues burst forth following Hurricane Katrina in August 2005. Once again, an Ohio hatemonger made national news. Scott Morris, the Ohio leader of the Sons of Confederate Veterans, issued a provocative statement on behalf of his Southern heritage group. Morris denounced Katrina victims as "vile criminals" and "pestilent vermin" and warned that "these leeches will go on to pollute the communities [where] they're relocated."[234]

The National Socialist Movement invaded Toledo on October 15, 2005. The movement, also called America's Nazi Party, marched to support Tom Szych, a white Toledo resident who claimed to be hassled by a Black gang, the Dexter Boyz. Nazis had promoted the rally heavily through the local media, and antifascist activists had gathered from around the Midwest. The neo-Nazis had a permit to walk a mile but only completed a quarter of a mile along the route before city officials canceled the march for public safety reasons.[235] The sight of police escorting the Nazis to the starting point of their march outraged the protesters. A confrontation between police and demonstrators followed the march that had occurred in a Black neighborhood on the north side of town.

As the crowd grew to nearly 600, eggs and other items were tossed at the Nazis, who shielded their faces with their white power signs. The police responded by riding their horses into the crowd to protect the Nazis. Police singled out a youth wearing a Cincinnati Reds hat, arresting him without explanation.[236] Angry youth from the neighborhood gathered rocks to throw at the Nazis. Two police squad cars arrived and attempted to secure the intersection. They were met by a hail of rocks and quickly drove away with smashed windows. More police responded with a show of force: gas-mask-wearing bicycle police, cops in riot gear, tear gas, rubber bullets, flash bangs, pepper spray, and tasers.

The neighborhood response was varied. Some residents pleaded with people to not throw rocks, while others yelled "Everybody get a rock!" Some people seemed appalled by the violence; a woman held a sign that read "Stop acting foolish. All we humans have hurt one another!!! Repent. Learn to love and forgive." A sign on a chain-link fence read "Peace on our Streets" with an anti-Nazi symbol.

Toledo Mayor Jack Ford attempted to address the crowd with a megaphone, but his words were inaudible over the noise. Some said they heard him saying that if they did not disperse, there would be mass arrests. Ford later claimed on news reports that someone in the crowd threatened to shoot him, so he left. No other attempts were made to communicate with the crowd.

City officials deemed the street battle a "riot." The *Toledo Blade* reported that "angry crowds attacked emergency workers, burned down a bar, and looted two convenience stores." Dan Donaldson, National Socialist regional director, explained the reason for the march to the *Blade*: "There is somebody out there for white people's interests and white people's rights. There's somebody who cares."[237]

Although the year 2000 was a low point for hate groups in Ohio, hate groups grew nationally by 33 percent over the first half-decade of the millennium. A 5 percent increase centered around anti-immigrant groups. Ohio fell back to eighth place in hate groups in the country, with 31 active groups. The only state in the Northern old Union with more than Ohio was New Jersey. Ohio Klan groups held steadfast with 12 chapters, topping the ten known neo-Nazi organizations in the state at the time.[238]

With new and cheaper recording technology available, there was a surge of racist music labels, including one in Lancaster, Ohio. ISD Records was named in honor of the neo-Nazi band Screwdriver's lead singer, Ian Stuart Donaldson, who died in a 1993 car crash. The label evolved from a music company founded by the British neo-Nazi skinhead group Blood and Honor to a Lancaster production company run by a spin-off group, Combat 18. ISD Records had in their fold one of the most sought-after hate bands, Blue Eyed Devils, known for their single "Vandalized and Victimized." The label's website linked directly to the Blood and Honor Radio Network that streamed nothing but hate music 24/7 over the internet.[239]

In Logan, Ohio, on the property of Ohio State Skinhead Kevin Kislingbury, the Vinlander Social Club hosted the inaugural meeting of their Official Blood and Honour Council. The October 22, 2005, unity meeting of the white supremacists was attended by 60 representatives from more than a dozen skinhead crews. They established new leadership, called the Council of 28. Also present at the meeting were members of the Imperial Klan of America and the National Alliance.[240]

The Council of 28 met again in May 2006 at a compound owned by the Imperial Klan of America, in Kentucky. Following the meeting, their legendary consumption of alcohol led to an altercation with Steve Boswell, the Missouri coordinator of the National Socialist Movement. The Vinlanders, including the Ohio State Skinheads (OSS), took offense at being defined as "just a social club." Boswell, who uttered those words, was violently assaulted. He posted photos of his bruised, lacerated, and battered face on the internet, leading to a decline in OSS's membership.[241]

More racist incidents were documented in central and northeastern Ohio. A letter advocating abortions for pregnant Black women was sent to 350 Ohio State University dormitory rooms in April 2006. The racist group responsible was never identified.[242] The letters KKK and words "White Power" were spray-painted on July 4, 2006, inside the residence of a white female police officer in Cleveland who was married to a Latino man. In Elyria 11 days later, a letter appeared in a Black man's mailbox mentioning the KKK and telling him to clean up his residence.[243]

J. Kenneth Blackwell, Ohio's 2006 Republican gubernatorial candidate, campaigned with a man widely viewed as one of America's leading white supremacists. Blackwell had served as Ohio's treasurer from 1994 to 1999. He was also the first Black man to be a major party nominee for Ohio governor. He toured the state on October 4, 2006, with Larry Pratt, author of *Armed People Victorious,* which advocated for the creation of militant right-wing militias. Pratt had spoken and shared platforms in the past with Ku Klux Klan and neo-Nazi Aryan Nation members. He was forced to take a leave of absence from Pat Buchanan's 1996 presidential campaign over charges of white supremacist and anti-Semitic views. Pratt's 150,000-member Gun Owners of America group was proudly to the right of the National Rifle Association.[244]

According to the *Columbus Dispatch,* Pratt said he couldn't be a racist because he was campaigning with Blackwell, a Black man. Blackwell was "our kind of guy," said Pratt, in reference to Blackwell's support of gun owners' rights.[245] Blackwell's campaign spokesperson, attorney Eric Seabrook, conceded on October 8 to Khari Enaharo radio show listeners on 98.9 FM that Pratt was a white supremacist, but stressed that "it was all about the gun rights issue."

But this was not the first time Blackwell had lined up with extreme right-wing backers boasting racist and anti-Semitic roots. Earlier in 2006 Blackwell had posted a picture of himself on his website addressing the Council for National Policy. After a public uproar, Blackwell removed his CNP photo from the site. Blackwell lost the election to Democrat Ted Strickland, 36.6 percent to 60.5 percent.

Once again, in 2007 hate groups experienced a steady 5 percent growth nationally. Overall, active hate groups increased 48 percent from their low point in the year 2000. Ohio dropped to number nine as ten Klan and ten neo-Nazi groups dominated the state's 28 total hate groups.[246] Racial incidents continued to occur in the Buckeye State. In July 2008 Earl McLearran pled guilty to ethnic intimidation after hurling racial slurs and threatening to burn down a Black family's house in Dayton if they didn't move out of the neighborhood.[247] Dayton appeared in the news again in August 2008 when a 16-year-old male was charged with aggravated arson and burglary for setting fire to a Black woman's house.[248]

Many white supremacists viewed the Obama presidential campaign as having a silver lining. "Obama will be a signal, a clear signal for millions of our people. Whether Obama wins or loses in

November, millions of European Americans will inevitably react with new awareness of their heritage and the need for them to defend and advance it," former Klan leader David Duke stated.[249] Obama's campaign and subsequent election spurred a massive resurgence of right-wing hate groups.[250] Fear of a Black president also spawned a second wave of militia groups. The first wave surged in the 1990s and saw the rise and fall of self-professed patriot groups after Tim McVeigh's 1995 Oklahoma City bombing.

Amid fears that Obama was from Kenya and that he would legalize all undocumented immigrants, racial incidents flourished. In Mt. Vernon, Ohio, a group of young white males in May 2009 put a noose around a half-Latino man's neck and dragged him while shouting racial and ethnic slurs. One of the 18-year-old perpetrators pleaded no contest to ethnic intimidation and was given a ten-day jail sentence.[251] Another noose was left along with a note in a Black family's yard in Fairview Park, near Cleveland, in 2009. The note was signed by the Aryan Knights of Fairview Park and demanded the Black family leave town.

"Rage on the Right," a 2010 SPLC report, found that a shocking 363 new patriot groups formed in Obama's first year as president, a 244 percent increase. Eighty-five of them were full-blown armed militias.[252]

At Nelsonville, Ohio's, Hocking College in January 2010, a threatening message scrawled on a restroom wall warned that Black students would be killed on February 2.[253] Four skinheads, three of them members of the US Army, beat up a homeless man in Cincinnati. Private Riley Feller and Michael Hesson were both charged with felonious assault in connection to the April 10 beating.[254] Daniel Lee Jones, a neo-Nazi from Portland, Oregon, pled guilty to mailing a noose to a NAACP official in Lima, Ohio, in May 2010. The NAACP had been critical when a police officer shot a Black man in Lima. Jones also mailed racist flyers to other Lima residents.[255]

In September 2010 alone, three racist incidents in Ohio made the news. In Cleveland, Ronald Pudder was indicted on federal hate crime charges of arson and damaging a church. He had set fire to the entrance of a predominantly Black church. A Highland Heights resident, 22-year-old Northern Kentucky University college student, Adam Reide, was charged with four counts of criminal mischief for allegedly writing racist comments all over campus. In Columbus, "9-11" was spray-painted on windows and countertops at a Muslim-owned market. Cash and a laptop computer were also stolen, and several display cases vandalized.[256]

Between the years 2000 and 2010, active hate groups in the US increased from 602 to 1,002. Ohio fell to tenth with 32 active groups. At this time Ohio had 27 patriot groups, including 12 militias. Generally, patriot groups define themselves as opposed to the New World Order. Armed militias were more problematic than patriot groups. The Confederate States Home Guard protected Chillicothe, Ohio. The Constitutional Militia of Clark County defended their area. In northwest Ohio the North Coast Citizens Militia was armed and vigilant. The Northeastern Ohio Defense Force 3BN stood ready in Lisbon. They were aided by local militias in Kenton, Zanesville, Lebanon, St. Paris, Ashtabula County, and Belmont County.[257]

With the year 2010 ending and militias rising, an email was sent to the Islamic Association of Cincinnati saying, "You should know that you are not wanted in Cincinnati . . . we don't want you here. Mohammad is a joke. Go back to your desert. Beware. We may just declare jihad on you."[258] As rumors spread that President Obama was a Muslim born in Kenya, a jihad against American Islamists was unleashed. Former House Speaker Newt Gingrich compared Muslims to Nazis, and US Representative Louie Gohmert (R-TX) warned that Muslim women were being brought to America to birth future terrorists.[259]

At the height of the militia movement in the 1990s, there were 858 antigovernment patriot groups. There were only 149 patriot groups in the last year of the Bush administration. By 2011 there were 1,274 groups with 334 known militias. In addition to Obama's election, the 2008 economic crash played a distinct role in the militia group increase.[260] Still, the more traditional cross-burnings happened in Ohio. A cross with the words "KKK will make you pay" appeared in front of a Black family's house in Marengo in March 2011.[261]

As the new year of 2012 rang in, a residence in Hilliard occupied by an Egyptian immigrant's son was set ablaze. Several months earlier it had been painted with anti-Islamic and anti-Arab slurs.[262] As Obama ran for re-election, so-called patriot groups prospered. Ohio moved from 27 to 34 patriot groups and added a 13th militia group. Yet a more disturbing trend was the centralization of various militias as the Ohio Minutemen Militia. They were located in Fremont and in four other regions of the state, and had a statewide armed organization.[263]

The question of how deeply racism had permeated the state emerged when new reports revealed that civil servants, like firemen from northeastern Ohio, were engaging in Nazi rituals. Shawnee Township Fire Chief Todd Truesdale's 45th birthday inspired his fellow firefighters to throw him a party with a Nazi-themed birthday cake. Decorating the cake were the words "German Fire Dept" encircling a swastika. On the left corner sat a tall replica of an oven, also with a swastika on the side, and decorations made of frosting depicting presumably Jewish people marching toward the oven.

Platoon Chief Paul Way, a 28-year veteran of Ohio's Shawnee Township Fire Department, filed a civil rights claim in 2012 against Chief Truesdale and the fire department. In his suit, Way described a culture where Township firefighters saluted their chief Nazi-style with the cry "Heil Hitler!" Truesdale documented the Nazi salute in many photos.[264] Firefighters even gave Truesdale the Nazi salute in front of township trustees, according to court findings. Following Way's complaint, and after consulting with Truesdale, the trustees placed Way on administrative leave.

At Way's disciplinary hearing, a local attorney acting as his hearing officer found that the township trustees and the Fire Chief did not commit any serious violations that exposed the department or any persons in the general public to risk. It was all fun and games. According to a federal judge's opinion, "Photographs showed firefighters engaging in misconduct in the station, in public areas, at fire sites, on the fire truck, during training, and at department social events." In addition, the court found that "the use of homophobic slurs also was routine in the Department." The court went on to say that "such slurs also appeared on birthday cakes for the firefighters."[265]

Court records indicated that "Truesdale himself often referred to Way as a 'faggot,' though he knew Way's son was gay." On Way's birthday, the department presented him with a cake with the words "Happy Birthday, Fag."[266] When Way complained about the fire department's racist, anti-Semitic, and homophobic culture, he was fired. Shawnee Township settled with Way in 2016. Todd Truesdale remained fire chief.

High-tech hate groups and their adversaries reached new heights as computer technology progressed in 2013, according to a Southern Poverty Law Center Intelligence Report titled "Cyber-Commandos." A revamped Anti-Racist Action found that most of its work was being done online. When Ohio's white supremacists were outed in

1994, private investigators had to be hired. Now both the ARA and the racists were busy outing, or "doxing," each other online.[267]

There still appeared to be spontaneous hate activities at the local level. In Oakwood, Ohio, a Jewish family's home was vandalized in late February and again in early March 2013. "Go away Jews" was painted on their house. At the liberal Oberlin College, homophobic and racist slurs appeared on posters in March 2013. Even more shocking, a report that someone wearing a hood and robe resembling a Klan outfit was seen near the college's African American Heritage Center.[268] Two months later, in Mansfield, Bibles with racial slurs written inside were left at the homes of 16 Black people.[269]

Richard Schmidt, a 48-year-old Toledo neo-Nazi, received national attention in December 2013. He had been barred from owning weapons due to a felony manslaughter conviction for murdering a Latino man outside a bar in 1989. Nevertheless, in 2013 he was caught with 18 weapons and an estimated 40,000 rounds of ammunition while tracking Black and Jewish community leaders in Detroit, according to a report by NBC News's Michael Isikoff. Schmidt was given a six-year sentence, which was criticized by many as far too lenient.[270]

Finally, after four years of astounding growth, the number of hate groups fell sharply in 2013. Experts attributed it to legal crackdowns on antigovernment patriot groups and to "the failure of various nightmarish radical predictions to materialize, the co-opting by politicians of the extreme right's issues, and the re-election of President Obama."[271] Ohio stood tenth in the country in 2013, with five KKK and six neo-Nazi groups active in the state.

The number of active hate groups continued to drop in 2014. Ohio stayed in the top tier, with nine such organizations, but only two Klan chapters remained: the Original Knight Riders of the Ku Klux Klan and the Loyal White Knights of the Ku Klux Klan, both based in Columbus.[272] The Loyal White Knights of the Ku Klux Klan were visible in Hillsboro, Ohio, where they left recruitment flyers on parked-car windshields downtown.[273] A Southern Poverty Law Center study titled "Age of the Wolf" concluded that lone-wolf racists and leaderless racist attacks were becoming more predominant.[274]

Still, one of Ohio's neo-Nazi groups, the National Socialist Movement, held a rally in Toledo on April 18, 2015, to commemorate the riot from ten years earlier.[275]

The re-emergence of Ohio's Kenneth Blackwell on Trump's presidential transition team surprised many. Blackwell had been working for the anti-LGBT group the Family Research Council. He was also named to the now-defunct President's Commission on Election Integrity, along with longtime anti-immigrant activist and attorney Kansas Secretary of State Kris Kobach. Kobach is well known for his controversial voter list, claiming that many Black, Latino, and Asian individuals are registered multiple times to vote illegally in many different states.

At the close of 2016, the Southern Poverty Law Center issued its annual report on hate groups in America. Their methodology only counted groups with active members on the ground, rather than just websites. Hate groups rose from 892 in 2015 to 917 in the aftermath of the Trump election victory. Ohio ranked eighth, at 35 hate groups. In the SPLC's analysis, "Trump's run for office electrified the radical right which saw in him a champion of the idea that America is fundamentally a white man's country."[276]

The SPLC summarized factors fueling the rise in hate groups: "A surge in right-wing populism, stemming from the long unfolding effects of globalization and the movement of capital and labor that it spawned, brought a man many considered to be a racist, misogynist, and xenophobe into the most powerful political office in the world." The SPLC pointed out that Trump's victory mirrored similar currents in Europe where globalization, immigration, and refugees energized an array of extreme right-wing national political movements. SPLC's report concluded that "after half a century of being increasingly relegated to the margins of society, the radical right entered the political mainstream last year in a way that had seemed virtually unimaginable since George Wallace ran for president in 1968."[277]

Trump's election empowered lone-wolf attacks in Ohio. An interracial couple returned home from visiting their daughters in Chicago to find their Cincinnati house trashed in early December 2016. The couple, married 34 years, found swastikas spray-painted on their walls along with the words "White Power" and "Die Nigger." The *Washington Post* reported that the couple's son had committed suicide in 2010 and that "he was treated very racist because he was a biracial young man." Every room in the house had been vandalized. Cement had been poured in their bathtub and stove, railings and walls were kicked in, and a ceiling collapsed.[278] Cincinnati Mayor John Cranley issued a statement: "This crime is not only an attack on an innocent family, it is an attack on our values."[279]

The Unite the Right march and rally in Charlottesville, Virginia, on August 12, 2017, ended when Ohio neo-Nazi Alex Fields Jr. drove his Dodge Challenger into a crowd of counterprotesters, killing Heather Heyer and injuring 19 other people. Fields faced ten felony indictments, including first-degree murder. Fields had driven from Ohio to Virginia to participate in the right-wing event. He had previously moved with his mother from northern Kentucky to Maumee, Ohio, near Toledo, for her job.[280]

Within two weeks of the Charlottesville tragedy, neo-Nazis and white supremacists descended on two of Ohio's historically liberal college towns, Wooster and Yellow Springs. Wooster College is a progressive liberal arts college, and Yellow Springs is the site of perhaps the US's most well-known left-wing peace college, Antioch.

A few days before the Charlottesville rally, Wooster/Orrville NAACP President John Clay received a text image of a KKK flyer from a concerned resident. The flyer identified the East Coast Knights of the True Invisible Empire and insisted that "White Pride Doesn't Mean Hate . . . God Bless the Ku Klux Klan." The flyer was distributed with candy inside a small Ziploc bag.[281] Clay told WKYC Channel 3 that "it kind of shot fear through my heart because it's 2017 and we're still having to deal with this."[282]

In the early morning of August 28, 2017, an Antioch College student out jogging came across flyers from two different neo-Nazi groups posted on several stop signs. The flyers bore the names of either Identity Europa or National Vanguard. Surprisingly, the flyers were not recruitment propaganda; rather, they contained neo-Nazi slogans, supported white supremacy, and expressed hatred toward gays and feminists.[283]

The Mockingbird website reported that a professor noticed "a pickup truck with prominent stickers for a so-called Three Percent Militia group called the West Ohio Minutemen idling in a downtown parking lot."[284] Heavily armed Three Percent militia groups emerged in Ohio during the Trump campaign, dedicated to protecting his supporters' free speech. The intimidating paramilitary group has carried assault rifles on to the Ohio Statehouse grounds in violation of state law. But, in the aftermath of the Charlottesville incident, this was the first time they were linked to neo-Nazi actions. The Mockingbird website argued that the presence of the militia and the neo-Nazi flyers was significant: "Nationally this event is ground breaking in that it is not the so-called defense of Confederate 'heritage' symbols but an actual attack on a historically abolitionist town both at night and in broad daylight by armed right wing groups that have never previously worked together in public."[285]

KKK flyers were also dropped off at an individual's home in Green Township, just outside of Cincinnati, mere days after Charlottesville. The flyer warned of a "bastardized population" and asserted that "Racial purity is America's security." A few days later, cars in Green Township were spray-painted with "KKK" and a racial slur.[286]

The infamous Central Ohio neo-Nazi website *The Daily Stormer* played a provocative role before and after the Charlottesville rally. Andrew Anglin, a Linworth High School graduate living in Worthington, a Columbus suburb, registered the *Daily Stormer* website in March 2013. On Independence Day in 2013, the site launched, replacing Anglin's previous site, *Total Fascism.* Anglin named his site in honor of Hitler's *Der Sturmer.*[287] Matthew Heimbach, leader of the Traditionalist Worker Party with an Ohio base, spoke in defense of Fields: "The Jews will use their guns to try to stop us, but also their pigs and courts to try to break our spirits." Anglin weighed in, writing, "Here's the deal: Fields did nothing wrong."[288]

"The Daily Stormer had become arguably the leading hate site on the internet, far surpassing Stormfront, whose message boards had brought white nationalism into the digital age back in the 1990s," wrote the *Atlantic,* which described Anglin as "the publisher of the world's biggest neo-Nazi website."[289] As of April 2017, the site ranked 13,137th globally and 5,597th within the US, according to Alexa.[290]

The Daily Mail reported that racist mass murderer Dylann Roof, who shot nine Black people in a Charleston, South Carolina, church in 2015, posted on the website. The SPLC "compared the text of Roof's manifesto, which was discovered on his website The Last Rhodesian Saturday, to comments and posts made by user AryanBlood1488 on the site The Daily Stormer and found striking similarities."[291] As the *Atlantic* put it, "Dylann Roof became a hero to Anglin's readers, who honored him with 'Bowl Cut' memes."

After Anglin defamed Heather Heyer and praised the Charlottesville tragedy, he was subject to such intense pressure that he and his website temporarily disappeared. The *Huffington Post* ran an article on December 19 titled "America's Most Notorious Neo-Nazi Is On the Lam: Won't You Come Home Andrew Anglin." The article called him the "King of the Nazi trolls" and claimed that someone had seen him two days earlier in a Meijer store in Reynoldsburg, Ohio.[292] *Cleveland.com* reported that "Ohio's pale prince of extremism has gone underground" after the *Daily Stormer* was tied to the Charlottesville incident.[293]

The limit of free speech versus advocacy of violence is outlined in the US Supreme Court decision *Brandenburg v. Ohio*. Clarence Brandenburg, an Ohio farmer, was known for his advocacy of violence against Blacks and Jews. The court ruled that Brandenburg's racist and anti-Semitic ravings did not incite people to imminent lawless action, in part because of their vague and general nature. The rule is the more speech specifically targets an individual, the less protected it becomes.

Before Andrew Anglin came to national notoriety in August 2017, ARA had called attention to him in his hometown on January 14. A resurrected Columbus chapter of Anti-Racist Action protested on a cold January day just a few blocks north of Old Worthington. The 50 protesters called their action a "Demonstration Against Hate from Worthington to Whitefish." ARA sought to shine the spotlight on Morningstar Ministries and its ties to the *Daily Stormer* website. Greg Anglin, the force behind the ministry, grew up in Worthington and raised his son Andrew there as well. The elder owns and rents several properties in the Columbus area. Andrew listed his father's Christian counseling office as the street address for alt-right supporters to send their cash donations.

Andrew had just announced that he was organizing a demonstration in Whitefish, Montana, hometown of neo-Nazi leader Richard Spencer. A week after the protest, the Montana demonstration was called off and the Worthington address disappeared from the website.

Andrew Anglin is one of the new breed of racists in today's society. He is a white, upper-middle-class suburban millennial who subscribes to alt-right beliefs, supports Donald Trump, and is an avowed neo-Nazi. Andrew wrote on the *Daily Stormer* website, "The rat kikes from the SPLC called up the owner of the building started making threats, so the building company was going to cancel his lease if I didn't stop using the mailbox there."[294]

Olivia Flak, an ARA organizer, told the *Columbus Free Press* that "the address is down but the site is still up. We want to continue to put pressure on the alt-right." That very site would be a key organizing tool to unite the white supremacists and alt-right, as it did for the rally in Charlottesville. Anglin said of Charlottesville, "This was our Beer Hall Putsch," in reference to Hitler's failed 1923 coup attempt.[295]

Anglin faced three lawsuits that were pending in three different federal courts. One suit involved an internet harassment campaign in Montana. Anglin had run an anti-Semitic campaign against the Jews in Whitefish, Montana. His lawyers put forth the novel idea that Anglin couldn't be legally served or sued in a US federal court not only because he couldn't be found but because he was not a resident or citizen of Ohio. His lawyer argued that Anglin is "not a citizen of any state but a 'stateless' individual." Andrew is registered to vote in Ohio.[296]

During the *Stormer*'s attack on Tanya Gersh, a Jewish realtor from Whitefish, the site's webmaster, Andrew Auernheimer, sent her a message: "You fucking wicked kike whore. This is Trump's America now." When Whitefish Police Chief Bill Dial likened Anglin's anti-Semitic campaign to domestic terrorism, the *Atlantic* saw it as "a sign of just how emboldened the alt-right had become."[297] In 2015 Andrew Anglin had endorsed Trump on the *Daily Stormer* website. In his look back at 2017 on the site, he wrote: "Donald Trump as President had some super highs and some super lows . . . the best part was when he defended us over Charlottesville."

Following the Charlottesville hate rally, the *New York Times* went in search of sympathizers supporting the new neo-Nazi movement and found Tony Hovater in New Carlisle, Ohio: "He is the Nazi sympathizer next door, polite and low-key at a time the old boundaries of accepted political activity can seem alarmingly in flux." The newspaper focused on Hovater because he wasn't a leader but "a committed foot soldier—an organizer, an occasional podcast guest on a website called Radio Aryan, and a self-described 'social media villain.'"[298]

Hovater also helped found the Traditionalist Worker Party, one of the right-wing extremist groups that marched in Charlottesville. The group claims to oppose racism but has participated in white supremacist events throughout the US, according to the Anti-Defamation League, and sells Nazi swastika armbands on its website.[299]

The *New York Times* noted, "There are times when it can feel toxic to openly identify as a far-right extremist in the Ohio of 2017. But not always. He said the election of President Trump helped open a space for people like him, demonstrating that it is not the end of the world to be attacked as the bigot he surely is." Hovater said, "You can just say, 'Yeah, so?' And move on," the *Times* reported.[300]

The SPLC also pointed to the Trump presidency in energizing "White Supremacists and other hatemongers." Trump shocked the nation by stating, "but you also had people that were very fine people, on both sides" about those marching at Charlottesville. "The racist rally and the deadline violence in Charlottesville illustrated the growing strength of a white supremacist that's been emboldened by the xenophobic campaign and, now, the divisive presidency of Donald Trump," stated the SPLC's assessment.[301]

"The national leader of a Ku Klux Klan group active in the Dayton area said he is glad anti-racist counter-protester Heather Heyer was killed and others injured when an Ohio man allegedly drove his car into them at a Charlottesville, Va., rally of right-wing groups on Saturday," reported the *Dayton Daily News*. Imperial Wizard Chris Baker of the Loyal White Knights of the Ku Klux Klan elaborated for the *News*, "Because even though he done it by accident, he was still on the white side and he accidentally hit a bunch of antifascists. So to me any time an antifascist dies, that's a point in my book. I'm happy about it." After proclaiming Hail Victory, Baker explained: "We're not a hate group, we're more of a civil rights organization now."[302]

One of the rising stars of racism, Richard Spencer, organized a tour of major universities and found himself at odds with the institutions' administrations. In October 2017 Spencer filed suit against The Ohio State University for refusing to rent space on campus to him for a speaking event. The university sent a letter to Spencer's tour organizer, Cameron Padgett, stating that Spencer presented a substantial risk to public safety. Spencer had previously spoken at the University of Florida in Gainesville, where the governor had declared a state of emergency and the university had paid $600,000 to provide security. Still, a neo-Nazi was assaulted, and a white supremacist arrested, for shooting at protesters with an intent to kill.[303] It was Richard Spencer who texted to a reporter in Charlottesville, "I'd be near campus tonight, if I were you," alerting him to the Nazi-style torchlight parade held on August 11.[304]

In the year following the Charlottesville incident, the *New York Times* noted, "the number of hate groups in the US rose for the fourth year in a row in 2018, pushed to a record high by a toxic combination of political polarization, anti-immigrant sentiment and technologies that help spread propaganda online." The *Times* article reported on SPLC data showing a 30 percent jump in hate crimes since 2014. This statistic matches an FBI hate crime report also noting a 30 percent increase in reported hate crimes between 2015 and 2017. The Anti-Defamation League (ADL) reported that in the year 2018, 50 people were killed as a result of hate crimes.[305]

The *Times* reported that Heidi Beirich, Director of the SPLC Intelligence Project, which tracks hate group activity in the US, points to "an increase in extremist activity" that began "in the earliest days of the 2016 presidential election when anxieties over immigration helped propel President Trump to the White House." Beirich stated that before Trump's campaign, the number of hate groups had fallen in the previous three years under the Obama administration.[306] In Beirich's assessment, "Trump has made people in the white supremacist movement move back into politics and the public domain. He is a critical aspect of this dynamic, but he is not the only reason why the ranks of hate groups are growing. The ability to propagate hate in the online space is key."[307]

Beirich points to an almost 50 percent increase in white nationalist groups, from 100 to 148, in 2018. One such white nationalist group, the neo-Nazi Patriot Front, boldly flyered Indianola Avenue in the gay- and lesbian-friendly liberal Clintonville neighborhood of Columbus on Monday, February 26, in the middle of the day. A battle over the flyers ensued as Clintonville residents tore them down and white nationalists replaced them. Between February 26 and March 3, the Patriot Front flyered Clintonville four times in addition to previously flyering the suburbs of Dublin, Hilliard, Westerville, and Worthington. In Westerville, the neo-Nazi National Socialist Movement left leaflets at residents' homes and wrote graffiti spelling out the word "Jew" at a Jewish family's home.[308]

Over 60 antiracist activists staged a demonstration on Saturday, March 3, 2019, with signs stating "No Nazis Allowed," "No to White Nationalism," and "End White Supremacy," among other sentiments. Brakton Bragg, a Patriot Front spokesperson, explained his organization's view: "The nation is the property of the founding stock and no one else." The Front's flyer stated, "Our goals do not end with a candidate in an office or a bill signed into law. Our horizon is set on absolute victory. Resurrection through insurrection."[309]

The Patriot Front is a splinter group formed at the time of the Charlottesville rally that uses a bold strategy linking neo-Nazi networks with well-armed militia men and "fence-sitting" alt-righters attracted to violent street action.[310]

Across the nation, the ADL documented 1,187 cases of white supremacist propaganda efforts in 2018, a 182 percent increase from 2017, when there were only 421 incidents. Andrew Anglin's Ohio-based Daily Stormer Book Club was responsible for nearly a tenth of all on-campus neo-Nazi group flyering incidents.[311] The SPLC called Anglin's website, *Daily Stormer,* "the leading extremist website in the country." A jury awarded a $4.1 million verdict against the neo-Nazi website in June 2019 for falsely accusing Dean Obeidallah, a Sirius XM radio talk-show host, of terrorism. Columbus-based US District Court Judge Edward Sargus Jr. entered a default verdict on Obeidallah's behalf, noting that Anglin's statements were not protected speech under the First Amendment.[312] Still, the opinions reflected by Anglin's website are indicative of certain sentiments held by people in Ohio. The axiom that "Ohio is the most southern of northern states" still survives.

Neo-Nazi posters popped up all over the Buckeye State in 2018 and 2019. Case Western Reserve University was bombarded with neo-Nazi flyers after the midterm election. Flyers contained a link to the Daily Stormer's website.[313] Wright State University administrators ordered white supremacist flyers removed from the Dayton-area campus in February 2018.[314]

Neo-Nazi posters made headline news in Circleville, Ohio, in February 2019. The posters, incorporating the colors of the US flag, urged people in the central Ohio town to "Keep America American. Report any and all illegal aliens. They are criminal." Radio station Magic 95.5 FM reported that a Circleville Patriot Front member, Richard, offered, "We object to the term 'hate group,'" and stated that the Front instead is dedicated to the creation of a white ethno-state. "We think diversity is not good for anyone. We are a very traditionalist pro-white, anti-Jewish organization. We are against minorities generally. We feel that everyone is better off in their own corner."[315]

More than a dozen antigovernment Three Percent armed militiamen showed up at the Ohio Statehouse on Saturday, March 25, 2017, to protect Trump supporters. These so-called Three Percenters are so named because they believe that all you need is three percent of the population to take up arms in order to overthrow a corrupt government. The Three Percenters began as a backlash to President

Obama. One of the organization's founders is Michael Brian Vanderboegh, a prominent Christian Oath Keeper from Alabama. The militia were dressed in camouflage and armed with AR-15s, the civilian version of the US military weapon. This is precisely the merger of Trump supporters with extreme right-wing organizations dreamed of by white supremacists and neo-Nazis.[316]

In mid-March 2019, Trump commented to the alt-right outlet Breitbart: "I can tell you I have the support of the police, the support of the military, the support of the Bikers for Trump—I have the tough people, but they don't play it tough—until they go to a certain point, and then it would be very bad, very bad."[317]

Emerging from the Charlottesville tragedy, 17-year-old Thomas Rousseau devised a new strategy to rebrand the white supremacist movement and tie it to President Trump's anti-immigrant rhetoric. He named his new group the Patriot Front. The organization's manifesto is: "A nation within a nation is our goal. Our people face complete annihilation as 'culture and heritage are attacked from all sides.'"[318]

One of the peculiar slogans chanted at Charlottesville was "Jews will not replace us!" along with the Nazi slogan from the Third Reich "Blood and Soil!" As Rousseau explained at a University of Texas white supremacy rally held after Charlottesville, "A corrupt, ruthless, global, and tyrannical elite has usurped your democracy and turned it into a weapon, first to enslave and then to replace you."[319]

A high school journalist during the 2016 presidential election, Rousseau was a dedicated Trump supporter.[320] The SPLC files document that Rousseau led members of Vanguard America at the violent and deadly 2017 "Unite the Right" Charlottesville rally. Ohioan James Alex Fields Jr. marched with Vanguard America and carried a shield with that organization's emblem at the rally. Several photos captured Rousseau standing near Fields, the man convicted of murder and given a life sentence in June 2019 on 29 hate crime charges for the death of antifascist activist Heather Heyer when he drove his car into a crowd of antifa protesters in Charlottesville.[321]

As a consequence of the Charlottesville incident, Vanguard America disbanded. Rousseau rebranded Vanguard American as the Patriot Front and seized on iconic American images such as George Washington, Andrew Jackson, Robert E. Lee, and George Patton.[322] Rousseau's tactic, pushing white supremacy as patriotism, is centered around prepackaged propaganda flyers and video postings. His goal is to avoid large rallies and build smaller, local chapters that organize on college campuses and in small-town America.[323]

Two of Rousseau's slogans reflect the underlying white supremacist beliefs among the emerging and well-armed alt-right. The vision of salvation through a white power apocalypse lives on in Ohio and elsewhere. Sympathizers and supporters can download a Patriot Front flyer that says "Resurrection through Insurrection," a goal of both the Front and the Three Percenters.

Earlier in this book, the role of white supremacist ideology was spelled out during the conquest of Native Americans in the Buckeye State. Rousseau and his "patriots" have a flyer for that as well. They show a map of the US with the words "Conquered Not Stolen."

In mainstream Ohio politics, the most obvious white supremacist ploy is the purging, or deregistering, of minority voters. Back in 2004 George W. Bush's margin of victory over his opponent John Kerry was only 118,000 votes. *Columbus Free Press* investigations uncovered that 305,000 voters had been eliminated from the voting rolls. This included nearly a quarter of all voters in Cleveland, a city that voted 81 percent Democratic, and, according to the 2000 census, whose Black population was 50.96 percent. Heavily Democratic Toledo and the urban Black districts in Cincinnati had also been targeted for purging voters.[324]

Millions of Ohio voters have tried to vote on Election Day over the past 15 years, only to find their names erased from the poll books.

The American Civil Liberties Union (ACLU) sued the state of Ohio and Ohio Secretary of State Jon Husted to protect voters' rights to remain registered. At the crux of the ACLU's lawsuit were 385,065 registered Ohioans who were refused absentee ballots in 2016 because they had failed to vote in the 2012 or 2014 federal elections.

The US Supreme Court decided that the Secretary of State has broad powers over voting in Ohio.

Ohio's notorious "use it or lose it" rule allows the Secretary of State to remove voters from the rolls if they haven't voted in a federal election in a two-year period, even if they cast a vote in a state or local election during the same period. Of course, the chances of being purged are far more likely if voters are in urban Democratic counties or precincts.

Between the 2004 and 2008 presidential elections, an extensive study conducted by the *Columbus Free Press* examining all voter registration rolls in the states' 88 counties found that 1.25 million had been scrubbed from the rolls. Again, these purged voters were overwhelmingly from Democratic precincts.

The now-defunct welfare rights organization ACORN and the Obama campaign had to engage in a massive project to reregister the voters before Election Day.

In the run-up to the 2012 presidential election, the *Columbus Free Press* exposed the fact that 1.1 million voters had been purged, according to public records. The purges were highest in poor, minority, and urban precincts.[325]

In 2016 Ohio Secretary of State Jon Husted was responsible for purging more than a million voters. Moreover, the *Columbus Dispatch* found that Husted refused to mail absentee ballot forms to over one million registered voters, primarily in urban areas. One reason given was that they had moved. An analysis by the *Columbus Free Press* found that 568,456 of these registered voters had moved within the Buckeye State and were still eligible to vote at their new addresses.[326] This targeting of Black voters is a new form of Jim Crow.

Perhaps the best analysis of why white supremacy must be tracked and studied is reflected in the words of James Ridgeway, author of the seminal book *Blood in the Face: The Ku Klux Klan, Aryan Nations, Nazi Skinheads, and the Rise of a New White Culture*:

> Up until recently, the far right has been viewed by mainstream politicians and voters as an irrelevant force, playing out its fantasies on the fringes of the normal body politic. But during the 1990s, the fringe movement has steadily gained currency among a wider audience.[327]

When Ridgeway offered this assessment, he was referring to Reagan's 1980 and 1984 campaigns and his presidency during the '80s. Recall Reagan opened his 1980 campaign in Philadelphia, Mississippi, best known as the site of the notorious murder of three civil rights workers in 1964. The slaying of James Chaney, Mickey Schwerner, and Andrew Goodman was captured in the movie *Mississippi Burning*. Reagan, in search of "George Wallace-inclined voters," embraced the theme of states' rights, the phrase white southerners had used for more than a century to justify Jim Crow segregation.[328]

While Reagan endorsed Nixon's so-called southern strategy to woo white "Dixiecrat" voters to the GOP, Trump's more obvious solicitation of alt-right nationalist ideologues is far more dangerous and potentially disruptive than Reagan's appeal to states' rights. Trump's inflammatory xenophobic rhetoric reached new lows with his July 14, 2019, tweet aimed at progressive Democratic congresswomen: "Why don't they go back and help fix the totally broken and crime infested places from which they came."[329] Trump's tweet came out the same day his administration announced that it would be conducting some of the largest roundups of undocumented immigrants in US history.

One of the congresswomen in question, Alexandria Ocasio-Cortez, issued the following statement: "It's important to note that the President's words . . . telling four American Congresswomen of color 'go back to your own country,' are hallmark language of white supremacists. Trump feels comfortable leading the GOP into outright racism, and that should concern all Americans."[330] Trump was unrepentant about his remarks and made clear that they would be at the centerpiece of his 2020 re-election campaign.

The normally staid *Columbus Dispatch* blasted the following headline following Trump's August 1 presidential rally in Cincinnati: "Rally has racial tinge." Trump's target was not the four congresswomen but our major Asian rival. The president proclaimed, "We will be taxing the hell out of China."[331]

We began this book by defining what we mean by the use of the term *white supremacy*. Trump's rallies reflect the third form of white supremacy, where beliefs held by mainstream native-born whites in the supposed inferiority of other ethnic and racial groups are reflected in everyday racist attitudes.

Ohio once again made national news when James Patrick Reardon of Mahoning County was arrested and charged with aggravated menacing. He had posted a video on social media that showed him firing a gun and mentioning a local Jewish community center. He captioned the video "Police identify the Youngstown Jewish Family Community shooter as local white nationalist Seamus O'Rearedon." Reardon used the alias "Seamus O'Rearedon" in the movement.[332]

Reardon's activities exemplified the first type of white supremacy that we outlined in the beginning of this text, where a specific racist ideology promotes the idea that persons of European descent, particularly from northern Europe, are superior to people of other races.

Anti-Semitic incidents reached a record high in 2019, according to the ADL, in a report released in May 2020. CEO Jonathan

Greenblatt of the ADL expects 2020 to be even worse due to the COVID-19 pandemic that is fueling anti-Semitic conspiracy theories. "Anti-Semitism is a virus. It's like a disease, and it persists. . . . It never seems to go away. There truly is no single antidote or cure," Greenblatt said. He attributed the record high of 2019 to the "normalization of anti-Semitic tropes" and to the "charged politics of the day."[333]

Overall, the ADL found that white supremacist propaganda distribution had more than doubled nationwide in 2019. Where does Ohio fit into this specific type of white supremacist surge? Ohio's numbers were even more startling, with a 442 percent increase in white supremacist propaganda distribution. Ohio went from 26 incidents in 2018 to 141 in 2019. Columbus had 27 incidents, more than the entire state during the previous year.[334]

A crowd of 500 to 600 antiracist protesters drowned out a mere nine members of the Indiana-based Honorable Sacred Knights of the KKK in Dayton on May 25, 2019 (see Figure 2.5). The Klan's hopes of recruiting in the highly segregated city were unproductive due to the police barriers that kept them hundreds of yards away from anyone who could hear them. Dayton's Mayor, Nan Whaley, acknowledged the inequality between Black and white residents. "Dayton is still too segregated and still too unequal. This is unacceptable and something we must keep focused on to change every single day," Whaley told the *Dayton Daily News*.[335]

As the COVID-19 pandemic spread in 2020, so did the white supremacist virus. The Proud Boys appeared at the Ohio Statehouse at an April 18 anti-lockdown rally. Their tactic was to spew anti-Asian bigotry and the notion that the Chinese government had deliberately infected the US population with the coronavirus, according to the Southern Poverty Law Center.[336] *Dispatch* photographer Adam Cairns photographed T. J. Philips at an Akron-area "Open Ohio" protest sporting a Proud Boys tattoo on his forearm. Philips wore a black-and-gold Proud Boys jacket with a matching "Make America Great Again" cap on his head.[337]

On April 20, as protesters with "Open Ohio" signs rallied against the stay-at-home order, Ohio Governor Mike DeWine denounced white supremacist signs held by protesters as "disgusting" and "vile." One sign bore the image of a rat wearing a Star of David with the phrase "The Real Plague."[338] The 36-year-old bald white man holding the "Real Plague" sign was Matthew Paul Slatzer, from

FIGURE 2.5. Antiracist protester at the Dayton rally. Credit: Paul Becker, *Columbus Free Press* photographer, 2019.

Canton, a member of the neo-Nazi National Socialist Movement. Slatzer is also known for entering a convenience store in Stow, Ohio, on May 3, 2020, with a machete and a hatchet, saying that he was going to Kent State to look for Jews.[339] He was wearing "a black T-shirt with a Nazi symbol and swastika, black tactical boots and had a Nazi tattoo on the back of his head. He told the clerk he was a member of the Aryan Brotherhood," said the *Cleveland Jewish News*. Slatzer has since been arrested on weapons charges after an incident in a Canton bar.[340]

The COVID-19 pandemic of 2020 generated numerous scientific studies on its impact on the US population. The second definition of white supremacy outlined in the beginning of this text referred to a system of structural or systemic racism in which white people possess privileges that others lack. In May 2020 the Franklin County Public Health Department officially declared racism a public health crisis as a result of the pandemic. This declaration was the first of its kind in Ohio, driven, in part, by the pandemic that highlighted racial disparities in health care delivery and treatment. Public health officials acknowledged a disparity within their agency on how services were provided based on race. The declaration noted that Black residents of Columbus and Franklin County "make up a disproportionate share of coronavirus infections and hospitalizations."[341] A headline in the *Dispatch* confirmed the analysis: "More local blacks get virus, are hospitalized."[342]

Various scholars liken the effect of the 2020 pandemic on the Black population to the original sin of white supremacy—the genocidal removal of Native Americans from the Ohio territory. The epidemics brought by conquistadors and European settlers beginning in 1492 ultimately resulted in the death of 70 to 90 percent of the Native American population. Smallpox entered the Ohio Valley and Great Lakes region between 1756 and 1757, mostly because of Native American involvement in the colonial war between the British and the French. The *Atlantic* argued that disease has never been just disease for Native Americans. Jeffrey Ostler, professor of history at the University of Oregon, offered that "Native communities' vulnerability to epidemics is not a historical accident, but a direct result of oppressive policies and ongoing colonialism."[343]

The topic of racism pushed the COVID-19 virus from top headlines around the world when the graphic video of a Black man, George Floyd, being killed by Minneapolis police on May 25, 2020, went viral on social media. Floyd's death reignited massive Black Lives Matter protests throughout the country, including all areas of Ohio. The movement's fury was aimed at the systematic violence perpetrated on the Black community by white, urban law enforcement officers.

Numerous police and corrections officers have been exposed as members of white supremacist groups in recent news reports. The Federal Bureau of Investigation (FBI) documented in 2006 that US police forces had a white supremacist problem. A heavily redacted version of the report titled "White Supremacist Infiltration of Law Enforcement" was widely circulated on the internet. The report warns of white supremacist groups like the Ku Klux Klan infiltrating law enforcement. The report documents how avowedly racist organizations call on their members to become part of the "thin blue line."

Long-standing chants by antiracist groups reflect this: "Blue by day, white by night" and "The cops and the Klan go hand in hand." A Connecticut police officer was outed as a Proud Boy. An estimated quarter of the police force of Fruitland Park, Florida, were revealed to be KKK members.[344]

In the aftermath of Floyd's death, 28 members of Congress are calling on the FBI and the Department of Justice to release the completely unredacted document, according to the *Daily Beast*.[345]

Underscoring the urgency of releasing the report is a document published in late April 2020 by the Tech Transparency Project. Their study revealed 125 Facebook groups promoting the idea of the "boogaloo"—a far-right word used to describe civil war.[346] "More than sixty percent of the [boogaloo] groups were created in the last three months, as COVID-19 quarantines took hold in the U.S., and they attracted tens of thousands of members in the last thirty days," according to the report. It notes, "Organizations that study far right groups, including the Anti-Defamation League (ADL) and Institute for Strategic Dialogue have found that the boogaloo has ties to white supremacist movements." Rumors circulated on social media that "Boogaloo Bois" and other right-wing allies may try to disrupt Columbus' Fourth of July Black Lives Matters demonstrations. The Anti-Defamation League reported on June 2, 2020 extremist anti-Semitic Brian Andrew Grossman attended Black Lives Matters protests in Columbus and shared his videos online.[347]

White supremacist social DNA still runs deep in small-town Ohio. In Shelby, Ohio, on June 24, 2020, police arrested Gregory S. Dick for yelling racial slurs at 50 peaceful Black Lives Matter marchers. "KKK, this is a KKK town brother. Get your Black ass outta here," Dick yelled during the town's June 10 march. Dick was charged with disorderly conduct.[348]

Bethel, Ohio, made international news following an attack on a handful of Black Lives Matter demonstrators by 800 counter-protesters, including four motorcycle gangs, in the small southwestern Ohio town. The British newspaper the *Guardian*, as well as the *Washington Post* and *New York Times*, reported on Bethel, a town with 2,800 residents, only one half of one percent of whom are Black, according to the US Census. "Counter-protesters harassed group of peaceful demonstrators with rifles, bats and racial slurs in mostly white town of Bethel," described the *Guardian*.[349]

The *Dispatch* described what one Bethel resident watched from her porch: "Dozens of her neighbors walk by with bats in their hands or guns strapped to their sides. They were married couples, friends and relatives, young people and old, all heading up Union Street toward the center of town." What drove this activity was rumors "about busloads of coming to her town to join small Black Lives Matter protests . . . Word was that hundreds could be arriving from Cincinnati or Columbus or Detroit." The *Dispatch* estimated that there were actually only 80 to 100 actual Black Lives Matters protesters, the vast majority of them locals.[350]

The rapid re-emergence of white supremacists during the pandemic lockdown and following the death of George Floyd is the result of various forces, among them the actions of President Trump. A whole series of activities indicate that the President is "dog whistling" to the white supremacists. He is not speaking "in code." He is far more direct, in the tradition of George Wallace.

Critics argued that Trump's re-election campaign rally in Tulsa, Oklahoma, was intended to foment racist sentiments. As *Time* put it, politely, "Trump's Tulsa Rally Highlights His Record of Racial Division."[351] Trump originally selected June 19, 2020, for the rally, a day known as Juneteenth, commemorating the day the final slaves were liberated by the Union Army in Texas. After an outcry from the Black community, the rally was moved to June 20. Tulsa remained a controversial location. In 1921 there was a notorious "race massacre" there, when white mobs attacked the Black population, burning down the Black "Wall Street"—one of the wealthiest Black communities in America. Hundreds of Black people were killed, over 800 injured, and 6,000 interned.[352] On Sunday, June 28, 2020, the President tweeted a video of one of his supporters chanting "White Power!" The tweet was later deleted.[353]

There are conflicting messages from the president and other elected officials during these chaotic times. Black Lives Matter protesters' actions and demands resulted in racist symbols being removed from many aspects of society, such as Confederate war statues and flags, and even the Aunt Jemima character from pancake syrup bottles. In Columbus, statues of the city's namesake—conquistador and founder of the New World slave trade—were quickly removed from outside City Hall and Columbus State Community College.

At the same time, the Ohio legislature considered a resolution declaring racism a public health crisis but failed to bring it to a hearing before their 2020 summer break. According to Patch.com, State Senator Tim Huffman of Tipp City wondered whether the "colored population—do not wash their hands as well as other groups? Or wear a mask? Or do not socially distance themselves? Could that just be maybe the explanation of why there's a higher incidence?"[354]

The question of race and mask-wearing was soon answered at the virtually all-white antimask protest on Saturday, July 18, 2020, at the Ohio Statehouse. The protest morphed into a Stand for America 2020 rally that attracted hundreds of semi-automatic-rifle-carrying and pistol-bearing "patriots" shouting "Give me liberty or give me death!" Death was more likely, as the Ohio Health Department reported 20 deaths from the virus that day and 1,679 new cases.[355] Each side was armed, although the Anti-Racist Action and Black Lives Matter counterprotester contingent was heavily outgunned, but there was no shootout.

White supremacists were plentiful. The Proud Boys provided security, Three Percent militia were present, people flashed the white supremacist "OK" hand sign, and a young man carried a sign saying "Racism does not exist" while wearing a "White History Month" T-shirt (see Figure 2.6). A Proud Boys' security vest included a "RWDS" patch—short for "Right Wing Death Squad." Boogaloo Boys wearing Hawaiian shirts and carrying weapons tried to join the Anti-Racist Action / Black Lives Matter counterprotest, but their presence sparked conflict about which side they were on.

The strategy of the white supremacists at this rally was one of a popular front. They were united in supporting Trump and opposing masks, but white supremacists logos were not as visible. One counterprotester observed, "Those symbols are no longer necessary to those people because they have been replaced by pro-Donald Trump flags, Confederate flags, militia insignia and Hawaiian shirts—but above all, sadly, by the flag of the US—which together with the word Freedom in certain hands and in certain mouths are equivalent to the most abject fascist symbols."[356]

The event had an eerie feel, invoking the late Weimar Republic, when there were street clashes between the left and the right-wing white supremacists. So bizarre was the gathering of nearly a thousand armed right-wingers that the British *Daily Mail* covered the event in an article titled "Hundreds of Anti-Mask Protesters

FIGURE 2.6. Stand for America protester. Credit: Paul Becker, *Columbus Free Press* photographer, 2020.

Protected by Armed Militia and Bikers Gather at the Ohio Statehouse Saying Face Coverings Are 'Propaganda' and Holding 'I will not wear someone else's fear' Signs."[357] An open battle between the forces of the alt-right and the ARA appeared almost inevitable. In some ways, the antimaskers are similar to Holocaust deniers. A certain anti-intellectualism pervades their analysis, and the presence of signs denouncing George Soros gave it a tinge of anti-Semitism. As outlined by Hofstadter in *The Paranoid Style in American Politics,* numerous conspiracy theories touted on signage and in speeches at the rally displayed disbelief in science and the threat of the virus.[358]

The COVID-19 virus, George Floyd's death, and the Black Lives Matter demonstrations opened up a historic dialogue about white privilege, racism, and inequality. There remains, however, deeply embedded racist sentiments across Ohio, and other states, fueled by the specter of white supremacy embodied in Trump's re-election campaign.

NOTES

Notes to "Then: A History of Racism and Bigotry in Ohio"

1. Ohio's state social studies standards call for the state's history to be taught almost exclusively in the fourth grade. Ohio history is not covered in any structured way after that unless a particular Ohio-related topic happens to coincide with another strand or standard. Ohio State Social Studies Standards can be retrieved from http://education.ohio.gov/Topics/Learning-in-Ohio/Social-Studies.
2. For an analytical approach to the concept of everyday racism, see Philomena Essed, *Understanding Everyday Racism: An Interdisciplinary Theory* (Los Angeles: Sage), 1991.
3. Philip Freneau, "The Pilgrim, No. VIII," *Freeman's Journal* (Philadelphia), January 9, 1782, 1.
4. Rob Harper, "State Intervention and Extreme Violence in the Revolutionary Ohio Valley," *Journal of Genocide Research* 10, no. 2 (2008): 234.
5. Jeffrey Ostler, "'To Extirpate the Indians': An Indigenous Consciousness of Genocide in the Ohio Valley and Lower Great Lakes, 1750s–1810," *The William and Mary Quarterly* 72, no. 4 (2015): 589.
6. There are many excellent accounts of the Gnadenhutten Massacre, but see especially Peter Silver, *Our Savage Neighbors: How Indian War Transformed Early America* (New York: Norton), 2008.
7. Arthur St. Clair to Henry Knox, October 26, 1788, in *The St. Clair Papers: The Life and Public Services of Arthur St. Clair,* edited by William Henry Smith (Cincinnati: Robert Clarke & Co., 1882), 2:93.
8. Levi Woodward et al., "Public Notice" (Cincinnati, 1794), in *The St. Clair Papers,* edited by William Henry Smith (Cincinnati: Robert Clarke & Co., 1882), 329.
9. Kristopher Maulden, "A Show of Force: The Northwest Indian War and the Early American State," *Ohio Valley History* 16, no. 4 (2016): 21.
10. George W. Manypenny, *Our Indian Wards* (Cincinnati: Robert Clarke & Co., 1880), xv.

11. Stephen J. Middleton, *The Black Laws in the Old Northwest: A Documentary History* (Santa Barbara, CA: ABC-CLIO, 1993), 15.
12. Ibid.
13. Ibid., 16.
14. Ibid., 16–18.
15. Ibid., 34.
16. Ibid., 34–35.
17. Ohio Department of Commerce, "History of BBS" (Columbus, OH), https://www.com.ohio.gov/documents/bbst_BBSAbout.pdf.
18. Nikki M. Taylor, "Reconsidering the 'Forced' Exodus of 1829: Free Black Emigration from Cincinnati, Ohio to Wilberforce, Canada," *Journal of African American History* 87 (Summer 2002): 287.
19. *Liberty Hall,* August 25, 1825, as quoted in Richard C. Wade, "The Negro in Cincinnati, 1800–30," *Journal of Negro History* 39, no. 1 (1954), 46.
20. John Malvin, *Autobiography of John Malvin* (Cleveland: Leader Printing Co., 1879), 11–12.
21. Ibid., 22.
22. Ibid., 24.
23. Taylor, "Reassessing the 'Forced' Exodus of 1829," 291.
24. David A. Gerber, *Black Ohio and the Color Line, 1860–1915* (Urbana: University of Illinois Press, 1976), 10.
25. "The citizens of Portsmouth are adopting measures to free the town of its colored population," *Portsmouth Courier,* January 21, 1831, Ohio History Center, Portsmouth N287, Ohio History Connection, Columbus, Ohio, http://www.sciotohistorical.org/items/show/108. Earlier accounts by historians like Carter Woodson and Nelson Evans placed the date in 1830, but historian Andrew Feight did the archival work to verify the 1831 date.
26. Andrew Feight, "'Black Friday': Enforcing Ohio's "Black Laws" in Portsmouth, Ohio," *Scioto Historical Society,* http://www.sciotohistorical.org/items/show/108.
27. *Ohio State Journal,* February 1, 1832, as quoted in Frank U. Quillin, *The Color Line in Ohio: A History of Race Prejudice in a Typical Northern State* (Ann Arbor: University of Michigan, 1913), 30.
28. Frank F. Mathias, "John Randolph's Freedmen: The Thwarting of a Will," *The Journal of Southern History* 39 no. 2 (May 1973): 264.
29. American Colonization Society, "Annual Report of the American Colonization Society," *The African Repository and Colonial Journal* 23 (1847): 70.
30. Mathias, 269–70.
31. "John Randolph's Negroes," *St. Mary's Sentinel,* as quoted in *The Liberator,* August 7, 1846, 1.
32. "John Randolph's Slaves," *Sidney Aurora,* as quoted in *The Liberator,* August 7, 1846, 1.
33. Mathias, 263.
34. "Ohio Resolutions," *The Liberator,* April 18, 1839, 1.
35. Stephen Middleton, *The Black Laws: Race and the Legal Process in Early Ohio* (Athens: Ohio University Press, 2005), 155.
36. James Loudon, in *Report of the Debates and Proceedings of the Convention for the Revision of the Constitution of the State of Ohio. 1850–51,* vol. 1 (Columbus: S. Medary Printing, 1851), 337.
37. Kevin F. Kern and Gregory S. Wilson, *Ohio: A History of the Buckeye State* (Malden, MA: Wiley, 2014), 212.
38. Betty M. Culpepper, "The Negro and the Black Laws of Ohio, 1803–1860" (master's thesis, Kent State University, 1966), 75.

39. Jonathan L. Entin, "An Ohio Dilemma: Race, Equal Protection, and the Unfulfilled Promise of a State Bill of Rights," *Cleveland State Law Review* 51 (2004): 398.
40. See especially Jacob T. Mach, "'Having Given Them Bayonets, We Will Not Withhold the Ballot'—Republicans and Black Suffrage in Reconstruction Ohio, 1865–1867" (master's thesis, Bowling Green State University, 2020).
41. Ibid, 399.
42. *Acts of the State of Ohio,* vol. 58 (Columbus: Richard Nevins, State Printer, 1861), 6.
43. "A Case of Miscegenation," *Perrysburg Journal,* January 25, 1890, 1.
44. *Cleveland Gazette,* August 30, 1884, 1.
45. "To Cincinnati Went the Strange Pair Who Were Refused a License," *Cincinnati Enquirer,* May 27, 1904, 2.
46. "Squire Refused to Marry Negro and White Woman," *Cincinnati Enquirer,* January 31, 1912, 16.
47. *Civil Rights Cases,* 109 U.S. 3 (1883).
48. "What Prejudice Did," *Cleveland Gazette,* June 4, 1887, 1.
49. "Will Not Work With Colored Miners," *Cleveland Gazette,* August 11, 1888, 1.
50. Steven J. Ross, *Workers on the Edge: Work, Leisure, and Politics in Industrializing Cincinnati, 1788–1890* (New York: Columbia University Press, 1985), 72.
51. Eileen Muccino, "Irish Filibusters and Know Nothings in Cincinnati," *Ohio Valley History* 10, no. 3 (Fall 2010): 3.
52. Lyman Beecher, *Dr. Beecher's Plea for the West* (Cincinnati: Truman and Smith, 1835), 175.
53. Ibid., 95.
54. "Know Nothingism," *Canton Repository,* August 22, 1854, 1.
55. Muccino, 4.
56. Ibid., 13.
57. Stephan F. Brumberg, "The Cincinnati Bible War (1869–1873) and Its Impact on the Education of the City's Protestants, Catholics, and Jews," *American Jewish Archives Journal* 54, no. 2 (2002): 12.
58. Ibid., 12.
59. Ibid., 23.
60. Veritas, "Catholicism and Modern Democracy," *Athens Messenger,* April 15, 1875, 6.
61. Joseph Patterson Smith, ed., *History of the Republican Party in Ohio* (Chicago: Lewis Publishing, 1898), 1:589.
62. Versalle F. Washington, *Eagles on Their Buttons: A Black Regiment in the Civil War* (Columbia: University of Missouri Press, 1999), 12.
63. "Letters to the People, No. 6," *Portsmouth Times,* July 19, 1862, 1.
64. "Turning the Tables," *Tiffin Weekly Tribune,* July 16, 1862 (originally published in *Toledo Commercial*), 1.
65. Frank R. Levstik, "The Toledo Riot of 1862: A Study of Midwest Negrophobia," *Northwest Ohio Quarterly* 44 (Autumn 1972): 105.
66. "Strike among the Stevedores," *Toledo Blade,* July 8, 1862, 3.
67. Ibid.
68. Ibid.
69. "The Riot," *Toledo Blade,* July 9, 1862, 3.
70. Ibid.
71. "The Desperation of Politicians," *Toledo Blade,* July 10, 1862, 2.
72. S. E., "The Toledo Riot," *Napoleon North-West,* July 11, 1862, 1.
73. Lee Williams, "Concentrated Residences: The Case of Black Toledo, 1890–1930," *Phylon* 43, no. 2 (2nd qtr. 1982): 168.
74. Lafcadio Hearn, "Levee Life: Haunts and Pastimes of the Roustabouts," *Cincinnati Commercial,* March 17, 1876. As cited in *Children of the Levee,* edited by O. W. Frost (Lexington: University of Kentucky Press, 1957), 60.

75. *Cincinnati Daily Gazette,* July 11, 1862, 2.
76. National Museum of African American History and Culture, "Blackface: The Birth of an American Stereotype," https://nmaahc.si.edu/blog-post/blackface-birth-american-stereotype.
77. "Burnt Cork Artists Give Annual Show," *New Philadelphia Daily Times,* March 8, 1907, 1.
78. "Minstrel Men Again Carry Off Honors in Annual Production," *New Philadelphia Daily Times,* April 21, 1911, 1.
79. "Port Clinton Jaycees See No Slurs in Production of Minstrel Program," *Sandusky Register,* January 27, 1964, 9.
80. Ibid.
81. "Public Letters by Our Readers," *Mansfield News Journal,* February 18, 1964, 4.
82. State of Ohio, "Amendment and Legislation: Proposed Constitutional Amendments, Initiated Legislation, and Laws Challenged by Referendum, Submitted to the Electors" (Columbus: Ohio Secretary of State), https://www.sos.state.oh.us/globalassets/elections/historical/issuehist.pdf.
83. Marilyn Kaye Howard, "Black Lynching in the Promised Land: Mob Violence in Ohio, 1876–1916" (PhD diss., The Ohio State University, 1999).
84. Ibid., 150.
85. Jack S. Blocker Jr., "Race, Sex and Riot: The Springfield, Ohio Race Riots of 1904 and 1906 and the Sources of Anti-Black Violence in the Lower Midwest," *Ohio Valley History* 6, no. 1 (Spring 2006): 29.
86. "The Akron Riot," *The Independent,* August 30, 1900, 1.
87. "Peck Pardoned," *Mount Vernon Democratic Banner,* May 9, 1913, 1.
88. "Confessed to the Awful Crime," *Akron Daily Democrat,* August 22, 1900, 1.
89. "Canton Militia Goes to Akron to Suppress Riot," *Stark County Democrat,* August 24, 1900, 1.
90. "Remarkable Bravery Shown by the Firemen," *Akron Daily Democrat,* August 23, 1900, 1.
91. "The Situation Is Well in Hand," *Akron Daily Democrat,* August 23, 1900, 1.
92. Blocker Jr., 28.
93. Ibid., 32.
94. Some historians divide the third phase of the Klan into three smaller segments: a civil rights–era Klan from 1945 to 1970, the David Duke era from 1975 to 1985, and the millennial (or "internet") Klan of the mid-1990s into the twenty-first century.
95. John C. Lester, *Ku Klux Klan: Its Origin, Growth and Disbandment* (New York: Neale, 1905), 60.
96. Leonard Dinnerstein, *The Leo Frank Case* (Athens: University of Georgia Press, 2008), 3–4.
97. Kenneth T. Jackson, *The Ku Klux Klan in the City, 1915–1930* (New York: Oxford University Press, 1992), 10; Charles C. Alexander, "The Ku Klux Klan as a Business Organization 1915–1930," *The Business History Review* 39, no. 3 (Autumn, 1965): 352.
98. David M. Chalmers, *Hooded Americanism: The History of the Ku Klux Klan* (New York: Doubleday Books, 1968), 175.
99. "Mrs. Alexander Defends Action," *Sandusky Star Journal,* August 31,1925, 1.
100. Shawn Lay, *Hooded Knights on the Niagara: The Ku Klux Klan in Buffalo, New York* (New York: New York University Press, 1995), 4.
101. Ku Klux Klan, Inc., *America for Americans* (Atlanta, GA: 1922), 7.
102. Thomas R. Pegram, *One Hundred Percent American: The Rebirth and Decline of the Ku Klux Klan in the 1920s* (Lanham, MD: Rowman & Littlefield, 2011), 76–77.
103. Josh Adams and Vincent J. Roscigno, "White Supremacists, Oppositional Culture and the World Wide Web," *Social Forces* 84, no. 2 (December 2005): 759–78.

104. Michael E. Brooks, *The Ku Klux Klan in Wood County, Ohio* (Mount Pleasant, SC: The History Press, 2014).
105. "Ku Klux Klan Drew a Mammoth Crowd," *Bowling Green Daily Sentinel-Tribune,* October 5, 1923, 1.
106. Tom Rice, "'The True Story of the Ku Klux Klan': Defining the Klan through Film," *Journal of American Studies* 42, no. 3 (December 2008): 471.
107. "Reasons Why Bible Reading Should Be Practiced in the Public School," *Wood County Republican,* September 18, 1924, 1.
108. "Ohio State Konklave Is Attended by 75,000," *Indianapolis Fiery Cross,* July 20, 1923, 1.
109. "75,000 Attend Klan Konklave," *Massillon Evening Independent,* August 31, 1925, 1; "Klan Chieftain Is Threatened," *Athens Sunday Messenger,* August 30, 1925, 1.
110. "Klan Takes Up Bryan's Fight on Evolution," *Defiance Crescent News,* August 21, 1925, 1.
111. Andrew Palella, "The Black Legion: J. Edgar Hoover and Fascism in the Depression Era," *Journal for the Study of Radicalism* 12, no. 2 (2018): 81.
112. George Morris, *The Black Legion Rides* (New York: Workers Library Publishers, 1936), 6.
113. John M. Carlisle, "Black Legion Chief Speaks," *The Detroit News,* May 27, 1936, 2.
114. "Relief Books Are Closed to State Probers," *Lima News,* July 24, 1935, 1–2.
115. Peter H. Amann, "Vigilante Fascism: The Black Legion as an American Hybrid," *Comparative Studies in Society and History* 25, no. 3 (July 1983): 503.
116. Ibid.
117. Ibid., 507.
118. Amann, "Vigilante Fascism," 496.
119. "Caliban in America," *The Nation,* June 10, 1936, 728.
120. "Black Legion Life Termers Eligible for Michigan Parole," *The Lima News,* May 30, 1954.
121. "Many Means of Torture Used by Black Knights to Put Men Out of the Way," *Circleville Herald,* June 13, 1936, 1.
122. Amann, "Vigilante Fascism," 496.
123. "Effinger Admits He Is Leader of Patriotic Group," *Lima News,* March 11, 1938, 1.
124. For a lengthier discussion on the inadequacy of the "overt-to-covert" or "racial progress" narratives, see Ibram X. Kendi, *Stamped from the Beginning: The Definitive History of Racist Ideas in America* (New York: Bold Type Books, 2016).
125. "'60s Rights Crusade Swells, Urge State Probe," *Ohio Sentinel,* February 20, 1960, 3.
126. "Excitement Created in Walnut Street Theater Lobby When Negro Was Refused Admission, and Police Took Hand," *Cincinnati Enquirer,* March 5, 1909, 11.
127. See, for example, Adia Harvey Wingfield, "The Modern Mammy and the Angry Black Man: African American Professionals' Experiences with Gendered Racism in the Workplace," *Race, Gender & Class* 14, no. 1 (2007): 196–212.
128. "Excitement," *Cincinnati Enquirer,* March 5, 1909, 11.
129. "Theater Closed, Manager Faces Charge at Xenia," *Defiance Crescent News,* February 2, 1943, 1.
130. "Pool Opening Await Decision in Courts," *Hamilton Daily News Journal,* May 9, 1949, 1.
131. "Panelists Propose Attitudes to Better Race Relations," *Elyria Chronicle Telegram,* November 11, 1957, 1.
132. "Sports in Review," *Dover Daily Reporter,* November 12, 1960, 32.
133. Nina Mjagkij, "The Cincinnati Urban League," in *Race and the City: Work, Community, and Protest in Cincinnati, 1820–1970,* edited by Henry Louis Taylor (Champaign: University of Illinois Press, 1993), 286.
134. Ibid.

135. "Edward L. Schott, Head of Amusement Park, Sets Forth Position," *Cincinnati American Israelite,* January 13, 1955, 1.
136. "The Coney Island Case," *Cincinnati Enquirer,* April 21, 1956, 4.
137. "Threaten Newsman for Taking Photos at Segregated Church Affair," *Ohio Sentinel,* June 18, 1960, 3.
138. "Segregation Ends at Coney Island," *Cincinnati Enquirer,* May 30, 1961, 1.
139. "Cincinnati Amusement Park Agrees to Integrate After Long Hard Fight," *Ohio Sentinel,* June 1, 1961, 3.
140. "Soldiers, Sailors Orphan Home Jim Crow Reported Near End," *Ohio Sentinel,* August 18, 1956, 3.
141. "Want 'Separate' Hospital, Says Rev. H. Beecher Hicks," *The Ohio State News,* April 8, 1950, 3.
142. Michael Jones-Correa, "The Origins and Diffusion of Racial Restrictive Covenants," *Political Science Quarterly* 115, no. 4 (Winter 2000–2001): 544.
143. Marian Morton, "Deferring Dreams: Racial and Religious Covenants in Shaker Heights, Cleveland Heights and East Cleveland, 1925 to 1970," *Teaching Cleveland,* February 27, 2010, 4.
144. "Injunction Against the Recording of Deeds Containing Racial Covenants: The Last of the Racial Covenant Cases?—*Mayers v. Ridley,*" *Maryland Law Review* 403 (1974): 407.
145. Edward M. Miggins, "No Crystal Stair: The Cleveland Public Schools and the Struggle for Equality, 1900–1930," *Journal of Urban History* 40, no. 4 (2014): 682.
146. "Cleveland Segregation Tied to Housing Policy," *Washington Court House Record Herald,* April 16, 1964, 9.
147. "Board to Ask Rehearing on Case," *Hillsboro Press Gazette,* January 13, 1956, 1–2.
148. "Judge to Ignore Segregation Rule," *Logan Daily News,* January 5, 1956, 1.
149. "Burning Cross Is Burned in Hillsboro Negro's Yard," *Van Wert Times Bulletin,* October 21, 1955, 1.
150. "Gives Answer on Teachers," *Massillon Evening Independent,* June 2, 1954, 3.
151. "Columbus School Head Is New OSU President," *Findlay Republican-Courier,* June 26, 1956, 1.
152. Leonard N. Moore, "The School Desegregation Crisis of Cleveland, Ohio, 1963–1964: The Catalyst for Black Political Power in a Northern City," *Journal of Urban History* 28, no. 2 (January 2002): 135.
153. Ibid., 136–37.
154. Ibid., 136.
155. Ibid., 138.
156. Ibid., 146.
157. Ibid., 146–47.
158. Records of the Ohio Knights of the Ku Klux Klan, "The Knights of the Ku Klux Klan Are Continuing Their Fight" (flyer), Center for Archival Collections, MS 731, box 2.
159. "Klan Has 'Americanism' Rally at Bund Camp; Members of Both Orders Mingle in Jersey," *New York Times,* August 19, 1940, 1.
160. "Stetson Kennedy, 94; Infiltrated the Klan and Exposed It," *New York Times,* August 30, 2011, A17.
161. "Klan Disbands as National Body; Claimed 5,000,000 Roll in 1920s," *New York Times,* June 5, 1944, 21.
162. "Klan Is Accused of a Revolt Plot: Georgia Charges It Seeks to Take Over Key Agencies—Sues to Revoke Charter," *New York Times,* June 21, 1946, 46.
163. Michael Newton, *White Robes and Burning Crosses: A History of the Ku Klux Klan from 1866* (Jefferson, NC: McFarland, 2014), 91.
164. "Athens County Negro Family Terrorized by Rowdies Burning Cross," *Coshocton Tribune,* January 18, 1949, 1.

165. "Athens County Cross Burning Is a Mystery," *Logan Daily News,* January 19, 1949, 1.
166. "Athens Burning Cross Work of KKK in Ohio," *The Ohio State News,* January 29, 1949, 9.
167. "Crowd Demanding that Negro Family Move Burns Cross in Front of Home," *Coshocton County Democrat,* August 15, 1956, 1.
168. "Threat to Ohio Negroes: Ku Klux Klan Cross Is Burned on Family's Front Lawn," *New York Times,* August 16, 1956, 27.
169. "Crowd Demanding that Negro Family Move Burns Cross in Front of Home," *Coshocton County Democrat,* August 15, 1956, 1.
170. "Fiery Cross Lights Lawn of Candidate Albritton," *Dayton Daily News,* May 3, 1960, 1.
171. "Another Hurdle Is Cleared by Spunky Dave Albritton," *Dayton Daily News,* November 9, 1960, 1.
172. US House of Representatives, Committee on Un-American Activities (hereafter cited as HUAC), *Activities of Ku Klux Klan Organizations in the United States* (Washington, DC: Office of the Clerk—US Capitol, 1966), 1575–80, 3274, 3281.
173. John Drabble, "The FBI, COINTELPRO-WHITEHATE, and the Decline of Ku Klux Klan Organizations in Alabama, 1964–1971," *Alabama Review* 61, no. 1 (2008): 4.
174. "70 Persons at KKK Rally," *Cambridge Daily Jeffersonian,* July 3, 1967, 13.
175. Ibid.
176. Ibid.
177. HUAC, *The Present-Day Ku Klux Klan Movement* (Washington, DC: US Government Printing Office, 1967), 159.
178. Ibid., 34.
179. "KKK in Ohio Wants to Remain a Mystery," *Washington Court House Record Herald,* April 10, 1965, 20.
180. "Ohio Klan Unit Issued Papers," *Steubenville Herald Star,* October 8, 1964, 11.
181. HUAC, *Activities of Ku Klux Klan Organizations in the United States,* 3364.
182. "Predicts Riots in Cincinnati," *Hamilton Daily News Journal,* September 2, 1966, 30.
183. "Klan Rally Set for This State," *Greencastle (IN) Daily Banner,* November 4, 1965, 2.
184. HUAC, *Activities of Ku Klux Klan Organizations in the United States,* 1488.
185. "Scott Handed Jail Sentence," *Xenia Daily Gazette,* December 19, 1967, 1.
186. "FBI Checks on Ku Klux Klan Jury Threat," *Findlay Republican Courier,* December 29, 1967, A2.
187. "Predicts Riots in Cincinnati," *Hamilton Daily News Journal,* September 2, 1966, 30.
188. "Mystery Witness Waits to Tell of Ohio KKK," *Middletown Journal,* February 11, 1966, 1.
189. "Youth Plots Killing of Luther King at Bidding of KKK," *Van Wert Times Bulletin,* February 11, 1966, 2.
190. "Mystery Witness Waits to Tell of Ohio KKK," *Middletown Journal,* February 11, 1966, 1.
191. HUAC, *Activities of Ku Klux Klan Organizations in the United States,* 3367.
192. Ibid., 3427.
193. "Ohio Police Agent Tells of Klan Plots," *Steubenville Herald Star,* February 11, 1966, 17.
194. "Mystery Witness Waits to Tell of Ohio KKK," *Middletown Journal,* February 11, 1966, 1.
195. HUAC, *Activities of Ku Klux Klan Organizations in the United States,* 3365.
196. Ibid., 3366.
197. "Federal Explosives Laws," US Department of Justice, Bureau of Alcohol, Tobacco, Firearms and Explosives, 180–194, http://www.gpo.gov/fdsys/pkg/USCODE-2011-title18/pdf/USCODE-2011-title18-partI-chap40.pdf.

198. HUAC, *Activities of Ku Klux Klan Organizations in the United States,* 3365.
199. "Ohio Klansmen Planning Rally," *Findlay Republican Courier,* August 3, 1965, 2.
200. HUAC, *The Present-Day Ku Klux Klan Movement,* 34.
201. "Ex-Chicago Klan-Cop Is Arrested," *Circleville Herald,* August 24, 1968, 2.
202. "Klan-Cop Gets Reduced Fine, Suspended Sentence," *Circleville Herald,* August 27, 1968, 1.
203. "Arrest Klan Leader in Cincinnati," *Massillon Evening Independent,* August 7, 1964, 12.
204. Ohio Revised Code Ann. § 2923.13.
205. US Supreme Court, *Brandenburg v. Ohio,* 395 U.S. 444 (1969).
206. "White People Group Off to Weak Start," *Newark Advocate,* July 15, 1963, 12.
207. "Cincinnati School Board Is Picketed," *Middletown Journal,* August 16, 1963, 8.
208. "Cleveland Segregation Tied to Housing Policy," *Washington Court House Record Herald,* April 16, 1964, 9.
209. "King Tells Cleveland Followers to Vote," *Dover Daily Reporter,* July 29, 1965, 22.
210. National Association for White People, *American People* 1, no. 6 (SEP 1964): 6. Gordon Hall and Grace Hoag Collection of Dissenting and Extremist Printed Propaganda, Box 76–6, Folder HH727, John Hay Library, Brown University, Providence (hereafter cited as Hall–Hoag Collection).
211. "White Group Founder Set to Ditch Plan," *Washington Court House Record Herald,* September 23, 1964, 13.
212. "Silent March Attracts 650," *Wilmington News Journal,* March 23, 1964, 3.
213. "Charges Filed Against Pickets," *Coshocton Tribune,* September 14, 1963, 1.
214. "Charges Filed in Barber Shop Demonstration," *Hamilton Daily News Journal,* September 14, 1963, 2.
215. "The Fearmongers," *Life,* February 7, 1964, 71.
216. Ibid., 72.
217. National Association for White People, "Special Notice to Trustees and Chapter Officers," *American People* 1, no. 6 (September 1964): 5. Hall–Hoag Collection, Box 76–6, Folder HH727.
218. "NAAWP Officers Oust Founder," *Coshocton Tribune,* October 6, 1964, 5.
219. HUAC, *Activities of Ku Klux Klan Organizations in the United States,* 3462.
220. Ibid., 3465.
221. "Fear of Exposure Haunts Cleveland Members of Klan," *Akron Beacon Journal,* February 10, 1966, 16.
222. "Sheriff's Slated Visit Denounced," *Steubenville Herald Star,* February 4, 1966, 13.
223. "Clark Substitutes Termed 'Just as Controversial,'" *Willoughby News Herald,* February 15, 1966, 12.
224. "Racial Powder Keg," *Wall Street Journal,* March 14, 1967, 1, 16.
225. "Won't Identify Akron Aides," *Akron Beacon Journal,* March 12, 1967, 8.
226. "Group Seeks Ouster of Carl Stokes," *Middletown Journal,* November 24, 1967, 11.
227. "Group Told: Stokes Recall," *Akron Beacon Journal,* August 5, 1968, 38.
228. "Asks High Court Oust Rep. Stokes," *Akron Beacon Journal,* May 1, 1970, 7.
229. Ohio Supreme Court, *Annable v. Stokes* (1970), 24 Ohio St.2d 32, 262 N. E.2d 863.
230. "Rights Group Charges Discrimination by Firm," *Ohio Mansfield News Journal,* July 1, 1969, 16.
231. "American Party Adopt Platform," *Steubenville Herald Star,* April 15, 1969, 5.
232. "Ohioan Banned from Vote Bid," *Steubenville Herald Star,* March 23, 1971, 40.
233. "Interview with a Nazi," *Golden Gater* (San Francisco State College), November 4, 1964, 3.
234. Ibid.
235. "Antioch Vile, Nazi Chants; Students Listen, Exit Silently," *Dayton Daily News,* October 15, 1964, 22.

236. "Interview with a Nazi," *Golden Gater* (San Francisco State College), November 4, 1964, 3.
237. "Antioch Vile, Nazi Chants; Students Listen, Exit Silently," *Dayton Daily News,* October 15, 1964, 22.
238. "American Nazi Party Head Eyes Virginia Governor Post," *East Liverpool Review,* April 15, 1965, 16.
239. "Rockwell Addresses 2,800 Students at Ohio University: Is Ridiculed," *Jewish Telegraphic Agency Daily News Bulletin,* April 20, 1965, 3.
240. "Columbus Fears More Trouble as New OSU Sit-Ins are Promised," *Cincinnati Enquirer,* May 2, 1965, 8-G.
241. "U.S. Nazi Party Head Eyes Governorship of Virginia," *Sandusky Register,* April 15, 1965, 3.
242. "2,800 Silent as U.S. Nazi Talks at O.U.," *Marion Star,* April 15, 1965, 17.
243. "Columbus Fears More Trouble as New OSU Sit-Ins Are Promised," *Cincinnati Enquirer,* May 2, 1965, 8-G.
244. Student editorial, *Ohio University Post,* April 19, 1965, n280.
245. "BGSU Quiet for Rockwell," *Toledo Blade,* April 1, 1967, 4.
246. "Rockwell Urges Fight for White Majority," *B-G News,* April 4, 1967, 1–5.
247. "Audience Indifferent to Rockwell," *B-G News,* April 4, 1967, 5.
248. Ibid.
249. "The Silent Treatment," *B-G News,* March 31, 1967, 2.
250. Fred Zackel, "Reminder of Hitler," *B-G News,* March 31, 1967, 2.
251. "He Fails to Conquer," *B-G News,* April 4, 1967, 5.
252. "The Transcript of Hate Message," *Akron Beacon Journal,* July 6, 1970, A2.
253. "American Nazi Party Branch Opens Headquarters in Area," *Cincinnati Enquirer,* June 14, 1971, 29.
254. "Gun Charges Filed in Case," *Hamilton Journal News,* March 22, 1971, 20.
255. "Nazis Solicit Police, Deputies," *Akron Beacon Journal,* April 28, 1969, B1.
256. "Falls Neo-Nazi Leader Arrested," *Akron Beacon Journal,* January 29, 1970, D1.
257. "Find Neo-Nazi Guilty on Two Charges," *Akron Beacon Journal,* March 5, 1970, E1.
258. "Suspected Bomber Tries Suicide," *Mansfield News Journal,* March 18, 1971, 17.
259. "State Board Upholds Ex-Mental Patient's Firing," *Akron Beacon Journal,* October 8, 1976, B3.
260. "Mute Faces Weapons Charge," *Akron Beacon Journal,* December 28, 1968, A7.
261. "Guns Ordered Returned," *Mansfield News Journal,* May 4, 1973, 33.
262. US Federal Bureau of Investigation (cited hereafter as FBI), *Memorandum from FBI Director to SACs in New York and Washington DC concerning National Youth Alliance* (airtel), May 5, 1969, 2.
263. Seymour Martin Lipset, *Rebellion in the University* (New York: Little, Brown, 1971), 122.
264. FBI, *Washington Field Office Report on National Youth Alliance,* July 13, 1971, 27.
265. Ibid., 37.
266. "White Student Group Admits Racist Goals," *Cincinnati Enquirer,* March 13, 1971, 24.
267. "'Brown Shirt' Supporters, New Approach Explained," *University of Cincinnati News Record,* May 25, 1971, 2.
268. "Student Linked to Withrow Unrest to Have Security Guard at School," *Cincinnati Enquirer,* February 25, 1970, 13.
269. Ken Hoop, "Moore's Fan Mail," *University of Cincinnati News Record,* January 26, 1971, 2.
270. Ken Hoop, "Liberal Dictators and a Bordello Nation," *University of Cincinnati News Record,* April 19, 1974, 4.

271. Michael Collins Piper and Ken Hoop, "The Great Sedition Trial of 1944," *Barnes Review* 6 (November–December 1999), https://barnesreview.org/product/the-barnes-review-novemberdecember-1999-a-mockery-of-justice-the-great-sedition-trial-of-1944/.
272. *American Free Press,* April 10 & 17, 2017, https://issuu.com/presspad/docs/i22848.
273. "Right Wing Organization Professes 7 Priorities," *University of Cincinnati News Record,* February 8, 1972, 2.
274. "The Lunatic Fringe," *BG News,* February 4, 1969, 2.
275. "Disturbed by Bigoted Remarks," *BG News,* February 6, 1969, 2.
276. "Black Culture Week in Review," *BG News,* February 11, 1969, 8. The individuals disrupting the film discussion were identified as "supporters of former Alabama Governor George C. Wallace."
277. Bowling Green State University, "Campus Enrollment 1914–2013," https://www.bgsu.edu/content/dam/BGSU/libraries/documents/cac/Enrollment-Data-1914-2013.pdf.
278. Robert Michael Carlock, "A New (Bowling Green State) University: Educational Activism, Social Change, and Campus Protest in the Long Sixties" (master's thesis, Bowling Green State University, 2019), 86.
279. "Blacks Seated on Council," *BG News,* February 21, 1969, 1.
280. "Technicality Unseats BSU Reps," *BG News,* February 28, 1969, 1.
281. "Look for Place to Call 'Ours,'" *BG News,* February 12, 1969, 2.
282. "Everyone Has 'Soul,'" *BG News,* February 12, 1969, 2.
283. Ibid.
284. Carlock, 35.
285. "NYA Wants 'Law, Order,'" *BG News,* February 27, 1969, 4.
286. Ibid.
287. Ibid.
288. Martin J. Molloy, "Claims NYA Misrepresented," *BG News,* March 11, 1969, 2.
289. Ronald Doughty, "No Choices or Rights on Racial Question," *BG News,* February 26, 1970, 2.
290. "Racist Leaflet Irks BSU," *BG News,* March 6, 1969, 1.
291. "Racist Leaflets," *BG News,* March 7, 1969, 2.
292. "NYA No Longer Functioning," *BG News,* April 29, 1969, 3.
293. "J. B. Stoner, 81: Unbowed White Supremacist," *Atlanta Journal-Constitution,* April 27, 2005.
294. *The Thunderbolt* (October 1958), National States' Rights Party documents, 1958, 1963–64, Box 11, Folder 1, MS-290, Anti-Semitism Collection, American Jewish Archives, Cincinnati, Ohio.
295. *The Thunderbolt* (February 1959), National States' Rights Party documents, 1959, Box 11, Folder 3, MS-290, Anti-Semitism Collection, American Jewish Archives, Cincinnati, Ohio.
296. FBI, *Memorandum from FBI SAC-Louisville to SAC-Birmingham regarding 1960 surveillance of NSRP meetings,* pp. D–L.
297. *The Thunderbolt* (February 1960), National States' Rights Party documents, 1960, Box 11, Folder 3, MS-290, Anti-Semitism Collection, American Jewish Archives, Cincinnati, Ohio.
298. *The Thunderbolt* (April 1960), National States' Rights Party documents, 1960, Box 11, Folder 3, MS-290, Anti-Semitism Collection, American Jewish Archives, Cincinnati, Ohio.
299. "Nominating Convention Cut Short," *Dayton Journal Herald,* March 21, 1960, 2.
300. "Faubus Named Presidential Candidate by States Righters," *Dayton Daily News,* March 20, 1960, 1.

301. *The Thunderbolt* (April 1960), National States' Rights Party documents, 1960, Box 11, Folder 3, MS-290, Anti-Semitism Collection, American Jewish Archives, Cincinnati, Ohio.
302. National States' Rights Party, *The Thunderbolt,* 1961–62, Box 11, Folder 2, MS-290, Anti-Semitism Collection, American Jewish Archives, Cincinnati, Ohio.
303. FBI, *Savannah field office report—Racial Matters: National States' Rights Party,* March 30, 1967, 2.
304. "Hate Newspaper Hits Wilmington," *Dayton Daily News,* June 2, 1962, 10.
305. "Charter Foe Defends His Views on Negroes, Jews, and Catholics," *Dayton Daily News,* October 31, 1961, 14.
306. "Preacher, 17 Members Named in Suit," *Dayton Daily News,* November 22, 1961, 17.
307. "Showdown Nears in Church Fight," *Dayton Daily News,* December 6, 1961, 33.
308. "Faction-Split Church Holds Quiet Services," *Dayton Daily News,* December 18, 1961, 26.
309. "Judge Acts to End Congregation Tiff," *Dayton Daily News,* April 25, 1965, 6.
310. "Appeals Court to Probe Church Strife Decision," *Dayton Daily News,* May 14, 1965, 27.
311. FBI, *Birmingham field office report—National States' Rights Party,* April 14, 1965, 53.
312. FBI, *Memorandum from SAC-Dallas to SAC-Savannah. National States' Rights Party,* January 6, 1967.
313. "Senators Get States' Rights Petitions," *Dayton Daily News,* May 11, 1964, 21.
314. "Negroes Blasted by States' Rightist," *Dayton Daily News,* June 21, 1964, A2.
315. "States' Righters Picket Home of Rep. McCulloch," *Cincinnati Enquirer,* August 9, 1964, 32.
316. "States' Rights Candidate Lashes FBI, Hoover at Local Meeting," *Cincinnati Enquirer,* August 22, 1964, 10.
317. "States' Righters Move into Ohio," *Dayton Daily News,* August 19, 1964, 20.
318. "Negro Will Be Sent Back, Racist Says," *Dayton Daily News,* October 6, 1964, 23.
319. "Violence Not Answer, King Says," *Dayton Daily News,* November 30, 1964, 20.
320. "Council Guns Turn On Hate Peddlers," *Cincinnati Enquirer,* April 29, 1965, 1.
321. "Council Prohibits Display of Bigots' Material Here," *Cincinnati American Israelite,* January 27, 1966, 18.
322. "'Hate' Group Headquarters Raided," *Cincinnati Enquirer,* May 9, 1965, 6.
323. "City 'Hate' Law Ruled Violation of State, Federal Constitutions," *Cincinnati Enquirer,* June 14, 1966, 23.
324. "4 Seized on 'Hate Law' Charges," *Indianapolis Star,* July 30, 1965, 1.
325. "'Won't Quit,' Say Hate Sheet Distributors," *Indianapolis News,* July 30, 1965, 1.
326. "Deafening Quietness Noted at NSRP Office," *Dayton Journal Herald,* November 16, 1965, 28.
327. "States Righters Flop Comically, Win Seldom," *Dayton Daily News,* April 18, 1966, 22.
328. "Negro-Hater Lynch in Town," *Dayton Daily News,* August 26, 1966, 3.
329. "Rightists Plan Six Rallies," *Dayton Daily News,* August 24, 1966, 58.
330. Ibid.
331. FBI, *Savannah field office report—Racial Matters: National States' Rights Party,* March 30, 1967, 11.
332. Ibid., 10.
333. FBI, *White Extremist Organizations: Part II—National States' Rights Party,* May 1970, 9.
334. "States Rights Party Steps Up Kentuckiana Activity," *Louisville Courier-Journal,* September 4, 1968, B1.

335. FBI, *White Extremist Organizations: Part II—National States' Rights Party,* May 1970, 10.
336. "Dayton Men to Blame, Says Berea Mayor," *Dayton Journal Herald,* September 3, 1968, 1.
337. FBI, *White Extremist Organizations: Part II—National States' Rights Party,* May 1970, 10.
338. "Security Tight at Racial Hearing," *Dayton Daily News,* September 10, 1968, 19.
339. FBI, *White Extremist Organizations: Part II—National States' Rights Party,* May 1970, 11.
340. FBI, *Report on the National Convention of the National States' Rights Party, Jacksonville Florida, June 7 and 8, 1969,* June 16, 1969, 6–7.
341. FBI, *White Extremist Organizations: Part II—National States' Rights Party,* May 1970, 11.
342. FBI, *Memorandum from SAC-Louisville to FBI director regarding 20–21 JUN 1970 National States' Rights Party convention,* June 25, 1970, 5.
343. FBI, *Memorandum from SAC-Chicago to FBI director regarding 20–21 JUN 1970 National States' Rights Party convention,* July 8, 1970, 5.
344. FBI, *Atlanta field report—National States' Rights Party,* March 15, 1973, 8.
345. Ibid., 56.

Notes to "Now: Present-Day Hate Groups in Ohio"

1. Co-author Bob Fitrakis has covered white supremacist movements in Ohio for more than 30 years for such publications as the *Free Press, Columbus Guardian,* and *Columbus Alive* and has served as a court-certified expert witness on hate groups. In notes that refer back to this reference, that citation is referring to the previous coverage of these issues by the co-author with the specific articles referenced listed in the bibliography.
2. Southern Poverty Law Center, "The Alt-Right and Extremism on Campus," in *Hate and Extremism in 2017,* 2017, 30.
3. Chloe Angyal, "Heather Heyer Was the Alt-Right's Worst Nightmare," *Huffington Post,* August 16, 2017, https://www.huffingtonpost.com/entry/heather-heyer-was-the-alt-rights-worst-nightmare_us_59946c02e4b04b193362484b.
4. Alan Feuer, "Planners of Deadly Charlottesville Rally Are Tested in Court," *New York Times,* February 12, 2018, https://www.nytimes.com/2018/02/12/us/charlottesville-lawsuit-far-right-heather-heyer.html.
5. Southern Poverty Law Center, "The Alt-Right and Extremism on Campus," 29.
6. Martin A. Lee, *The Beast Reawakens* (New York: Little, Brown, 1997), n. pag.
7. Bob Fitrakis and Judy Gentry, "A Detour Through Hate on the Information Superhighway," presented at the Ohio Association of Two Year Colleges, Edison Community College, October 24, 1997, 1.
8. Douglas A. Blackmon, "The Pioneer Fund Tried to Spread 'Natural Endowments' of Top Pilots," *Wall Street Journal,* August 17, 1999, https://www.wsj.com/articles/SB934843314555163550.
9. William L. Pierce, "Equality: Man's Most Dangerous Myth," *National Vanguard* 68, 1979, https://nationalvanguard.org/2010/09/equality-mans-most-dangerous-myth/.
10. Steven J. Gould, *The Mismeasure of Man* (New York: Norton, 1981), 11.
11. Barry Mehler, "Madge Thurlow Macklin," in *Notable American Women: The Modern Period,* edited by Barbara Sicherman and Carl Hurd Green (Cambridge, MA: Harvard University Press, 1980), 451–52.

12. Jo Thomas, "Extent of University Work for C.I.A. Is Hard to Pin Down," *New York Times,* October 9, 1977, https://www.nytimes.com/1977/10/09/archives/extent-of-university-work-for-cia-is-hard-to-pin-down-research.html.
13. Michael Barkun, *Religion and the Racist Right: The Origins of the Christian Identity Movement* (Chapel Hill: University of North Carolina Press, 1994), n. pag.
14. Anti-Defamation League, "Danger: Extremism: The Major Vehicles and Voices on America's Far-Right Fringe," pamphlet, New York, 1996, n. pag.
15. Fitrakis and Gentry, 1.
16. Andrew H. Malcolm, "Outspoken Talk Show Host Slain Outside Denver Home," *New York Times,* June 20, 1984, https://www.nytimes.com/1984/06/20/us/outspoken-talk-show-host-slain-outside-denver-home.html.
17. Robert Jimison, "How the FBI Smashed White Supremacist Group The Order," *CNN,* August 21, 2018.
18. Fitrakis and Gentry.
19. John Craig, "Cheyne Kehoe Turns Himself In Brother Still On Run After Shootout With Ohio Troopers," June 17, 1997, https://www.spokesman.com/stories/1997/jun/17/cheyne-kehoe-turns-himself-in-brother-still-on/.
20. Jo Thomas, "Bank Robbery Trial Offers a Glimpse of a Right-Wing World," *New York Times,* January 9, 1997.
21. AP, "Hate Groups Growing in the United States," *New York Times,* May 3, 1998, n. pag.
22. "The Alt-Right and Extremism on Campus," Hate and Extremism in 2017 booklet, 2017, 29.
23. Ibid., 30.
24. Ibid., 29.
25. Ibid., 32.
26. Paul A. Gilje, *Rioting in America* (Bloomington: Indiana University Press, 1996), 171.
27. Jim McNamara, interview with *Columbus Free Press,* January 24, 2018.
28. Ibid.
29. Jim Hiser, "Niggers and Jews, Nazis in Columbus," *Columbus Free Press,* June 4–July 1, 1975, 11.
30. Ibid.
31. Ibid.
32. Ibid.
33. Lance Ryder, "Press Obsessed with Statehouse Melee," *Columbus Free Press,* July 13–August 30, 1977, 1.
34. Ibid.
35. Ibid.
36. Ibid.
37. David Mann, interview with Bob Fitrakis, February 17, 2018.
38. Ibid., 1.
39. Jeff Coleman, "Jury Frees Anti-Klanners," *Columbus Free Press,* January 11–February 7, 1978, 1.
40. D. C. Andrews, "Klops Klobber Klanners," *Columbus Free Press,* October 5–November 1, 1977, 3.
41. Ibid., 3.
42. Jeff Coleman, "Jury Says Police Attacked, Beat Anti-Klan Picketers," *Columbus Free Press,* April 12–May 9, 1978, 1.
43. David Mann, interview with Bob Fitrakis, February 17, 2018.
44. Ibid., 1.
45. Ibid.

46. Ibid.
47. Ibid.
48. Ibid.
49. David Mann, interview with Bob Fitrakis, February 17, 2018.
50. Andrews, "Klops Klobber Klanners," 3.
51. Ibid.
52. Ibid.
53. Free Press Staff, "Klan Sets Ohio Meet," *Columbus Free Press,* July 10–August 10, 1979, 1.
54. Jeff Coleman, "Klan Builds in Ohio," *Columbus Free Press,* August 7–September 10, 1979, 1.
55. Ibid.
56. Ibid.
57. Associated Press, "Protesters in Ohio Leave before Klan Rally Begins," *New York Times,* July 23, 1979, 12.
58. Coleman, "Klan Builds in Ohio," 1.
59. Jim McNamara, interview with *Columbus Free Press,* January 24, 2018.
60. Free Press Staff, "Columbus Group to Counter Fascism," *Columbus Free Press,* October 10–November 5, 1979, 2.
61. Ibid.
62. Jim McNamara, interview with Bob Fitrakis, January 24, 2018.
63. Free Press Staff, "Columbus Group to Counter Fascism," 2.
64. Neil Livingston, "Black Cops Charge F.O.P.-Klan Ties," *Columbus Free Press,* November 7–December 3, 1979, 1.
65. Communist Workers Party, "Smash the Klan with Correct Understanding and Armed Self-Defense," *Workers Viewpoint Organization,* November 1, 1979.
66. McNamara, interview with Fitrakis, January 24, 2018.
67. Bob Hart, "Nazis Silenced in Cincy," *Columbus Free Press,* May 28–June 24, 1980, 1.
68. Ibid.
69. Ibid.
70. Barry Braunschurtz, "Middletown Takes On Klan," *Columbus Free Press,* June 25–July 29, 1980, 2.
71. Free Press Staff, "Family Menaced," *Columbus Free Press,* September 3–30, 1980, 1.
72. Free Press Staff, "Police Ignore Shooting by Ku Klux Klan," *Columbus Free Press,* September 3–30, 1980, 13.
73. Jaime Fuller, "What the Neshoba County Fair says about Southern politics," *Washington Post,* July 31, 2014, https://www.washingtonpost.com/news/the-fix/wp/2014/07/31/what-the-neshoba-county-fair-says-about-southern-politics/.
74. Bob Herbert, "Righting Reagan's Wrongs?" *New York Times,* November 13, 2007, http://www.nytimes.com/2007/11/13/opinion/13herbert.html.
75. Rick Perlstein, "Exclusive: Lee Atwater's Infamous 1981 Interview on the Southern Strategy," *The Nation,* November 13, 2012, https://www.thenation.com/article/exclusive-lee-atwaters-infamous-1981-interview-southern-strategy/.
76. Adele Shank, "Reagan," *Columbus Free Press,* September 3–30, 1980, 12.
77. "Fascism to Be Targeted," *Columbus Free Press,* September 3–30, 1980, 12.
78. Patrick Thornton and Page Hall, "Rights of Fascists Debated," *Columbus Free Press,* October 19–November 25, 1980, 2.
79. Ibid.
80. Ibid.
81. Ibid.
82. Anti-Racist Action, "A History of Anti-Racist Action," 2009, antiracistaction.org/history/.

83. "Covering the KKK," *Athens News,* July 2, 2017, https://www.athensnews.com/news/local/covering-the-kkk/article_871d4c26-5f46-11e7-ab5e-23d15357ed1b.html.
84. Jim Phillips, "Jackson Murder Suspect Hosted Klan in 1987," *Athens News,* March 26, 1990, 1.
85. Jim Phillips, "Hate Group Rallies with Klan at Area Gathering: Skinheads Find Common Ground with Racist Group," *Athens News,* May 30, 1989, 1.
86. Jim Phillips, "Klan Rally," *Athens News,* June 29, 1987, 3.
87. Ibid.
88. Ibid.
89. Free Press Readers Forum, *Columbus Free Press,* June 1980, 4.
90. Russ Bellant, *Old Nazis, the New Right, and the Republican Party* (Boston: South End Press, 1991).
91. Paul Delaney, "Ol' South Raises Its Ugly Head in Lott, Barr," *Baltimore Sun,* January 17, 1999, https://www.baltimoresun.com/news/bs-xpm-1999-01-17-9901160366-story.html.
92. Greg Noble, "From the Vault: Ku Klux Klan Erected Cross on Cincinnati's Fountain Square in 1992," *WCPO,* August 24, 2017, https://www.wcpo.com/news/our-community/from-the-vault/from-the-vault-ku-klux-klan-erects-cross-on-cincinnatis-fountain-square-in-1992.
93. Bob Fitrakis, "Strange Encounter with the Klan," *Columbus Free Press,* May 1993.
94. Ibid.
95. Ibid.
96. Ibid.
97. Ibid.
98. Ibid.
99. Ibid.
100. Ibid.
101. Ibid.
102. Ibid.
103. Ibid.
104. Ibid.
105. Ibid.
106. Ibid.
107. Cornell McCleary, "Ignore Them," *Columbus Free Press,* October 1993, 10.
108. Mike Dittmer, "Unity Day Includes Gays and Lesbians," *Columbus Free Press,* October 1993, 10.
109. Andy Allen, "Don't Let Them Recruit," *Columbus Free Press,* October 1993, 11.
110. Bob Fitrakis, "When the Klan Kame to Kolumbus," *Columbus Alive,* November 1993.
111. Ibid.
112. Ibid.
113. Ibid.
114. Ibid.
115. Ibid.
116. Ibid.
117. Ibid.
118. Ibid.
119. Ibid.
120. "KKK Outnumbered at Ohio Rally," *Journal Times,* October 24, 1993, https://journaltimes.com/news/national/kkk-outnumbered-at-ohio-rally/article_e62d28fc-a43b-5a46-998e-43e80740ed56.html.

121. Cornell McCleary, "Taking On the Ku Klux Klowns," *Columbus Free Press,* January 1994, 4.
122. Ibid., 5.
123. Free Press Staff, "Klan Activities Met with Protest," *Columbus Free Press,* April 1994, 28.
124. Ibid.
125. Michael Cooper, "What Happened When the Ku Klux Klan Came to Springfield 23 Years Ago?," *Springfield News-Sun,* August 17, 2017, http://www.springfieldnewssun.com/news/crime--law/what-happened-when-the-klux-klan-came-springfield-years-ago/MEkJuQSthuKww6Jg4nSVkL/.
126. Anti-Racist Action, "Grand Titan Jailed in Ohio," *Columbus Free Press,* Summer 1994, 6.
127. Ibid.
128. Ibid.
129. Ibid.
130. Andrew Welsh-Huggins, "Klan's 'Free' Speech Costs Cities," *Associated Press,* October 9, 1999, https://apnews.com/article/5ee58ac3d5b7ba809843dd0e6207d48e.
131. Ibid.
132. Anti-Racist Action, "Klan Kross Krunched," *Columbus Free Press,* January 1995, 19.
133. Ibid.
134. Anti-Racist Action, "ARA Shorts," *ARA News,* February 5, 1995, 6.
135. Ibid., 19.
136. Ibid., 20.
137. Anti-Racist Action, "An Intro to ARA," 1997, 2.
138. Anti-Racist Action, "ARA Shorts," *ARA News,* February 5, 1995, 6.
139. Mark Fisk, "Been Caught Spitting," *ARA News,* February 5, 1995, 23.
140. Greg Maynard, "National Antifascist Conference Touches Down at North High," *Columbus Free Press,* October 1995, 8.
141. Murray Chass, "Baseball; Ex-A's Employee Cites Schott Racial Remarks," *New York Times,* November 26, 1992, n. pag.
142. Robert Fitrakis, "Whiny Dems and Jews," *Columbus Alive,* May 28, 1996, n. pag.
143. Ibid.
144. Ibid.
145. Ibid.
146. Ibid.
147. Robert Fitrakis, *Fitrakis Files: Spooks, Nukes, and Nazis* (Columbus: Columbus Alive, 2003), 152.
148. Russ Bellant, *The Coors Connection: How Coors Family Philanthropy Undermines Democratic Pluralism* (Boston: South End Press, 1991), n. pag.
149. Mark Potok, "Revealed: Conway, Bannon Members of Secretive Group," *Southern Poverty Law Center,* August 31, 2016, https://www.splcenter.org/hatewatch/2016/08/31/revealed-conway-bannon-members-secretive-group.
150. Bob Fitrakis and Harvey Wasserman, "Why did J. Kenneth Blackwell seek, then hide, his association with super-rich extremists and e-voting magnates?," *Columbus Free Press,* Spring 2006, 8.
151. Bob Fitrakis, "Speaker Pro Temper," *Columbus Alive,* April 2, 1997, n. pag.
152. Associated Press, "Baton Rouge Organization Brought Together Conservatives, Rebels with AM-US-Iran-Contras Rdp," *Associated Press,* January 9, 1987, https://apnews.com/article/8702d71ee621c4db254f52a37964bbd9.
153. Bellant, *Old Nazis, The New Right, and the Republican Party,* n. pag.
154. Ibid.
155. Fitrakis, "Speaker Pro Temper," n. pag.

156. Southern Poverty Law Center, "Roger Pearson," January 30, 2018, https://www.splcenter.org/fighting-hate/extremist-files/individual/roger-pearson.
157. Fitrakis, "Speaker Pro Temper," n. pag.
158. Potok, "Revealed: Conway, Bannon Members of Secretive Group."
159. Robert Fitrakis, *Fitrakis Files: Spooks, Nukes, and Nazis* (Columbus: *Columbus Alive,* 2003), 157.
160. Ibid, 208.
161. Ibid.
162. Fitrakis, "Speaker Pro Temper," n. pag.
163. Ibid.
164. Fitrakis, *Fitrakis Files: Spooks, Nukes, and Nazis* (Columbus: Columbus Alive, 2003), 181.
165. Ibid.
166. Ibid.
167. Ibid, 190.
168. Bob Fitrakis, "Aryan Nations' Buckeye Battle Cry," *Columbus Alive,* March 5, 1997, 8.
169. Ibid.
170. Jo Thomas, "Bank Robbery Trial Offers a Glimpse of a Right-Wing World," *New York Times,* January 9, 1997, http://www.nytimes.com/1997/01/09/us/bank-robbery-trial-offers-a-glimpse-of-a-right-wing-world.html.
171. Fitrakis, "Aryan Nations' Buckeye Battle Cry," 8.
172. Ibid., 9.
173. Ibid., 8.
174. Ibid.
175. Barkun, 220.
176. Tom Morganthau and Steven Shabad, "The View from the Far Right," *Newsweek,* April 30, 1995, https://www.newsweek.com/view-far-right-181446.
177. Fitrakis, "Aryan Nations' Buckeye Battle Cry," 9.
178. William Pierce, *The Turner Diaries* (Washington DC: National Vanguard Books, 1978).
179. Ibid.
180. Ibid., 8.
181. Ibid., 9.
182. Ibid.
183. Ibid., 8.
184. John Craig, "Cheyne Kehoe Turns Himself In, Brother Still On Run after Shootout with Ohio Troopers," *The Spokesman,* June 17, 1997, http://www.spokesman.com/stories/1997/jun/17/cheyne-kehoe-turns-himself-in-brother-still-on/.
185. Bob Fitrakis, "Those Crazy Kehoes," *Columbus Alive,* August 13, 1977, n. pag.
186. Bob Fitrakis, "He Ain't Chevie, He's My Brother," *Columbus Alive,* February 4, 1998, n. pag.
187. Peter Simi and Robert Futrell, *American Swastika: Inside the White Power Movement's Hidden Spaces of Hate* (New York: Roman & Littlefield, 2010), 103.
188. Bill Morlin, "McVeigh in Spokane before Bombing? Innkeeper Links Kehoe, McVeigh in Months before Oklahoma City Blast," *The Spokesman,* January 16, 1998, http://www.spokesman.com/stories/1998/jan/16/mcveigh-in-spokane-before-bombing-innkeeper-links/.
189. Associated Press, "3 Charged with Plotting Aryan Republic," *New York Times,* December 14, 1997, http://www.nytimes.com/1997/12/14/us/3-charged-with-plotting-aryan-republic.html.

190. Associated Press, "Murder, Robbery, Polygamy—A Supremacist Plot?" *Deseret News,* December 14, 1997, https://www.deseret.com/1997/12/14/19351224/murder-robbery-polygamy-a-supremacist-plot.
191. Fitrakis, "He Ain't Chevie, He's My Brother," *Columbus Alive,* February 4, 1998, n. pag.
192. Ibid.
193. The Center for New Community, "Beyond a Dead Man's Deeds: The National Alliance after William Pierce," August 2002, newcom.org.
194. Ibid., 36.
195. Fitrakis, "Ohio History X," n. pag.
196. Ibid.
197. Fitrakis, *Fitrakis Files: Spooks, Nukes, and Nazis* (Columbus: Columbus Alive, 2003), 209.
198. Ibid, 210.
199. Anti-Racist Action, Fifth Annual Anti-Racist Action Conference program, October 1–18, 1998.
200. Anti-Racist Action, "An Intro to ARA," 1997.
201. Jim McNamara, "Fear and Loathing in Las Vegas," *Columbus Free Press,* Autumn 1998, 38.
202. Anti-Racist Action, "Death in the Desert," *Anti-Racist News,* December 1998, 1.
203. Stuart Wexler, *America's Secret Jihad: The Hidden History of Religious Terrorism in the United States* (Berkeley, CA: Counterpoint, 2015), 2.
204. Fitrakis, "Aryan Nations' Buckeye Battle Cry," 9.
205. Bob Fitrakis, "White Man's Bible," *Columbus Alive,* August 19, 1999, n. pag.
206. Ibid.
207. Gary Gerhardt and Kevin Flynn, *The Silent Brotherhood: The Chilling Inside Story of America's Violent Anti-Government Militia Movement* (New York: Free Press, 1989), n. pag.
208. Fitrakis, "White Man's Bible," n. pag.
209. Bob Fitrakis, "Nazis in the Heartland," *Columbus Alive,* January 20, 2000, n. pag.
210. Ibid.
211. Ibid.
212. Ibid.
213. Ibid.
214. Southern Poverty Law Center, "Racist Council of Conservative Citizens Finds Home In Mainstream Politics," March 15, 1999, https://www.splcenter.org/fighting-hate/intelligence-report/1999/racist-council-conservative-citizens-finds-home-mainstream-politics.
215. Bob Fitrakis, "Ohio: Home of Hate," *Columbus Alive,* February 3, 2000.
216. Ibid.
217. David W. Martin, "White Power Outage," Cleveland Scene, March 7, 2002, https://www.clevescene.com/cleveland/white-power-outage/Content?oid=1478999.
218. Mark Potok, "The Year in Hate: A Period of Realignment and Rebuilding Follows a Tumultuous Year on the American Radical Right," Southern Poverty Law Center, 2003, 30.
219. Southern Poverty Law Center, "David Lane," https://www.splcenter.org/fighting-hate/extremist-files/individual/david-lane.
220. "For the Record," *Intelligence Report,* Summer 2003, 63.
221. Potok, "The Year in Hate," 36–37.
222. Fitrakis, *The Fitrakis Files: Spooks, Nukes and Nazis.*
223. David Holthouse, "Motley Crews," *Intelligence Report,* Fall 2006, 42.
224. Ibid.
225. David Holthouse, "Racist Skinheads," *Intelligence Report,* Fall 2006, 40.

226. Southern Poverty Law Center, "For the Record," *Intelligence Report,* Winter 2003, 47.
227. Potok, "The Year in Hate," 72.
228. Southern Poverty Law Center, "For the Record," *Intelligence Report,* Summer 2004, 48.
229. Southern Poverty Law Center, "For the Record," *Intelligence Report,* Spring 2005, 76.
230. Holthouse, "Motley Crews," 42.
231. Bob Moser, "Holy War: The Religious Right's Crusade Against Gays Heats Up," *Intelligence Report,* Spring 2005, 9.
232. Southern Poverty Law Center, "For the Record," *Intelligence Report,* Winter 2005, 56.
233. Southern Poverty Law Center, "For the Record," *Intelligence Report,* Fall 2005, 56.
234. Mark Potok, "The Blame Game," *Intelligence Report,* Fall 2005, 2.
235. Heidi Singer, "Nazis Spur Riot in Ohio," *New York Post,* October 16, 2005, https://nypost.com/2005/10/16/nazis-spur-riot-in-ohio.
236. Free Press Staff, "Rally by Hate Group Spurs Insurrection in Toledo, Ohio," *Columbus Free Press,* November–December 2005, http://freepress.org/article/rally-hate-group-spurs-insurrection-toledo-ohio.
237. Ryan Dunn, "Neo-Nazis Plan Return to Toledo for Demonstration: Black Leaders Urge Avoiding April 18 Rally," *Toledo Blade,* March 4, 2015, https://www.toledoblade.com/local/2015/03/04/Neo-Nazis-plan-return-to-Toledo-for-demonstration.html.
238. Southern Poverty Law Center, "The Year in Review," *Intelligence Report,* Spring 2007, 52.
239. T. K. Kim, "White Noise," *Intelligence Report,* Spring 2006, 46.
240. Ibid.
241. David Holthouse and Laurie Wood, "Burnout," *Intelligence Report,* Winter 2008, 50.
242. Southern Poverty Law Center, "For the Record," *Intelligence Report,* Fall 2006, 42.
243. Southern Poverty Law Center, "For the Record," *Intelligence Report,* Winter 2006, 72.
244. Bob Fitrakis and Harvey Wasserman, "Why Is the Man Who Stole Ohio Campaigning with a White Supremacist?," October 9, 2006, https://freepress.org/article/why-man-who-stole-ohio-campaigning-white-supremacist.
245. Alan Johnson and Catherine Candisky, "Blackwell to campaign with gun-rights backer," *Columbus Dispatch,* October 5, 2006.
246. David Holthouse and Mark Potok, "The Year in Hate," *Intelligence Report,* Spring 2008, 52.
247. Southern Poverty Law Center, "For the Record," *Intelligence Report,* Summer 2009, 63.
248. Southern Poverty Law Center, "For the Record," *Intelligence Report,* Winter 2008, 63.
249. Heidi Beirich and Mark Potok, "Silver Lining: For Many White Supremacists a Black President Might Not Be All That Bad a Thing," *Intelligence Report,* Fall 2008, 15.
250. Mark Potok, "Resurgence on the Right," *Intelligence Report,* Summer 2009, 2.
251. Southern Poverty Law Center, "For the Record," *Intelligence Report,* Fall 2009, 63.
252. Southern Poverty Law Center, "Meet the Patriots," *Intelligence Report,* Summer 2010, 31.
253. Southern Poverty Law Center, "For the Record," *Intelligence Report,* Summer 2010, 47.
254. Southern Poverty Law Center, "For the Record," *Intelligence Report,* Fall 2010, 48.
255. Southern Poverty Law Center, "The Blotter," *Intelligence Report,* Fall 2010, 9.
256. Southern Poverty Law Center, "For the Record," *Intelligence Report,* Winter 2010, 48.

257. Mark Potok, "The Year in Hate and Extremism," *Intelligence Report,* Spring 2011, 59.
258. Southern Poverty Law Center, "For the Record," *Intelligence Report,* Spring 2011, 68.
259. Robert Steinback, "Jihad against Islam," *Intelligence Report,* Summer 2011, 17.
260. Ibid., 39.
261. Southern Poverty Law Center, "For the Record," *Intelligence Report,* Summer 2011, 48.
262. Southern Poverty Law Center, "For the Record," *Intelligence Report,* Summer 2012, 48.
263. Mark Potok, "The Year in Review," *Intelligence Report,* Spring 2012, 38.
264. Bob Fitrakis, "The Nazis Next Door," *Columbus Free Press,* August 2017, 4.
265. Ibid.
266. Ibid.
267. Don Terry, "Cyber Commandos," *Intelligence Report,* Summer 2013, 33.
268. Ibid.
269. Southern Poverty Law Center, "For the Record," *Intelligence Report,* Fall 2013, 38.
270. David Neiwert, "Ohio Neo-Nazi's Sentence on Weapons Charges Draws Criticism," *Southern Poverty Law Center,* December 20, 2103, https://www.splcenter.org/hatewatch/2013/12/20/ohio-neo-nazis-sentence-weapons-charges-draws-criticism.
271. Mark Potok, "The Year in Hate and Extremism," *Intelligence Report,* Spring 2014, 37.
272. Southern Poverty Law Center, "For the Record," *Intelligence Report,* Spring 2015, 44.
273. Southern Poverty Law Center, "For the Record," *Intelligence Report,* Spring 2014, 68.
274. Ryan Lenz, "Age of the Wolf," *Intelligence Report,* Spring 2015, 25.
275. Southern Poverty Law Center, "For the Record," *Intelligence Report,* Summer 2015, 48.
276. Potok, "The Year in Hate and Extremism," *Southern Poverty Law Center,* 2017.
277. Ibid.
278. Cleve R. Wootson Jr., "'Raw Hatred': Vandals Break Into Interracial Couple's Home, Spray-Paint Slurs and Swastikas," *Washington Post,* December 5, 2016, https://www.washingtonpost.com/news/post-nation/wp/2016/12/05/raw-hatred-vandals-break-into-interracial-couples-home-spray-paint-slurs-and-swastikas/.
279. Brett Milam and Mallorie Sullivan, "Police: Person of Interest in Defaced Price Hill Home," *Cincinnati.com,* December 3, 2016, https://www.cincinnati.com/story/news/2016/12/03/price-hill-couple-returns-holiday-home-defaced-hate/94885624.
280. Sam Allard, "Charlottesville Killer, Ohio's James Alex Fields Indicted on Ten Counts," *Cleveland Scene,* December 19, 2017, https://www.clevescene.com/scene-and-heard/archives/2017/12/19/charlottesville-killer-ohios-james-alex-fields-indicted-on-10-counts.
281. Theresa Cottam, "Wooster Leaders Plan Unity Rally after KKK Recruiting Flyers Are Found in Community," *Akron Beacon Journal,* August 23, 2017, https://www.ohio.com/akron/news/local/wooster-leaders-plan-unity-rally-after-kkk-recruiting-fliers-found-in-community.
282. Amani Abraham, "KKK Flyers Found in Wooster, Community Planning Unity Day on Sunday," *WKYC,* August 23, 2017, http://www.wkyc.com/article/news/local/ohio/kkk-fliers-found-in-wooster-community-planning-unity-rally-on-sunday/466777521.
283. Gerry Bello, "Neo-Nazi and Three Percent Militia Unite to Terrorize Small Ohio Town," *Mockingbird Paper,* 2018, http://www.mockingbirdpaper.com/content/neo-nazis-and-three-percent-militia-unite-terrorize-small-ohio-town.
284. Ibid.
285. Ibid.

286. Breanna Edwards, "KKK Flyers Distributed across Green Township Ohio," *The Root,* August 18, 2017, https://www.theroot.com/kkk-flyers-distributed-across-green-township-ohio-1797970349.
287. Luke O'Brien, "The Making of an American Nazi," *The Atlantic,* December 2017, https://www.theatlantic.com/magazine/archive/2017/12/the-making-of-an-american-nazi/544119.
288. Michael Edison Hayden, "Neo-Nazi Peddling False Conspiracy That Alleged Charlottesville Killer James Fields Is a 'Prisoner of War,'" *Newsweek,* January 12, 2018, http://www.newsweek.com/neo-nazi-conspiracy-alleged-charlottesville-killer-james-fields-prisoner-war-778793.
289. Luke O'Brien, "America's Most Notorious Neo-Nazi Is On the Lam: Won't You Come Home Andrew Anglin," *Huffington Post,* December 19, 2017, https://www.huffingtonpost.com/entry/on-the-lam-with-andrew-anglin-americas-most-notorious-neo-nazi_us_5a33fb5ae4b01d429cc86842.
290. Andrew Anglin, "Daily Stormer's Top 20 Stories of 2017," *Daily Stormer,* December 31, 2017, https://dailystormer.name/daily-stormers-top-ten-stories-of-2017/
291. Snejana Farberov, " Revealed: Dylann Roof 'was active on white supremacist website for months posting same comments about minorities as in his hate-filled manifesto'," *DailyMail.com,* June 23. 2015, https://www.dailymail.co.uk/news/article-3136475/Dylann-Roof-active-white-supremacist-website-months-posting-comments-minorities-hate-filled-manifesto.html.
292. Ibid.
293. Stephen Koff, "Ohio's Most Visible Neo-Nazi Is Playing Hard to Get," *Cleveland.com,* December 29, 2017, http://www.cleveland.com/metro/index.ssf/2017/12/ohios_most_visible_neo-nazi_is.html.
294. Becca Pollard, "Community Puts Hitch in Worthington Neo-Nazi Fundraiser," *Columbus Free Press,* February 9, 2017, http://columbusfreepress.com/article/community-puts-hitch-worthington-neo-nazi-fundraising#overlay-context=article.
295. Ibid.
296. O'Brien, "America's Most Notorious Neo-Nazi Is On the Lam."
297. O'Brien, "The Making of an American Nazi."
298. Richard Fausset, "A Voice of Hate in America's Heartland," *New York Times,* November 25, 2017, https://www.nytimes.com/2017/11/25/us/ohio-hovater-white-nationalist.html.
299. Ibid.
300. Ibid.
301. Southern Poverty Law Center, "White Supremacists and Other Hatemongers Emboldened, Energized in the Trump Era," *Hate and Extremism in 2017,* 2017, 4.
302. Lynn Hulsey, "Groups Like the KKK Preach White Power But Shun 'Hate' Label," *Dayton Daily News,* August 18, 2017, http://www.mydaytondailynews.com/news/crime--law/groups-like-the-kkk-preach-white-power-but-shun-hate-label/U9JCYBPpBFHimNHlPObpdP.
303. Breanna Edwards, "Ohio State Is Being Sued after Refusing to Rent Space on Campus for White Supremacist Richard Spencer to Speak," *The Root,* October 23, 2017, https://www.theroot.com/ohio-state-being-sued-after-refusing-to-rent-space-on-c-1819764336.
304. Joe Heim, "Recounting a Day of Rage, Hate, Violence and Death," *Washington Post,* August 14, 2017, https://www.washingtonpost.com/graphics/2017/local/charlottesville-timeline/?utm_term=.be9820fa9af9.
305. Liam Stack, "Over 1,000 Hate Groups Are Now Active in United States, Civil Rights Group Says," *New York Times,* February 20, 2019, https://www.nytimes.com/2019/02/20/us/hate-groups-rise.html.

306. Ibid.
307. Ibid.
308. Jim Woods, "Police Look into Leaflets Left at Homes," *Columbus Dispatch,* August 22, 2017.
309. Bob Fitrakis, "Anti-racists Gather to Let Nazis Know: You Are Not Wanted in Clintonville," *Columbus Free Press,* March 4, 2018, https://columbusfreepress.com/article/anti-racists-gather-let-nazis-know-you-are-not-wanted-clintonville.
310. HateWatch Staff, "Meet 'Patriot Front': Neo-Nazi Network Aims to Blur Lines with Militiamen, the Alt-right," Southern Poverty Law Center HateWatch, December 12, 2017, https://www.splcenter.org/hatewatch/2017/12/11/meet-patriot-front-neo-nazi-network-aims-blur-lines-militiamen-alt-right.
311. Chris Mosby, "White Supremacists Target Ohio in Record Year for Propaganda," *Patch,* March 9, 2019, https://patch.com/Ohio/Cleveland/white-supremacists-target-Ohio-record-year-propaganda.
312. Associated Press, "Judge Awards $4.1 Million in Neo-Nazi Website Lawsuit," July 12, 2019.
313. Evan MacDonald, "Fliers Linking to Neo-Nazi Site Found on Case Western Reserve Campus," Cleveland.com, November 22, 2018, https://www.cleveland.com/education/2018/11/fliers-linking-to-neo-nazi-site-found-on-case-western-reserve-campus.html.
314. Max Filby, "Wright State Removes Neo-Nazi Groups Posters from Campus," *Dayton Daily News,* February 21, 2019, https://www.daytondailynews.com/news/wright-state-removes-neo-nazi-group-posters-from-campus/HoVKi1juC15fSSSozJrb9N/.
315. Th3Storm, "Racist Say What? Neo-Nazi Posters Causes Tension in Circleville," February 21, 2019,https://mycolumbusmagic.com/2395888/racist-say-what-neo-nazi-posters-causes-tension-in-circleville/.
316. Bob Fitrakis, notes from rally observation, March 25, 2017.
317. Justin Wise, "Trump suggests that it could get 'very bad' if military, police, biker supporters play 'tough,'" The Hill, March 19, 2019, https://thehill.com/homenews/administration/434110-trump-suggests-that-things-could-get-very-bad-if-military-police.
318. Southern Poverty Law Center, "Thomas Rousseau," https://www.splcenter.org/fighting-hate/extremist-files/individual/thomas-rousseau.
319. Ibid.
320. Ibid.
321. Ibid.
322. Ibid.
323. Ibid.
324. Robert J. Fitrakis and Harvey Wasserman, *The Strip and Flip Disaster of America's Stolen Elections* (Columbus: CICJ Books, 2017), 79.
325. Bob Fitrakis and Harvey Wasserman, "Mass Ohio Voter Purges Begin," *Columbus Free Press,* October 2, 2016.
326. Bob Fitrakis, "Ohio's New Jim Crow Goes Before the Supremes," *Columbus Free Press,* January 7, 2018.
327. James Ridgeway, *Blood in the Face: The Ku Klux Klan, Aryan Nations, Nazi Skinheads, and the Rise of a New White Culture (New York: Thunder's Mouth, 1990), 26.*
328. Jon Schwarz, "Seven Things about Ronald Reagan You Won't Hear at the Reagan Library GOP Debate," *The Intercept,* September 16, 2015.
329. Associated Press, "Trump: Progressive Congresswomen Should 'Go Back and Help Fix the Totally Broken Crime Infested Places From Which They Came'," July 14, 2019, https://ktla.com/news/nationworld/trump-to-progressive-congresswomen-go-back-and-help-fix-the-totally-broken-crime-infested-places-from-which-they-came/.

330. John Wagner and Rachel Blade, "Trump Rejects Criticism That His Weekend Tweet about Four Minority Lawmakers Was Racist, Says They 'Hate Our Country,'" *Washington Post,* July 15, 2019, https://www.washingtonpost.com/politics/trump-calls-on-minority-congresswomen-to-apologize-after-he-said-they-should-go-back-to-their-countries/2019/07/15/897f1ddo-a6ef-11e9-a3a6-ab670962db05_story.html.
331. Darrel Rowland, "Rally Has Racial Tinge," *Columbus Dispatch,* August 2, 2019.
332. Derrick Bryson Taylor, "Ohio Man Held after Threat to Jewish Hub," *New York Times,* August 19, 2019.
333. Michael Kunzelman, "Anti-Semitic Incidents in U.S. Hit Record High," *Columbus Dispatch,* May 13, 2020.
334. Anti-Defamation League, "ADL: White Supremacist Propaganda Distribution in Ohio Up 442% Over Last Year," February 18, 2020, https://cleveland.adl.org/news/adl-white-supremacist-propaganda-distribution-in-ohio-up-442-over-last-year/.
335. Cornelius Frolik and Wayne Baker, "Dayton Rallies Against KKK: 'This Ugly Chapter Is Over,' But Work to Be Done," *Dayton Daily News,* May 26, 2019, https://www.daytondailynews.com/news/local/dayton-rallies-against-kkk-this-ugly-chapter-over-but-work-done/m2q3WMtQe5ZPxlYCEL3W1M/.
336. Cassie Miller, "Anti-Lockdown Rallies Are Providing an Opening for the Proud Boys and Other Far-Right Extremists," *Southern Poverty Law Center,* April 27, 2020, https://www.splcenter.org/hatewatch/2020/04/27/anti-lockdown-rallies-are-providing-opening-proud-boys-and-other-far-right-extremists.
337. "Photos: Protests Over Stay-at-Home Orders at Ohio Statehouse," *Columbus Dispatch,* April 18, 2020, https://www.dispatch.com/photogallery/OH/20200418/PHOTOGALLERY/418009999/PH/1.
338. Meghan Roos, "Ohio Governor Condemns 'Disgusting' Anti-Semitic Sign at Coronavirus Lockdown Protest," *Newsweek,* April 23, 2020, https://www.newsweek.com/ohio-governor-condemns-disgusting-anti-semitic-sign-coronavirus-lockdown-protest-1499796.
339. Nick R. Martin, "Protest Problems," *The Informant,* June 1, 2020, https://www.informant.news/p/protest-problems.
340. Jane Kaufman, "Man Looking to Kill Jews Faces Unrelated Weapons Charges in Canton," *Cleveland Jewish News,* June 16, 2020, https://www.clevelandjewishnews.com/news/local_news/man-looking-to-kill-jews-faces-unrelated-weapons-charges-in-canton/article_dce4d710-affb-11ea-acc1-9ba311b8c9cc.html.
341. Mark Kovac, "County Health Officials Call Racism a Crisis," *Columbus Dispatch,* May 15, 2020.
342. Rita Price and Mark Ferenchik, "More Local Blacks Get Virus, Are Hospitalized," *Columbus Dispatch,* May 9, 2020.
343. Jeffrey Ostler, "Disease Has Never Been Just Disease for Native Americans," *The Atlantic,* April 29, 2020.
344. Associated Press, "Florida Town Stunned by News of Police Department's KKK Ties," *Tampa Bay Times,* July 21, 2014, https://www.tampabay.com/news/publicsafety/florida-town-stunned-by-news-of-police-kkk-ties/2189339/.
345. Kelly Weill, "Inside the New Push to Expose America's White Supremacist Cops," *Daily Beast,* June 29, 2020, https://www.thedailybeast.com/inside-the-new-push-to-expose-americas-white-supremacist-cops.
346. Cassie Miller, "The 'Boogaloo' Started as a Racist Meme," *Southern Poverty Law Center,* June 5, 2020, https://www.splcenter.org/hatewatch/2020/06/05/boogaloo-started-racist-meme.
347. Anti-Defamation League, "Small But Vocal Array of Right Wing Extremists Appearing at Protests," June 10, 2020, https://www.adl.org/blog/small-but-vocal-array-of-right-wing-extremists-appearing-at-protests.

348. Monroe Trombly, "Man Cited for Allegedly Yelling Slur at Protest," *Mansfield News Journal,* June 28, 2020.
349. Adrian Horton, "Hundreds of Armed Counter-Protesters Confront Black Lives Matter Rally in Ohio," *Guardian,* June 18, 2020, https://www.theguardian.com/us-news/2020/jun/18/hundreds-armed-counter-protesters-confront-black-lives-matter-event-bethel-ohio.
350. Dan Horn, "When Black Lives Matter Came to a Small Ohio Town," *Columbus Dispatch,* June 18, 2020.
351. Brian Bennett, "Trump's Tulsa Rally Highlights His Record of Racial Division," *Time,* June 20, 2020, https://time.com/5856316/donald-trump-tulsa-rally/.
352. The Oklahoma Commission to Study the Race Riot of 1921, "Final Report," February 28, 2001.
353. Zeke Miller, "Donald Trump Tweets Video with 'White Power' Chant, Then Deletes It," *Associated Press,* June 28, 2020, https://apnews.com/7eea48b80f14474b70579 67a9654c4f0.
354. Ohio Capital Journal / States Newsroom, "Ohio House Lawmakers Leave Racism Resolution on the Table," *Patch.com,* June 17, 2020, https://patch.com/ohio/across-oh/ohio-house-lawmakers-leave-racism-resolution-table.
355. Frances Mulraney, "Hundreds of Anti-mask Protesters Protected by Armed Militia and Bikers Gather at the Ohio Statehouse Saying Face Coverings Are 'Propaganda' and Holding 'I Will Not Wear Someone Else's Fear' Signs," *Daily Mail,* July 19, 2020.
356. Raul Arias, "Automatic Weapons in Abundance at Stand for America Rally," *Columbus Free Press,* July 19, 2020.
357. Mulraney, "Hundreds of Anti-mask Protesters."
358. Richard Hofstadter, *The Paranoid Style in American Politics* (New York: Knopf, 1965).

BIBLIOGRAPHY

Bibliography to "Then: A History of Racism and Bigotry in Ohio"

Primary Sources

ARCHIVAL MATERIALS

American Nazi Party documents. Box 1, Folder 10. MS-290. Anti-Semitism Collection. American Jewish Archives, Cincinnati, Ohio.

National Association for the Advancement of White People. "Special Notice to Trustees and Chapter Officers." In *American People* 1, no. 6 (September 1964). Gordon Hall and Grace Hoag Collection of Dissenting and Extremist Printed Propaganda, Box 76–6, Folder HH727, John Hay Library, Brown University, Providence.

National State's Rights Party documents, 1958–1962. Box 10, Folder 9. MS-290. Anti-Semitism Collection. American Jewish Archives, Cincinnati, Ohio.

National State's Rights Party documents. 1958, 1963–1964. Box 11, Folder 1. MS-290. Anti-Semitism Collection. American Jewish Archives, Cincinnati, Ohio.

National State's Rights Party. *The Thunderbolt*. 1961–1962. Box 11, Folder 2. MS-290. Anti-Semitism Collection. American Jewish Archives, Cincinnati, Ohio.

———. *The Thunderbolt*. n.d. Box 11, Folder 3. MS-290. Anti-Semitism Collection. American Jewish Archives, Cincinnati, Ohio.

Records of the Ohio Knights of the Ku Klux Klan. Bowling Green State University: Center for Archival Collections, MS 731.

NEWSPAPERS

Akron Beacon Journal, 1966–68, 1970, 1973, 1976.
Athens Messenger, 1875.
Athens Sunday Messenger, 1925.
Atlanta Journal-Constitution, 2005.
BG News [Bowling Green, OH], 1967, 1969–71.
Cambridge Daily Jeffersonian, 1967.
Canton Repository, 1854.
Cincinnati American Israelite, 1955, 1966.
Cincinnati Daily Commercial, 1876.
Cincinnati Enquirer, 1904, 1909, 1912, 1961, 1964–66, 1971.
Cincinnati Times and Cincinnati Daily Times, 1848–73.
Circleville Herald, 1936, 1968.
Cleveland Gazette, 1862–87.
Cleveland Plain Dealer, 1963.
Coshocton County Democrat, 1956.
Coshocton Tribune, 1949, 1963–64.
Dayton Daily News, 1960–62, 1964, 1966, 1968.
Dayton Journal Herald, 1960, 1964–65, 1966, 1968.
Defiance Crescent News, 1925.
Dover Daily Reporter, 1960, 1965.
East Liverpool Evening Review, 1965.
Elyria Chronicle Telegram, 1957.
Findlay Republican-Courier, 1956, 1965, 1967.
Golden Gater (San Francisco State College), 1964.
Greencastle (IN) Daily Banner, 1965.
Hamilton Daily News Journal, 1949, 1963, 1966.
Hillsboro Press Gazette, 1956.
Independent (New York), 1900.
Indianapolis News, 1965.
Indianapolis Star, 1965.
Jewish Telegraphic Agency Daily News Bulletin, 1965.
The Liberator, 1846.
Liberty Hall, 1821, 1825.
Lima News, 1935–38.
Logan Daily News, 1949, 1956.
Louisville Courier-Herald, 1968.

Mansfield News Journal, 1964, 1969, 1971, 1973.

Marion Star, 1965.

Massillon Evening Independent, 1925, 1954.

Middletown Journal, 1963, 1966, 1967.

Mount Vernon Democratic Banner, 1913.

Napoleon North-West, 1862.

The Nation, 1936.

Newark Advocate, 1963.

New Philadelphia Daily Times, 1907, 1911.

New York Times, 1940, 1944, 1946, 1956, 2011.

Ohio Sentinel, 1956, 1960–61.

Ohio State News, 1949–50.

Ohio University Post, 1965.

Perrysburg Journal, 1890.

Portsmouth Times, 1862.

Sandusky Register, 1964.

Sandusky Star Journal, 1925.

Steubenville Herald Star, 1964–66, 1969, 1971.

Toledo Blade, 1862, 1967.

Toledo Commercial, 1862.

University of Cincinnati News Record, 1971–1974.

Van Wert Times Bulletin, 1955, 1966.

Wall Street Journal, 1967.

Washington Court House Record Herald, 1964–65.

Willoughby News Herald, 1966.

Xenia Daily Gazette, 1967.

PUBLISHED MATERIALS

American Colonization Society. "Annual Report of the American Colonization Society." *The African Repository and Colonial Journal* 23 (1847): 65–86.

Beecher, Lyman. *Dr. Beecher's Plea for the West.* Cincinnati: Truman and Smith, 1835.

Dee, Christine, ed. *Ohio's War: The Civil War in Documents.* Athens: Ohio University Press, 2007.

Freneau, Philip. "The Pilgrim, No. VIII." *Freeman's Journal* (Philadelphia), January 9, 1782.

Hearn, Lafcadio. "Levee Life: Haunts and Pastimes of the Roustabouts." *Cincinnati Commercial,* March 17, 1876. In *Children of the Levee,* edited by O. W. Frost. Lexington: University of Kentucky Press, 1957.

Ku Klux Klan, Inc. *America for Americans*. Atlanta: Ku Klux Klan, Inc. 1922.

Library of Congress. Sign on restaurant, Lancaster, Ohio (1938). https://www.loc.gov/pictures/item/2017731352/.

Malvin, John. *Autobiography of John Malvin*. Cleveland: Leader Printing Co., 1879.

Manypenny, George W. *Our Indian Wards*. Cincinnati: Robert Clarke & Co., 1880.

Middleton, Stephen J. *The Black Laws in the Old Northwest: A Documentary History*. Santa Barbara, CA: ABC-CLIO, 1993.

Morris, George. *The Black Legion Rides*. New York: Workers Library Publishers, 1936.

Ohio History Connection. Depiction of Gnadenhutten Massacre. https://www.ohiomemory.org/digital/collection/p267401coll32/id/15843/rec/8.

———. Freehold surety bond from Miami County, 1837. https://www.ohiomemory.org/digital/collection/p267401coll32/id/20524/rec/4.

———. Ku Klux Klan Ladies' Auxiliary Centennial Float [photograph]. https://www.ohiomemory.org/digital/collection/p267401coll36/id/11967/rec/2.

———. Police dispersing crowd outside Gegner's Barber Shop, 1964. https://www.ohiomemory.org/digital/collection/p267401coll36/id/7937/rec/26.

Smith, Joseph Patterson, ed. *History of the Republican Party in Ohio*, vol. 1. Chicago: Lewis Publishing, 1898.

Smith, William Henry, ed. *The St. Clair Papers: The Life and Public Services of Arthur St. Clair, Soldier of the Revolutionary War, President of the Continental Congress and Governor of the North-Western Territory, with his Correspondence and Other Papers*. Cincinnati: Robert Clarke & Co., 1882.

Stowe, Harriet Beecher. "What Is to Be Done with Them?" *Independent*, August 21, 1862.

GOVERNMENT DOCUMENTS

Ohio Department of Commerce. "History of BBS." Ohio Department of Commerce, https://www.com.ohio.gov/documents/bbst_BBSAbout.pdf.

Ohio General Assembly. *Acts of the State of Ohio*, vol. 58. Columbus: Richard Nevins, State Printer, 1861.

State of Ohio. "Amendment and Legislation: Proposed Constitutional Amendments, Initiated Legislation, and Laws Challenged by Referendum, Submitted to the Electors." Ohio Secretary of State. https://www.sos.state.oh.us/globalassets/elections/historical/issuehist.pdf.

———. *Report of the Debates and Proceedings of the Convention for the Revision of the Constitution of the State of Ohio. 1850–51*, vol. 1. Columbus: S. Medary Printing, 1851.

United States Federal Bureau of Investigation. *Memorandum from FBI SAC-Louisville to SAC-Birmingham regarding 1960 surveillance of NSRP meetings*, pp. D–L.

———. *Birmingham field office report: National States' Rights Party*. April 14, 1965.

———. *Savannah field office report. Racial Matters: National States' Rights Party*. March 30, 1967.

———. *Memorandum from FBI Director to SACs in New York and Washington DC concerning National Youth Alliance* (airtel). May 5, 1969.

———. *White Extremist Organizations: Part II—National States' Rights Party.* May 1970.

———. *Memorandum from SAC-Dallas to SAC-Savannah. National States' Rights Party.* January 6, 1967.

———. *Report on the National Convention of the National States' Rights Party, Jacksonville Florida, June 7 and 8, 1969.* June 16, 1969.

———. *Memorandum from SAC-Louisville to FBI director regarding 20–21 JUN 1970 National States' Rights Party convention.* June 25, 1970.

———. *Memorandum from SAC-Chicago to FBI director regarding 20–21 JUN 1970 National States' Rights Party convention.* July 8, 1970.

United States House of Representatives, Committee on Un-American Activities. *Activities of Ku Klux Klan Organizations in the United States.* Washington, DC: Office of the Clerk—US Capitol, 1966.

———. *The Present-Day Ku Klux Klan Movement.* Washington, DC: US Government Printing Office, 1967.

DATABASES

1860 and 1870 censuses. National Historical Geographic Information System (NHGIS). https://www.nhgis.org/.

Secondary Sources

Adams, Josh, and Vincent J. Roscigno. "White Supremacists, Oppositional Culture and the World Wide Web." *Social Forces* 84, no. 2 (December 2005): 759–78.

Alexander, Charles C. "The Ku Klux Klan as a Business Organization 1915–1930." *The Business History Review* 39, no. 3 (Autumn, 1965), 348–67.

———. *The Ku Klux Klan in the Southwest.* Norman: University of Oklahoma Press, 1995.

Alexander, Michelle. *The New Jim Crow: Mass Incarceration in the Age of Colorblindness.* New York: The New Press, 2010.

Amann, Peter H. "Vigilante Fascism: The Black Legion as an American Hybrid." *Comparative Studies in Society and History* 25, no. 3 (July 1983): 490–524.

———. "A 'Dog in the Nighttime' Problem: American Fascism in the 1930s." *The History Teacher* 19, no. 4 (1986): 559–84.

Bertaux, Nancy. "Structural Economic Change and Occupational Decline among Black Workers in Nineteenth-Century Cincinnati." In *Race and the City: Work, Community, and Protest in Cincinnati, 1820–1970,* edited by Henry Louis Taylor Jr., 126–55. Urbana: University of Illinois Press, 1993.

Binnington, Ian. "Standing Upon a Volcano: Cincinnati's Newspapers Debate Emancipation, 1860–1862." *American Nineteenth Century History* 10, no. 2 (June 2009): 163–86.

Blee, Katherine. *Women of the Ku Klux Klan: Racism and Gender in the 1920s*. Berkeley: University of California Press, 1991.

Blocker, Jack S. Jr. "Race, Sex and Riot: The Springfield, Ohio Race Riots of 1904 and 1906 and the Sources of Anti-Black Violence in the Lower Midwest." *Ohio Valley History* 6, no. 1 (Spring 2006): 27–44.

Brooks, Michael E. *The Ku Klux Klan in Wood County, Ohio*. Mount Pleasant, SC: The History Press, 2014.

Brumberg, Stephan F. "The Cincinnati Bible War (1869–1873) and Its Impact on the Education of the City's Protestants, Catholics, and Jews." *American Jewish Archives Journal* 54, no. 2 (2002): 11–46.

Carlock, Robert Michael. "A New (Bowling Green State) University: Educational Activism, Social Change, and Campus Protest in the Long Sixties." Master's thesis, Bowling Green State University, 2019.

Cave, Alfred. *Sharp Knife: Andrew Jackson and the American Indians*. New York: Praeger, 2017.

Chalmers, David M. *Hooded Americanism: The History of the Ku Klux Klan*. New York: Doubleday Books, 1968.

Clinansmith, Michael S. "Hooded Americanism in Michigan." *Michigan History* 55, no. 3 (1971): 243–62.

Coffey, Brian, and J. Clark Gocker. "Racial Disparities in Mortgage Lending: The Example of Urban Ohio." *Social Justice* 25, no. 3 (73): 115–27.

Culpepper, Betty M. "The Negro and the Black Laws of Ohio, 1803–1860." Master's thesis, Kent State University, 1966.

Dinnerstein, Leonard. *The Leo Frank Case*. Athens: University of Georgia Press, 2008.

Drabble, John. "The FBI, COINTELPRO-WHITEHATE, and the Decline of Ku Klux Klan Organizations in Alabama, 1964–1971." *Alabama Review* 61, no. 1 (2008): 3–47.

Dvorak, Kenneth Robert. *Terror in Detroit: The Rise and Fall of Michigan's Black Legion*. PhD diss., Bowling Green State University, 2000.

Entin, Jonathan L. "An Ohio Dilemma: Race, Equal Protection, and the Unfulfilled Promise of a State Bill of Rights." *Cleveland State Law Review* 51 (2004): 395–413.

Evans, Nelson W. *History of Scioto County*. Portsmouth: Nelson W. Evans, 1901.

Feight, Andrew. "'Black Friday': Enforcing Ohio's 'Black Laws' in Portsmouth, Ohio." *Scioto Historical Society*, http://www.sciotohistorical.org/items/show/108.

Fisher, Kyle. "After Gnadenhütten: The Moravian Indian Mission in the Old Northwest, 1782–1812." *Journal of Moravian History* 17, no. 1 (May 9, 2017): 27–58.

Gerber, David A. *Black Ohio and the Color Line, 1860–1915*. Urbana: University of Illinois Press, 1976.

Giffin, William W. *African Americans and the Color Line in Ohio, 1915–1930*. Columbus: The Ohio State University Press, 2005.

Gordon, Linda. *The Second Coming of the KKK: The Ku Klux Klan of the 1920s and the American Political Tradition*. New York: Liveright, 2017.

Greer, James. "The Home Owners' Loan Corporation and the Development of the Residential Security Maps." *Journal of Urban History* 39, no. 2 (2013): 275–96.

Harding, Leonard. "The Cincinnati Riots of 1862." *Bulletin of the Cincinnati Historical Society* 25, no. 4 (1967): 229–39.

Harper, Rob. "State Intervention and Extreme Violence in the Revolutionary Ohio Valley." *Journal of Genocide Research* 10, no. 2 (2008): 233–48.

Hawley, George. *Making Sense of the Alt-Right.* New York: Columbia University Press, 2017.

Howard, Marilyn Kaye. "Black Lynching in the Promised Land: Mob Violence in Ohio, 1876–1916." PhD diss., The Ohio State University, 1999.

"Injunction Against the Recording of Deeds Containing Racial Covenants: The Last of the Racial Covenant Cases?—*Mayers v. Ridley.*" *Maryland Law Review* 403 (1974): 403–19.

Jackson, Kenneth T. *The Ku Klux Klan in the City, 1915–1930.* New York: Oxford University Press, 1992.

Jones-Correa, Michael. "The Origins and Diffusion of Racial Restrictive Covenants." *Political Science Quarterly* 115, no. 4 (Winter 2000–2001): 541–68.

Kendi, Ibram X. *Stamped from the Beginning: The Definitive History of Racist Ideas in America.* New York: Bold Type Books, 2016.

Kern, Kevin F., and Gregory S. Wilson. *Ohio: A History of the Buckeye State.* Malden, MA: Wiley, 2014.

Knepper, George S. *Ohio and Its People: Bicentennial Edition.* Kent: Kent State University Press, 2003.

Lay, Shawn. *Hooded Knights on the Niagara: The Ku Klux Klan in Buffalo, New York.* New York: New York University Press, 1995.

Lester, John C. *Ku Klux Klan: Its Origin, Growth and Disbandment.* New York: Neale, 1905.

Levstik, Frank R. "The Toledo Riot of 1862: A Study of Midwest Negrophobia." *Northwest Ohio Quarterly* 44 (Autumn 1972): 100–106.

Lipset, Seymour Martin. *Rebellion in the University.* New York: Little, Brown, 1971.

Loewen, James W. *Sundown Towns: A Hidden Dimension of American Racism.* New York: The New Press, 2018.

Lutholtz, William M. *Grand Dragon: D. C. Stephenson and the Ku Klux Klan in Indiana.* West Lafayette, IN: Purdue University Press, 1991.

Mach, Jacob T. "'Having Given Them Bayonets, We Will Not Withhold the Ballot'—Republicans and Black Suffrage in Reconstruction Ohio, 1865–1867." Master's thesis, Bowling Green State University, 2020.

Mathias, Frank F. "John Randolph's Freedmen: The Thwarting of a Will." *The Journal of Southern History* 39, no. 2 (May 1973): 263–72.

Maulden, Kristopher. "A Show of Force: The Northwest Indian War and the Early American State." *Ohio Valley History* 16, no. 4 (2016): 20–40.

McNergney Vinyard, JoEllen. *Right in America's Grassroots: From the KKK to the Michigan Militia.* Ann Arbor: University of Michigan Press, 2011.

McPherson, James M. *Battle Cry of Freedom: The Civil War Era.* New York: Oxford University Press, 1988.

McVeigh, Rory. *The Rise of the Ku Klux Klan: Right-Wing Movements and National Politics.* Minneapolis: University of Minnesota Press, 2009.

Michney, Todd M. "Race, Violence, and Urban Territoriality: Cleveland's Little Italy and the 1966 Hough Uprising." *Journal of Urban History* 32, no. 3 (March 2006): 404–28.

Middleton, Stephen. *The Black Laws: Race and the Legal Process in Early Ohio.* Athens: Ohio University Press, 2005.

Miggins, Edward M. "No Crystal Stair: The Cleveland Public Schools and the Struggle for Equality, 1900–1930." *Journal of Urban History* 40, no. 4 (2014): 671–98.

Mjagkij, Nina. "The Cincinnati Urban League." In *Race and the City: Work, Community, and Protest in Cincinnati, 1820–1970,* edited by Henry Louis Taylor, 280–94. Champaign: University of Illinois Press, 1993.

Moore, Leonard J. *Citizen Klansmen: The Ku Klux Klan in Indiana, 1921–1928.* Chapel Hill, University of North Carolina Press, 1997.

Moore, Leonard Nathaniel. "The School Desegregation Crisis of Cleveland, Ohio, 1963–1964: The Catalyst for Black Political Power in a Northern City." *Journal of Urban History* 28, no. 2 (January 2002): 135–57.

Morton, Marian. "Deferring Dreams: Racial and Religious Covenants in Shaker Heights, Cleveland Heights and East Cleveland, 1925 to 1970." *Teaching Cleveland,* February 27, 2010, 1–7.

Muccino, Eileen. "Irish Filibusters and Know Nothings in Cincinnati." *Ohio Valley History* 10, no. 3 (Fall 2010): 3–26.

National Museum of African American History and Culture, Smithsonian Institution. "Blackface: The Birth of an American Stereotype." https://nmaahc.si.edu/blog-post/blackface-birth-american-stereotype.

Newton, Michael. *White Robes and Burning Crosses: A History of the Ku Klux Klan from 1866.* Jefferson, NC: McFarland, 2014.

———. *The National States Rights Party: A History.* Jefferson, NC: McFarland, 2017.

Oluo, Ijeoma. *So You Want to Talk About Race.* New York: Seal Press, 2019.

Ostler, Jeffrey. "'To Extirpate the Indians': An Indigenous Consciousness of Genocide in the Ohio Valley and Lower Great Lakes, 1750s–1810." *The William and Mary Quarterly* 72, no. 4 (2015): 587–622.

Palella, Andrew. "The Black Legion: J. Edgar Hoover and Fascism in the Depression Era." *Journal for the Study of Radicalism* 12, no. 2 (2018): 81–105.

Pegram, Thomas R. *One Hundred Percent American: The Rebirth and Decline of the Ku Klux Klan in the 1920s.* Lanham, MD: Rowman & Littlefield, 2011.

Piper, Michael Collins and Ken Hoop. "The Great Sedition Trial of 1944." *Barnes Review* 6 (November–December 1999), https://barnesreview.org/product/the-barnes-review-novemberdecember-1999-a-mockery-of-justice-the-great-sedition-trial-of-1944/.

Poluse, Martin. "Archbishop Joseph Schrembs's Battle to Obtain Public Assistance for the Parochial Schools of Cleveland during the Great Depression." *The Catholic Historical Review* 83, no. 3 (July 1997): 428–51.

Quarles, Chester L. *The Ku Klux Klan and Related American Racialist and Antisemitic Organizations: A History and Analysis.* Jefferson, NC: McFarland, 1999.

Quillin, Frank U. *The Color Line in Ohio: A History of Race Prejudice in a Typical Northern State.* Ann Arbor: University of Michigan, 1913.

Rice, Tom. "'The True Story of the Ku Klux Klan': Defining the Klan through Film." *Journal of American Studies* 42, no. 3 (December 2008): 471–88.

Robinson, Marsha R., ed. *Purgatory between Kentucky and Canada: African Americans in Ohio.* London: Cambridge Scholars, 2013.

Roediger, David R. *How Race Survived US History: From Settlement and Slavery to the Obama Phenomenon.* New York: Verso, 2008.

Ross, Steven J. *Workers on the Edge: Work, Leisure, and Politics in Industrializing Cincinnati, 1788–1890.* New York: Columbia University Press, 1985.

Rowe, Jill E. "Mixing It Up: Early African American Settlements in Northwestern Ohio." *Journal of Black Studies* 39, no. 6 (July 2009): 924–36.

Schwalm, Leslie A. "'Overrun with Free Negroes': Emancipation and Wartime Migration in the Upper Midwest." *Civil War History* 50, no. 2 (2004): 145–74.

———. *Emancipation's Diaspora: Race and Reconstruction in the Upper Midwest.* Raleigh: University of North Carolina Press, 2009.

Shearer, Tobin M. *Two Weeks Every Summer: Fresh Air Children and the Problem of Race in America.* Ithaca, NY: Cornell University Press: 2017.

Stockwell, Mary. *The Other Trail of Tears: The Removal of the Ohio Indians.* Yardley, PA: Westholme, 2015.

Taylor, Nikki M. "Reconsidering the 'Forced' Exodus of 1829: Free Black Emigration from Cincinnati, Ohio to Wilberforce, Canada." *Journal of African American History* 87 (Summer 2002): 283–302.

———. *Frontiers of Freedom: Cincinnati's Black Community 1802–1868.* Athens: Ohio University Press, 2005.

Voegeli, V. Jacque. "A Rejected Alternative: Union Policy and the Relocation of Southern 'Contrabands' at the Dawn of Emancipation." *The Journal of Southern History* 69, no. 4 (November 2003): 765–90.

Wade, Richard C. "The Negro in Cincinnati, 1800-30." *Journal of Negro History* 39, no. 1 (1954), 9–51.

Wade, Wyn Craig. *The Fiery Cross: The Ku Klux Klan in America.* New York: Oxford University Press, 1998.

Washington, Versalle F. *Eagles on Their Buttons: A Black Regiment in the Civil War.* Columbia: University of Missouri Press, 1999.

Williams, Lee. "Concentrated Residences: The Case of Black Toledo, 1890–1930." *Phylon* 43, no. 2 (2nd qtr. 1982): 167–76.

Wingfield, Adia Harvey. "The Modern Mammy and the Angry Black Man: African American Professionals' Experiences with Gendered Racism in the Workplace." *Race, Gender & Class* 14, no. 1 (2007): 196–212.

Woodson, Carter G. *A Century of Negro Migration.* Washington, DC: Association for the Study of Negro Life and History, 1918.

Zeskind, Leonard. *Blood and Politics: The History of the White Nationalist Movement.* New York: Farrar, Straus and Giroux, 2009.

Bibliography to "Now: Present-Day Hate Groups in Ohio"

Primary Sources

NEWSPAPERS AND MAGAZINES

Akron Beacon Journal, 2017

Associated Press, 1979, 1997–98, 2001, 2014, 2019–20

Athens News, 1987, 1989–90, 2017

The Atlantic, 2017, 2020

Baltimore Sun, 1999

Cincinnati.com, 2016

Cincinnati Enquirer, 1999

Cleveland.com, 2017–18

Cleveland Jewish News, 2020

Cleveland Scene, 2017

Columbus Alive, 1993, 1996–2000

Columbus Dispatch, 2017, 2019–20

Columbus Free Press, 1975, 1977–80, 1993–95, 1998, 2004–5, 2016–18

Daily Beast, 2020

Daily Mail, 2020

Dayton Daily News, 2017, 2019

Deseret News, 1997

The Guardian, 2020

Huffington Post, 2017

The Informant, 2020

Intelligence Report, Southern Poverty Law Center, 2002–2017

The Intercept, 2015

Journal Times, 1993

Mansfield News Journal, 2020

Mockingbird Paper, 2018

The Nation, 2012

New York Post, 2005

New York Times, 1977, 1979, 1984, 1992, 1997–98, 2007, 2017–19

Newsweek, 1995, 2018, 2020

Patch.com, 2019–20

The Root, 2017

The Spokesman, 1997–98

Springfield News-Sun, 2017

Tampa Bay Times, 2014

Toledo Blade, 2015

Time, 2020

Wall Street Journal, 1999

Washington Post, 2016–17

INTERVIEWS

Mann, David. Interview with Bob Fitrakis. February 17, 2018.

McNamara, Jim. Interview with *Columbus Free Press.* January 24, 2018.

GOVERNMENT DOCUMENTS

The Oklahoma Commission to Study the Race Riot of 1921. "Final Report." February 28, 2001.

PUBLISHED MATERIALS

Jaime Fuller. "What the Neshoba County Fair says about Southern politics," *Washington Post,* July 31, 2014. https://www.washingtonpost.com/news/the-fix/wp/2014/07/31/what-the-neshoba-county-fair-says-about-southern-politics/.

Rowe, Gary Thomas, Jr. *My Undercover Years with the Ku Klux Klan.* New York: Bantam, 1976.

TV

ACTV, 1989–2002

CNN, 2018

NBC4i, 2015

WBNS 10TV, 2019

WCPO, 2017

WKYC, 2017

WEBSITES

https://archive.org/—Free Press Library

https://www.splcenter.org—Southern Poverty Law Center

http://www.stormfront.org

Secondary Sources

Abanes, Richard. *American Militias.* Downers Grove, Illinois: InterVarsity Press, 1996.

Alexander, Michelle. *The New Jim Crow: Mass Incarceration in the Age of Colorblindness.* New York: The New Press, 2012.

"The Alt-Right and Extremism on Campus." In *Hate and Extremism in 2017.* Southern Poverty Law Center, 2017.

Anderson, Carol. *White Rage: The Unspoken Truth of Our Racial Divide.* London: Bloomsbury, 2016.

Anti-Defamation League. "ADL: White Supremacist Propaganda Distribution in Ohio Up 442% Over Last Year." February 18, 2020. https://cleveland.adl.org/news/adl-white-supremacist-propaganda-distribution-in-ohio-up-442-over-last-year/.

———. "The Aryan Circle: Crime in the Name of Hate." October 2009.

———. "Danger: Extremism: The Major Vehicles and Voices on America's Far-Right Fringe." Pamphlet. New York, 1996.

———. *Vigilante Justice: Militias and "Common Law" Courts Wage War against the Government.* New York, 1997.

———. *The Web of Hate: Extremists Exploit the Internet.* New York, 1996.

Anti-Racist Action. "A History of Anti-Racist Action." Retrieved from antiracistaction.org/history.

Associated Press. "Hate Groups Growing in the United States." *New York Times,* May 3, 1998.

Bar-Zohar, Michael. *The Hunt for German Scientists.* London: Arthur Baker, 1967.

Barkun, Michael. *Religion and the Racist Right: The Origins of the Christian Identity Movement.* Chapel Hill: University of North Carolina Press, 1994.

Bellant, Russ. *Old Nazis, The New Right, and the Republican Party.* Boston: South End Press, 1991.

———. *The Coors Connection: How Coors Family Philanthropy Undermines Democratic Pluralism.* Boston: South End Press, 1991.

———. *The Religious Right in Michigan Politics.* Silver Spring, MD: American for Religious Liberty, 1996.

Berlet, Chip, and Matthew Lyon. *Too Close For Comfort.* Boston: South End Press, 1997.

Bonilla-Silva, Eduardo. *White Supremacy and Racism in the Post–Civil Rights Era.* Boulder, CO: Lynne Rienner, 2001.

Carto, Willis, ed. *Profiles in Populism.* Old Greenwich, CT: Flag Press, 1982.

Communist Workers Party. "Smash the Klan with Correct Understanding and Armed Self-Defense." *Workers Viewpoint Organization,* November 1, 1979.

Dees, Morris. *Hate on Trial.* New York: Villard, 1993.

Dees, Morris, with James Corcoran. *Gathering Storm.* New York: HarperCollins, 1996.

Denitch, Bogdan. *After the Flood: World Politics and Democracy in the Wake of Communism.* Hanover, NH: Wesleyan University Press, 1992.

Ezekiel, Raphael S. *The Racist Mind.* New York: Viking, 1995.

Feagin, Joe R., and Hernan Vera. *White Racism.* New York: Routledge, 1995.

Fitrakis, Bob, and Judy Gentry. "A Detour Through Hate on the Information Superhighway." Presented at the Ohio Association of Two Year Colleges, Edison Community College, October 24, 1997.

Fitrakis, Robert. *The Fitrakis Files: Spooks, Nukes, and Nazis.* Columbus: Columbus Alive, 2003.

Fitrakis, Robert J., and Harvey Wasserman. *The Strip and Flip Disaster of America's Stolen Elections.* Columbus: CICJ Books, 2017.

George, John, and Laird Wilcox. *Nazis, Communists, Klansmen and Others on the Fringe.* Buffalo, NY: Prometheus Books, 1992.

Gerhardt, Gary, and Kevin Flynn. *The Silent Brotherhood: The Chilling Inside Story of America's Violent Anti-Government Militia Movement.* New York: Free Press, 1989.

Gilje, Paul A. *Rioting in America.* Bloomington: Indiana University Press, 1996.

Gould, Steven J. *The Mismeasure of Man.* New York: Norton, 1981.

Hofstadter, Richard. *The Paranoid Style in American Politics.* New York: Knopf, 1965.

Institute of Jewish Affairs. *Antisemitism: World Report 1993.* London, 1993.

King, Dennis. *Lyndon LaRouche and the New American Fascism.* New York: Doubleday, 1989.

Kronenwetter, Michael. *United They Hate: White Supremacists in America.* New York: Walker, 1992.

Langer, Elinor. *A Hundred Little Hitlers.* New York: Henry Holt, 2003.

Lee, Martin A. *The Beast Reawakens.* 1997; New York: Little, Brown, 2003.

Lesher, Stephan. *George Wallace.* Reading, MA: Addison-Wesley, 1994.

Lerner, Michael. *The Socialism of Fools: Anti-Semitism on the Left.* Oakland, CA: Tikkun Books, 1992.

Macdonald, Andrew (William Luther Pierce). *The Turner Diaries.* Hillsboro, WV: National Vanguard Books, 1978.

Mehler, Barry. "Madge Thurlow Macklin." In *Notable American Women: The Modern Period,* edited by Barbara Sicherman and Carl Hurd Green, 451–52. Cambridge, MA: Harvard University Press, 1980.

Mintz, Frank P. *The Liberty Lobby and the American Right.* Westport, CT: Greenwood, 1985.

Novick, Michael. *White Lies, White Power.* Monroe, ME: Common Courage, 1995.

Pascoe, Peggy. *What Comes Naturally: Miscegenation Law and the Making of Race in America.* New York: Oxford University Press, 2009.

Pierce, William L. "Equality: Man's Most Dangerous Myth." *National Vanguard* no. 68, 1979. https://nationalvanguard.org/2010/09/equality-mans-most-dangerous-myth/.

Potok, Mark. "The Year in Hate: A Period of Realignment and Rebuilding Follows a Tumultuous Year on the American Radical Right." Southern Poverty Law Center, 2003.

Ridgeway, James. *Blood in the Face: The Ku Klux Klan, Aryan Nations, Nazi Skinheads, and the Rise of a New White Culture.* New York: Thunder's Mouth, 1990.

Robertson, Pat. *The New World Order.* New York: World, 1992.

Sargent, Lyman Tower. *Extremism in America*. New York: New York University Press, 1995.

Simi, Peter, and Robert Futrell. *American Swastika: Inside the White Power Movement's Hidden Spaces of Hate*. New York: Roman & Littlefield, 2010.

United States Commission on Civil Rights, Ohio Advisory Committee. *Hate Crime in Ohio: Ohio Advisory Committee to the United States*. Chicago: US Commission on Civil Rights, Midwestern Regional Office, 1995.

Walker, Samuel. *Hate Speech: The History of an American Controversy*. Lincoln, NE: University of Nebraska Press, 1994.

Wexler, Stuart. *America's Secret Jihad: The Hidden History of Religious Terrorism in the United States*. Berkeley, CA: Counterpoint, 2015.

Zatarain, Michael. *David Duke: Evolution of a Klansman*. Gretna, LA: Pelican, 1990.

INDEX